# THE TASKS OF PHILOSOPHY

How should we respond when some of our basic beliefs are put into question? What makes a human body distinctively human? Why is truth an important good? These are among the questions explored in this collection of essays by Alasdair MacIntyre, one of the most creative and influential philosophers working today. Ten of MacIntyre's most influential essays written over almost thirty years are collected together here for the first time. They range over such topics as the issues raised by different types of relativism, what it is about human beings that cannot be understood by the natural sciences, the relationship between the ends of life and the ends of philosophical writing, and the relationship of moral philosophy to contemporary social practice. They will appeal to a wide range of readers across philosophy and especially in moral philosophy, political philosophy, and theology.

ALASDAIR MACINTYRE is Senior Research Professor of Philosophy at the University of Notre Dame, a Member of the American Academy of Arts and Sciences, and a Fellow of the British Academy. His publications include *A Short History of Ethics* (1967), *After Virtue* (1981), *Dependent Rational Animals* (1999), and numerous journal articles.

# THE TASKS OF PHILOSOPHY

## Selected Essays, Volume 1

ALASDAIR MACINTYRE

*University of Notre Dame*

CAMBRIDGE
UNIVERSITY PRESS

CAMBRIDGE UNIVERSITY PRESS
Cambridge, New York, Melbourne, Madrid, Cape Town, Singapore, São Paulo

Cambridge University Press
The Edinburgh Building, Cambridge CB2 2RU, UK

Published in the United States of America by Cambridge University Press, New York

www.cambridge.org
Information on this title: www.cambridge.org/9780521670616

First published 2006

Printed in the United Kingdom at the University Press, Cambridge

*A catalogue record for this publication is available from the British Library*

ISBN-13 978-0-521-85437-5 hardback
ISBN-10 0-521-85437-7 hardback
ISBN-13 978-0-521-67061-6 paperback
ISBN-10 0-521-67061-6 paperback

Cambridge University Press has no responsibility for the persistence or accuracy of URLs for external
or third-party internet websites referred to in this publication, and does not guarantee that
any content on such websites is, or will remain, accurate or appropriate.

# Contents

# *Preface*

The earliest of these essays appeared in 1972, the latest as recently as 2002. In 1971 Colin Haycraft of Duckworth in London and Ted Schocken of Schocken Books in New York had published a collection of my earlier essays, *Against the Self-Images of the Age: Essays in Ideology and Philosophy*, in which I had set myself three goals. The first was to evaluate a variety of ideological claims, claims about human nature and history, about the human good and the politics of its realization, advanced from the standpoints of Christian theology, of some kinds of psychoanalytic theory, and of some dominant versions of Marxism, the second to argue that, although there were sound reasons for rejecting those particular ideological claims, they provided no support for the then still fashionable end of ideology thesis, defended by Edward Shils and others. Yet these negative conclusions would have been practically sterile, if I were unable to move beyond them. And, if I was to be able to move beyond them, I badly needed to find resources that would enable me to diagnose more adequately the conceptual and historical roots of our moral and political condition.

A third task in *Against the Self-Images of the Age* was therefore to reconsider some central issues in moral philosophy and the philosophy of action. Yet the effect of rereading these essays in 1971, when collected together in a single volume, was to make me painfully aware of how relatively little had been accomplished in that book and how much more I needed by way of resources, if I was to discriminate adequately between what still had to be learned from each of the standpoints that I had criticized and what had to be rejected root and branch. How then was I to proceed philosophically? The first of the essays in this volume, "Epistemological crises, dramatic narrative, and the philosophy of science," marks a major turning-point in my thinking during the 1970s.

It was elicited by my reading of and encounters with Imre Lakatos and Thomas Kuhn and what was transformed by that reading was my conception of what it was to make progress in philosophy or indeed in systematic thought more generally. Up to that time, although I should have learned otherwise from the histories of Christian theology and of Marxism, I had assumed that my enquiries would and should move forward in a piecemeal way, focusing first on this problem and then on that, in a mode characteristic of much analytic philosophy. So I had worked away at a number of issues that I had treated as separate and distinct without sufficient reflection upon the larger conceptual framework within which and by reference to which I and others formulated those issues. What I learned from Kuhn, or rather from Kuhn and Lakatos read together, was the need first to identify and then to break free from that framework and to enquire whether the various problems on which I had made so little progress had baffled me not or not only because of their difficulty, but because they were bound to remain intractable so long as they were understood in the terms dictated by those larger assumptions which I shared with many of my contemporaries. And I was to find that, by rejecting the conception of progress in philosophy that I had hitherto taken for granted, I had already taken a first step towards viewing the issues in which I was entangled in a new light.

A second step was taken when I tore up the manuscript of the book on moral philosophy that I had been writing and asked how the problems of modern moral and political philosophy would have to be reformulated, if they were viewed not from the standpoint of liberal modernity, but instead from the standpoint of what I took to be Aristotelian moral and political practice, and if they were understood as having resulted from a fragmentation of older Aristotelian conceptions of the practical life, a fragmentation produced by the impact of modernity upon traditions that had embodied such conceptions. What I discovered was that the dilemmas of high modernity and their apparently intractable character become adequately explicable *only* when viewed and understood in this way. This was the highly controversial claim that I first advanced in *After Virtue* (University of Notre Dame Press, Second Edition, 1981) and developed in subsequent books.

It is a claim that may seem to have a paradoxical character. For, if we inhabit a cultural, social, and moral order that we can only understand adequately from some point of view external to that order, how is it possible for us simultaneously to remain inhabitants of that order and yet to transcend its limitations? The answer is that the cultures of modernity are arenas of potential and actual conflict in which modes of thought and action from a variety of pasts coexist with and put in question some of the distinctive institutional forms and moral stances of individualist and corporate modernity. So from within modernity critiques of that same modernity from the standpoint of past traditions pose philosophical as well as political and moral questions.

Those who identify themselves with such critiques need to be able to say where they stand on a range of philosophical issues and to give adequate reasons for their commitments. Some of those issues are addressed in the next five essays. "Colors, cultures, and practices" is an enquiry into the range and significance of our agreements and disagreements in our color vocabularies, our perceptions of color, and our ascriptions of color. It begins from Wittgensteinian considerations about how language use is socially constituted and how agreements in our naming of colors within cultures is compatible with significant disagreements between cultures as to how colors are to be named. But these are preliminaries to asking what good reasons there might be for discriminating and classifying colors in one way rather than another and to arguing that the context for such reasoning is provided by practices, notably, for example, by the practice of the art of painting, in which the goods aimed at within some practice at some particular stage of its development may well provide us with grounds – generally and characteristically grounds that are only identified retrospectively – for attending to and discriminating colors in one way rather than another.

A good deal more needs to be said than is said in this essay. But even when this enquiry is carried no further forward, it involves a critical evaluation and rejection of the claims of a sophisticated cultural relativism. The reasons that we have for rejecting such claims have some bearing on the closely related issue of moral relativism and that relativism is confronted directly in "Moral relativism, truth, and justification," a paper written for a *Festschrift* published to celebrate the splendid philosophical work of Elizabeth Anscombe and Peter Geach on the occasion of their fiftieth wedding anniversary. What my argument is designed to bring out – and I draw upon some of Geach's insights and arguments in doing so – is the place of the concept of truth in our moral discourse and our moral enquiries. That place is such as to put the theoretical moral relativist at odds with the inhabitants of those cultures on whose moral and other practical claims he is passing a verdict. The inhabitants of every moral culture, it turns out, have already rejected relativism and the problems that relativism was designed to solve, problems arising from radical moral disagreements within and between cultures, need to be approached in a very different way.

The fourth and fifth essays are concerned with how we ought to understand human beings. For the last three hundred years the project of explaining human thought and action in natural scientific terms has been an increasingly influential aspect of the distinctively modern mind. The sciences to which appeal has been made have undergone large changes. But the philosophical questions posed by that project have remained remarkably the same. So Hegel's critique of the claims advanced by the pseudo-sciences of physiognomy and phrenology in the late eighteenth and early nineteenth century is still to the point. And in "Hegel on faces and skulls" I conclude that Hegel provided us with good reasons for rejecting the view that human attitudes and actions are explicable by causal generalizations of the kind provided by the relevant natural sciences, in our day neurophysiology and biochemistry. In "What is a human body?" I argue further that we all of us have and cannot but have a prephilosophical understanding of the human body that is incompatible with treating its movements as wholly explicable in natural scientific terms. This understanding is presupposed by, among other things, those interpretative practices that make it possible for us to understand and to respond to what others say and do. So that in and by our everyday lives we are committed to a denial of the basic assumptions of much contemporary scientific naturalism.

These five essays address familiar philosophical issues. The sixth is very different. Moral philosophers often take themselves to be articulating concepts that are at home in the everyday life and utterances of prephilosophical moral agents, plain persons. But what if the moral concepts that inform the social and cultural practices in which both philosophers and plain persons participate in their everyday social life are in fact significantly different from and incompatible with the moral concepts of the philosophers? What if the moral concepts embodied in everyday practice are not only different and incompatible, but such that the way of life to which they give expression makes it difficult, perhaps impossible to find genuine application for the moral concepts of the philosophers? In "Moral philosophy and contemporary social practice: what holds them apart?" I suggest that just these possibilities are realized in the social and cultural order of advanced modernity and that the conclusions advanced within moral philosophy by rights theorists of various kinds, by proponents of virtue ethics, and by utilitarians are unable, except on rare occasions, to have any effect on contemporary social realities. The practices of individualist and corporate modernity are well designed to prevent the arguments of moral philosophers, whatever their point of view, from receiving a hearing.

If this is so, then the task of moral philosophers is not only to participate in theoretical enquiry and debate. Theoretical enquiry on moral and political matters is always rooted in some form of practice and to take a standpoint in moral and political debate is to define oneself in relationship to the practices in which one is engaged and to the conflicts in which one is thereby involved. Yet the social and cultural order that we nowadays inhabit is one that prescribes for philosophy a severely limited place, that of a discipline suitable for educating a very small minority of the young who happen to have a taste for that sort of thing. Its modes of public life are inimical to philosophical questioning of those modes and their presuppositions. And philosophers who seek to be more than theorists, whatever their point of view, are either forced into struggle against this marginalization or are condemned to speak only to and with other philosophers and their generally minuscule public. In this situation therefore the questions arise more sharply than at certain other times: Why engage in philosophy? What ends does philosophical enquiry serve? And what kind of philosophy will enable one to move towards the achievement of those ends? These are questions that I address in the four final essays in this volume.

In "The ends of life, the ends of philosophical writing" my enquiry is about the different relationships that may hold between the ends that philosophers pursue in their lives and the ends that they pursue in their writings and about the difference between those philosophical texts that enable us to ask better questions about the ends of life and those that divert us from asking such questions. The case made in this essay is indeed a case for a particular kind of philosophy, but it is not a case for any one philosophical standpoint. Yet this was not because I do not speak and write from a particular point of view. I wrote these essays and I write now with the intentions and commitments of a Thomistic Aristotelian. What these commitments amount to I tried to say, at least in part, in "First principles, final ends, and contemporary philosophical issues," a revised and expanded version of my 1990 Aquinas Lecture at Marquette University.

In that essay I had three aims. First, I needed to spell out for myself the conception of progress in philosophical enquiry that my work now presupposed, a very different conception from that which I had rejected while at work on "Epistemological crises, dramatic narrative, and the philosophy of science." Secondly, I hoped to make the Thomist conceptions of first principles and final ends intelligible to at least some of my contemporaries who were and are deeply committed to a rejection of those conceptions. And, thirdly, I wanted to identify the consequences for the history of modern philosophy of such rejection. The emphasis of this essay is therefore on the extent and nature of the disagreements between on the one hand Thomists and on the other analytic and postmodernist philosophers. Yet this makes the need to find common ground for debate and enquiry between Thomists and such critics, and the need to argue, so far as possible, from premises that are widely shared, all the more urgent. For in philosophy it is only by being open to objections posed by our critics and antagonists that we are able to avoid becoming the victims of our own prejudices.

Yet it is not always possible to find such common ground and sometimes this is a consequence of the fact that no one engages in philosophy without being influenced by their extraphilosophical allegiances, religious, moral, political, and otherwise. What is important here is twofold: first, not to disguise such allegiances as philosophical conclusions and, secondly, to make their influence on one's philosophical work explicit. The first is a danger that threatens those who fail to recognize, for example, that atheism requires an act of faith just as much as theism does and that physicalism is as liable to be held superstitiously as any religious view. The second is necessary, if one is to clarify the relationship between one's philosophical and one's other commitments. The next two essays are in part concerned to achieve such clarification in respect of my own commitments as a Roman Catholic who is a philosopher. Both are responses to John Paul II's encyclical letter, *Fides et Ratio*.

That encyclical is concerned both to insist upon the autonomy of the philosophical enterprise and to identify those philosophical theses to which anyone who affirms the Catholic creeds is inescapably committed. There is clearly a tension between these two themes and in "Truth as a good" I address the nature of that tension and more particularly enquire what understanding of truth is consistent with the Catholic faith. In "Philosophy recalled to its tasks" I have a number of concerns, but most centrally that of the relationship between the enquiries of the academic philosopher and the questioning and self-questioning of plain persons about their own nature and about the nature of things which is central to every developed human culture. In the encyclical we hear the voice not only of the pope, John Paul II, but of the philosopher, Karol Woityla, and I engage with it not only as an expression of the church's *magisterium*, but as a significant contribution to a both philosophical and theological understanding of philosophy.

Finally, I need to acknowledge my debts, particularly to those who have been or are my colleagues and to those who have been or are my students in the departments and centers to which I belonged at the time that I was writing these essays: at Boston University, at the Center for Kulturforskning of Aarhus University, and at the University of Notre Dame, where since the year 2000 I have been both a member of the Philosophy Department and a fellow of the Center for Ethics and Culture. My late colleague Philip Quinn was especially helpful in commenting on "Colors, cultures, and practices." I must once again thank Claire Shely for extraordinary work in preparing this volume.

Everyone whose academic life has been as long as mine has has incurred a special kind of debt to those with whom they have engaged in philosophical discussions that have extended over quite a number of years. I name them here, both the dead and the living, knowing that nothing I say can express adequately my sense of what I owe to them: Eric John, Herbert McCabe, O.P., James Cameron, Harry Lubasz, Max Wartofsky, Bernard Elevitch, David Solomon, Hans Fink, Ralph McInerny. I add to their names that of my wife, Lynn Sumida Joy, in acknowledgment of a still greater debt.

# Acknowledgments

Of the essays in this first volume numbers 5, 8, and 9 were previously unpublished. I am grateful to the following for permission to reprint essays that have appeared elsewhere:

- the Director of the Hegeler Institute for the first essay, previously published in *The Monist* vol. 60, no. 4, October 1977, pp. 453–72 (copyright© 1977, THE MONIST, An International Quarterly Journal of General Philosophical Enquiry, Peru, Illinois, 61534);
- the University of Notre Dame for the second essay, first published in *Midwest Studies in Philosophy* 17, 1992, edited by P. A. French, T. E. Uehling, Jr., and H. K. Wettstein, pp. 1–23;
- the Four Courts Press, Blackrock, Co. Dublin, for the third and tenth essays, first published in *Moral Truth and Moral Tradition: Essays in Honor of Peter Geach and Elizabeth Anscombe,* 1994, pp. 6–24, and in *Thomas Aquinas Approaches to Truth,* 2002, edited by J. McEvoy and M. Dunne, pp. 141–57;
- Doubleday, a division of Random House Inc., for the fourth essay, first published in *Hegel: A Collection of Critical Essays,* 1972, pp. 219–36;
- the Director of the Center for Kulturforsknung at Aarhus University for the sixth essay, first published as *Arbejdspapir* 113, 1992;
- Marquette University Press for permission to reprint the eighth essay, first published as the 1990 Aquinas Lecture at Marquette University.

# PART I

# Defining a philosophical stance

# CHAPTER I

# Epistemological crises, dramatic narrative, and the philosophy of science

I

What is an epistemological crisis? Consider, first, the situation of ordinary agents who are thrown into such crises. Someone who has believed that he was highly valued by his employers and colleagues is suddenly fired; someone proposed for membership of a club whose members were all, so he believed, close friends is blackballed. Or someone falls in love and needs to know what the loved one *really* feels; someone falls out of love and needs to know how he or she can possibly have been so mistaken in the other. For all such persons the relationship of *seems* to *is* becomes crucial. It is in such situations that ordinary agents who have never learned anything about academic philosophy are apt to rediscover for themselves versions of the other-minds problem and the problem of the justification of induction. They discover, that is, that there is a problem about the rational justification of inferences from premises about the behavior of other people to conclusions about their thoughts, feelings, and attitudes and of inferences from premises about how individuals have acted in the past to conclusions expressed as generalizations about their behavior, generalizations which would enable us to make reasonably reliable predications about their future behavior. What they took to be evidence pointing unambiguously in some one direction now turns out to have been equally susceptible of rival interpretations. Such a discovery is often paralysing, and were we all of us all of the time to have to reckon with the multiplicity of possible interpretations open to us, social life as we know it could scarcely continue. For social life is sustained by the assumption that we are, by and large, able to construe each other's behavior, that error, deception, self-deception, irony, and ambiguity, although omnipresent in social life, are not so pervasive as to render reliable reasoning and reasonable action impossible. But can this assumption in any way be vindicated?

Consider what it is to share a culture. It is to share schemata which are at one and the same time constitutive of and normative for intelligible action by myself and are also means for my interpretations of the actions of others. My ability to understand what you are doing and my ability to act intelligibly (both to myself and to others) are one and the same ability. It is true that I cannot master these schemata without also acquiring the means to deceive, to make more or less elaborate jokes, to exercise irony and utilize ambiguity, but it is also, and even more importantly, true that my ability to conduct any successful transactions depends on my present-ing myself to most people most of the time in unambiguous, unironical, undeceiving, intelligible ways. It is these schemata which enable inferences to be made from premises about past behavior to conclusions about future behavior and present inner attitudes. They are not, of course, empirical generalizations; they are prescriptions for interpretation. But while it is they which normally preserve us from the pressure of the other-minds problem and the problem of induction, it is precisely they which can in certain circumstances thrust those very problems upon us.

For it is not only that an individual may rely on the schemata which have hitherto informed his interpretations of social life and find that he or she has been led into radical error or deception, so that for the first time the schemata are put in question, but also that perhaps for the first time they become visible to the individual who employs them. And such an individual may as a result come to recognize the possibility of system-atically different possibilities of interpretation, of the existence of alterna-tive and rival schemata which yield mutually incompatible accounts of what is going on around him. Just this is the form of epistemological crisis encountered by ordinary agents and it is striking that there is not a single account of it anywhere in the literature of academic philosophy. Perhaps this is a symptom of the condition of that discipline. But happily we do possess one classic study of such crises. It is Shakespeare's *Hamlet*.

Hamlet arrives back from Wittenberg with too many schemata available for interpreting the events at Elsinore of which already he is a part. There is a revenge schema drawn from the Norse sagas; there is a Renaissance courtier's schema; there is a Machiavellian schema about competition for power. But Hamlet not only has the problem of which schema to apply; he also has the other ordinary agents' problem: whom now to believe? His mother? Rosencrantz and Guildenstern? His father's ghost? Until he has adopted some particular schema as his own he does not know what to treat as evidence; until he knows what to treat as evidence he cannot tell which schema to adopt. Trapped in this epistemological circularity the general form of his problem is: "What is going on here?" Thus Hamlet's problem is close to that of the literary critics who have asked: "What is going on in *Hamlet?*" And it is close to that of directors who have asked: "What should be cut from Shakespeare's text and what should be included in my production so that the audience may understand what is going on in *Hamlet?*"

The resemblance between Hamlet's problem and that of the critics and directors is worth noticing; for it suggests that both are asking a question which could equally well be formulated as: "What is going on in *Hamlet?*" or "How ought the narrative of these events to be constructed?" Hamlet's problems arise because the dramatic narrative of his family and of the kingdom of Denmark, through which he identified his own place in society and his relationships to others, has been disrupted by radical interpretative doubts. His task is to reconstitute, to rewrite that narrative, reversing his understanding of past events in the light of present responses to his probing. This probing is informed by two ideals, truth and intelligibility, and the pursuit of both is not always easily reconciled. The discovery of an hitherto unsuspected truth is just what may disrupt an hitherto intelligible account. And of course while Hamlet tries to discover a true and intelligible narrative of the events involving his parents and Claudius, Gertrude and Claudius are trying to discover a true and intelligible narrative of Hamlet's investigation. To be unable to render oneself intelligible is to risk being taken to be mad, is, if carried far enough, to be mad. And madness or death may always be the outcomes which prevent the resolution of an epistemological crisis, for an epistemological crisis is always a crisis in human relationships.

When an epistemological crisis is resolved, it is by the construction of a new narrative which enables the agent to understand *both* how he or she could intelligibly have held his or her original beliefs *and* how he or she could have been so drastically misled by them. The narrative in terms of which he or she at first understood and ordered experiences is itself now made into the subject of an enlarged narrative. The agent has come to understand how the criteria of truth and understanding must be reformulated. He has had to become epistemologically self-conscious and at a certain point he may have come to acknowledge two conclusions: the first is that his new forms of understanding may themselves in turn come to be put in question at any time; the second is that, because in such crises the criteria of truth, intelligibility, and rationality may always themselves be put in question – as they are in *Hamlet* – *we* are never in a position to claim that now we possess the truth or now we are fully rational. The most that we can claim is that this is the best account which anyone has been able to give so far, and that our beliefs about what the marks of "a best account so far" are will themselves change in what are at present unpredictable ways.

Philosophers have often been prepared to acknowledge this historical character in respect of scientific theories; but they have usually wanted to exempt their own thinking from the same historicity. So, of course, have writers of dramatic narrative; *Hamlet* is unique among plays in its openness to reinterpretation. Consider, by contrast, Jane Austen's procedure in *Emma*. Emma insists on viewing her protégé, Harriet, as a character in an eighteenth-century romance. She endows her, deceiving both herself and Harriet, with the conventional qualities of the heroine of such a romance. Harriet's parentage is not known; Emma converts her into the foundling heroine of aristocratic birth so common in such romances. And she designs for Harriet precisely the happy ending of such a romance, marriage to a superior being. By the end of *Emma* Jane Austen has provided Emma with some understanding of what it was in herself that had led her not to perceive the untruthfulness of her interpretation of the world in terms of romance. *Emma* has become a narrative about narrative. But Emma, although she experiences moral reversal, has no more than a minor epistemological crisis, if only because the standpoint which she now, through the agency of Mr. Knightley, has come to adopt, is presented as though it were one from which *the* world as it is can be viewed. False interpretation has been replaced not by a more adequate interpretation, which itself in turn may one day be transcended, but simply by the truth. We of course can see that Jane Austen is merely replacing one interpretation by another, but Jane Austen herself fails to recognize this and so has to deprive Emma of this recognition too.

Philosophers have customarily been Emmas and not Hamlets, except that in one respect they have often been even less perceptive than Emma. For Emma it becomes clear that her movement towards the truth necessarily had a moral dimension. Neither Plato nor Kant would have demurred. But the history of epistemology, like the history of ethics itself, is usually written as though it were not a moral narrative, that is, in fact as though it were not a narrative. For narrative requires an evaluative framework in which good or bad character helps to produce unfortunate or happy outcomes.

One further aspect of narratives and their role in epistemological crises remains to be noticed. I have suggested that epistemological progress consists in the construction and reconstruction of more adequate narratives and forms of narrative and that epistemological crises are occasions for such reconstruction. But if this were really the case then two kinds of questions would need to be answered. The first would be of the form: how does this progress begin? What are the narratives from which we set out? The second would be of the form: how comes it, then, that narrative is not only given so little place by thinkers from Descartes onwards, but has so often before and after been treated as a merely aesthetic form? The answers to these questions are not entirely unconnected.

We begin from myth, not only from the myths of primitive peoples, but from those myths or fairy stories which are essential to a well-ordered childhood. Bruno Bettelheim has written:

Before and well into the oedipal period (roughly, the ages between three and six or seven), the child's experience of the world is chaotic . . . During and because of the oedipal struggles, the outside world comes to hold more meaning for the child and he begins to try to make some sense of it . . . As a child listens to a fairy tale, he gets ideas about how he may create order out of the chaos that is his inner life.[1]

It is from fairy tales, so Bettelheim argues, that the child learns how to engage himself with and perceive an order in social reality; and the child who is deprived of the right kind of fairy tale at the right age later on is apt to have to adopt strategies to evade a reality he has not learned how to interpret or to handle.

The child asks himself, "Who am I? Where did I come from? How did the world come into being? Who created man and all the animals? What is the purpose of life?" . . . He wonders who or what brings adversity upon him and what can protect him against it. Are there benevolent powers in addition to his parents? *Are* his parents benevolent powers? How should he form himself, and why? Is there hope for him, though he may have done wrong? Why did all this happen to him? What will it mean to his future?[2]

The child originally requires answers that are true to his own experience, but of course the child comes to learn the inadequacy of that experience. Bettelheim points out that the young child told by adults that the world is a globe suspended in space and spinning at incredible speeds may feel bound to repeat what they say, but would find it immensely more plausible to be told that the earth is held up by a giant. But in time the

---

1 Bruno Bettelheim, *The Uses of Enchantment* (New York: Alfred A. Knopf, 1976), pp. 74–75.
2 Ibid., p. 47.

young child learns that what the adults told him is indeed true. And such a child may well become a Descartes, one who feels that all narratives are misleading fables when compared with what he now takes to be the solid truth of physics.

Yet to raise the question of truth need not entail rejecting myth or story as the appropriate and perhaps the only appropriate form in which certain truths can be told. The child may become not a Descartes, but a Vico or a Hamann who writes a story about how he had to escape from the hold which the stories of his childhood and the stories of the childhood of the human race originally had upon him in order to discover how stories can be true stories. Such a narrative will be itself a history of epistemological transitions and this narrative may well be brought to a point at which questions are thrust upon the narrator which make it impossible for him to continue to use it as an instrument of interpretation. Just this, of course, happens to Descartes, who, having abjured history as a means to truth, recounts to us his own history as the medium through which the search for truth is to be carried on. For Descartes and for others this moment is that at which an epistemological crisis occurs. And all those questions which the child has asked of the teller of fairy tales arise in a new adult form. Philosophy is now set the same task that had once been set for myth.

II

Descartes's description of his own epistemological crisis has, of course, been uniquely influential. Yet Descartes radically misdescribes his own crisis and thus has proved a highly misleading guide to the nature of epistemological crises in general. The agent who is plunged into an epistemological crisis knows something very important: that a schema of interpretation which he has trusted so far has broken down irremediably in certain highly specific ways. So it is with Hamlet. Descartes, however, starts from the assumption that he knows nothing whatsoever until he can discover a presuppositionless first principle on which all else can be founded. Hamlet's doubts are formulated against a background of what he takes to be – rightly – well-founded beliefs; Descartes's doubt is intended to lack any such background. It is to be contextless doubt. Hence also that tradition of philosophical teaching arises which presupposes that Cartesian doubts can be entertained by anyone at any place or time. But of course someone who really believed that he knew nothing would not even know how to begin on a course of radical doubt;

for he would have no conception of what his task might be, of what it would be to settle his doubts and to acquire well-founded beliefs. Conversely, anyone who knows enough to know *that* does indeed possess a set of extensive epistemological beliefs which he is not putting in doubt at all.

Descartes's failure is complex. First of all he does not recognize that among the features of the universe which he is not putting in doubt is his own capacity not only to use the French and the Latin languages, but even to express the same thought in both languages; and as a consequence he does not put in doubt what he has inherited in and with these languages, namely, a way of ordering both thought and the world expressed in a set of meanings. These meanings have a history; seventeenth-century Latin bears the marks of having been the language of scholasticism, just as scholasticism was itself marked by the influence of twelfth and thirteenth-century Latin. It was perhaps because the presence of his languages was invisible to the Descartes of the *Discours* and the *Meditationes* that he did not notice either what Gilson pointed out in detail, how much of what he took to be the spontaneous reflections of his own mind was in fact a repetition of sentences and phrases from his school textbooks. Even the *Cogito* is to be found in Saint Augustine.

What thus goes unrecognized by Descartes is the presence not only of languages, but of a tradition, a tradition that he took himself to have successfully disowned. It was from this tradition that he inherited his epistemological ideals. For at the core of this tradition was a conception of knowledge as analogous to vision: the mind's eye beholds its objects by the light of reason. At the same time this tradition wishes to contrast sharply knowledge and sense-experience, including visual experience. Hence there is metaphorical incoherence at the heart of every theory of knowledge in this Platonic and Augustinian tradition, an incoherence which Descartes unconsciously reproduces. Thus Descartes also cannot recognize that he is responding not only to the timeless demands of skepticism, but to a highly specific crisis in one particular social and intellectual tradition.

One of the signs that a tradition is in crisis is that its accustomed ways for relating *seems* and *is* begin to break down. Thus the pressures of skepticism become more urgent and attempts to achieve the impossible, to refute skepticism once and for all, become projects of central importance to the culture and not mere private academic enterprises. Just this happens in the late middle ages and the sixteenth century. Inherited modes of ordering experience reveal too many rival possibilities of interpretation. It is no accident that there is a multiplicity of rival interpretations of both the thought and the lives of such figures as Luther and Machiavelli in a way that there is not for such equally rich and complex figures as Abelard and Aquinas. Ambiguity, the possibility of alternative interpretations, becomes a central feature of human character and activity. *Hamlet* was Shakespeare's brilliant mirror to the age, and the difference between Shakespeare's account of epistemological crises and Descartes's is now clear. For Shakespeare invites us to reflect on the crisis of the self as a crisis in the tradition which has formed the self; Descartes by his attitude to history and to fable has cut himself off from the possibility of recognizing himself; he has invented an unhistorical self-endorsed self-consciousness and tries to describe his epistemological crisis in terms of it. Small wonder that he misdescribes it.

Consider by contrast Galileo. When Galileo entered the scientific scene, he was confronted by much more than the conflict between the Ptolemaic and Copernican astronomies. The Ptolemaic system was itself inconsistent both with the widely accepted Platonic requirements for a true astronomy and with the perhaps even more widely accepted principles of Aristotelian physics. These latter were in turn inconsistent with the findings over two centuries of scholars at Oxford, Paris, and Padua about motion. Not surprisingly, instrumentalism flourished as a philosophy of science and Osiander's instrumentalist reading of Copernicus was no more than the counterpart to earlier instrumentalist interpretations of the Ptolemaic system. Instrumentalism, like attempts to refute skepticism, is characteristically a sign of a tradition in crisis.

Galileo resolves the crisis by a threefold strategy. He rejects instrumentalism; he reconciles astronomy and mechanics; and he redefines the place of experiment in natural science. The old mythological empiricist view of Galileo saw him as appealing to the facts against Ptolemy and Aristotle; what he actually did was to give a new account of what an appeal to the facts had to be. Wherein lies the superiority of Galileo to his predecessors? The answer is that he, for the first time, enables the work of all his predecessors to be evaluated by a common set of standards. The contributions of Plato, Aristotle, the scholars at Merton College, Oxford, and at Padua, and the work of Copernicus himself at last all fall into place. Or, to put matters in another and equivalent way: the history of late medieval science can finally be cast into a coherent narrative. Galileo's work implies a rewriting of the narrative which constitutes the scientific tradition. For it now became retrospectively possible to identify those anomalies which had been genuine counterexamples to received theories from those anomalies which could justifiably be dealt with by ad hoc explanatory devices or even ignored. It also became retrospectively possible to see how the various elements of various theories had fared in their encounters with other theories and with observations and experiments, and to understand how the form in which they had survived bore the marks of those encounters. A theory always bears the marks of its passage through time and the theories with which Galileo had to deal were no exception.

Let me cast the point which I am trying to make about Galileo in a way which, at first sight, is perhaps paradoxical. We are apt to suppose that because Galileo was a peculiarly great scientist, therefore he has his own peculiar place in the history of science. I am suggesting instead that it is because of his peculiarly important place in the history of science that he is accounted a peculiarly great scientist. The criterion of a successful theory is that it enables us to understand its predecessors in a newly intelligible way. It, at one and the same time, enables us to understand precisely why its predecessors have to be rejected or modified and also why, without and before its illumination, past theory could have remained credible. It introduces new standards for evaluating the past. It recasts the narrative which constitutes the continuous reconstruction of the scientific tradition.

This connection between narrative and tradition has hitherto gone almost unnoticed, perhaps because tradition has usually been taken seriously only by conservative social theorists. Yet those features of tradition which emerge as important when the connection between tradition and narrative is understood are ones which conservative theorists are unlikely to attend to. For what constitutes a tradition is a conflict of interpretations of that tradition, a conflict which itself has a history susceptible of rival interpretations. If I am a Jew, I have to recognize that the tradition of Judaism is partly constituted by a continuous argument over what it means to be a Jew. Suppose I am an American: the tradition is one partly constituted by continuous argument over what it means to be an American and partly by continuous argument over what it means to have rejected tradition. If I am an historian, I must acknowledge that the tradition of historiography is partly, but centrally, constituted by arguments about what history is and ought to be, from Hume and Gibbon to Namier and Edward Thompson. Notice that all three kinds of tradition – religious, political, intellectual – involve epistemological debate as a necessary feature of their conflicts. For it is not merely that different participants in a tradition disagree; they also disagree as to how to characterize their disagreements and as to how to resolve them. They disagree as to what constitutes appropriate reasoning, decisive evidence, conclusive proof.

A tradition then not only embodies the narrative of an argument, but is only to be recovered by an argumentative retelling of that narrative which will itself be in conflict with other argumentative retellings. Every tradition therefore is always in danger of lapsing into incoherence and when a tradition does so lapse it sometimes can only be recovered by a revolutionary reconstitution. Precisely such a reconstitution of a tradition which had lapsed into incoherence was the work of Galileo.

It will now be obvious why I introduced the notion of tradition by alluding negatively to the viewpoint of conservative theorists. For they, from Burke onwards, have wanted to counterpose tradition and reason and tradition and revolution. Not reason, but prejudice, not revolution, but inherited precedent, these are Burke's key oppositions. Yet, if the present arguments are correct, it is traditions which are the bearers of reason, and traditions at certain periods actually require and need revolutions for their continuance. Burke saw the French Revolution as merely the negative overthrow of all that France had been and many French conservatives have agreed with him, but later thinkers as different as Péguy and Hilaire Belloc were able retrospectively to see the great revolution as reconstituting a more ancient France, so that Jeanne D'Arc and Danton belong within the same single, if immensely complex, tradition.

Conflict arises, of course, not only within, but between traditions and such a conflict tests the resources of each contending tradition. It is yet another mark of a degenerate tradition that it has contrived a set of epistemological defences which enable it to avoid being put in question or at least to avoid recognizing that it is being put in question by rival traditions. This is, for example, part of the degeneracy of modern astrology, of some types of psychoanalytic thought, and of liberal Protestantism. Although, therefore, any feature of any tradition, any theory, any practice, any belief can always under certain conditions be put in question, the practice of putting in question, whether within a tradition or between traditions, itself always requires the context of a tradition. Doubting is a more complex activity than some skeptics have realized. To say to oneself or to someone else "Doubt all your beliefs here and now" without reference to historical or autobiographical context is not meaningless; but it is an invitation not to philosophy, but to mental breakdown, or rather to philosophy as a means of mental breakdown. Descartes concealed from himself, as we have seen, an unacknowledged background of beliefs, which rendered what he was doing intelligible and sane to himself and to others. But, supposing that he had put that background in question too, what would have happened to him then?

We are not without clues, for we do have the record of the approach to breakdown in the life of one great philosopher. "For I have already shown," wrote Hume,

> that the understanding, when it acts alone, and according to its most general principles, entirely subverts itself, and leaves not the lowest degree of evidence in any proposition, either in philosophy or common life . . .The *intense* view of these manifold contradictions and imperfections in human reason has so wrought upon me, and heated my brain, that I am ready to reject all belief and reasoning, and can look upon no opinion even as more probable or likely than another. Where am I, or what? From what causes do I derive my existence, and to what condition shall I return? Whose favour shall I court, and whose anger must I dread? What beings surround me? And on whom have I any influence? I am confronted with all these questions, and begin to fancy myself in the most deplorable condition imaginable, inviron'd with the deepest darkness and utterly depriv'd of the use of every member and faculty.[3]

We may note three remarkable features of Hume's cry of pain. First, like Descartes, he has set a standard for the foundations of his beliefs which could not be met; hence all beliefs founder equally. He has not asked if he can find good reason for preferring in the light of the best criteria of reason and truth available some among others out of the limited range of possibilities of belief which actually confront him in this particular cultural situation. Secondly, he is in consequence thrust back without any possibility of answers upon just that range of questions that, according to Bettelheim, underlie the whole narrative enterprise in early childhood. There is indeed the most surprising and illuminating correspondence between the questions which Bettelheim ascribes to the child and the questions framed by the adult, but desperate, Hume. For Hume by his radical skepticism had lost any means of making himself – or others – intelligible to himself, let alone to others. His very skepticism itself had become unintelligible.

There is perhaps a possible world in which "empiricism" would have become the name of a mental illness, while "paranoia" would be the name of a well-accredited theory of knowledge. For in this world empiricists would be consistent and unrelenting – unlike Hume – and they would

---

3 David Hume, *Treatise of Human Nature*, ed. L. A. Selby-Bigge (London: Oxford University Press, 1941), Bk. I, iv, vii, pp. 267–69.

thus lack any means to order their experience of other people or of nature. Even a knowledge of formal logic would not help them; for until they knew how to order their experiences they would possess neither sentences to formalize nor reasons for choosing one way of formalizing them rather than another. Their world would indeed be reduced to that chaos which Bettelheim perceives in the child at the beginning of the oedipal phase. Empiricism would lead not to sophistication, but to regression. Paranoia by contrast would provide considerable resources for living in the world. The empiricist maxims, such as "Believe only what can be based upon sense-experience" and Occam's razor, would leave us bereft of all generalizations and therefore of all attitudes towards the future (or the past). They would isolate us in a contentless present. But the paranoid maxims "Interpret everything which happens as an outcome of envious malice" and "Everyone and everything will let you down" receive continuous confirmation for those who adopt them. Hume cannot answer the question: "What beings surround me?" But Kafka knew the answer to this very well:

In fact the clock has certain personal relationships to me, like many things in the room, save that now, particularly since I gave notice – or rather since I was given notice – . . . they seem to be beginning to turn their backs on me, above all the calendar . . . Lately it is as if it had been metamorphosed. Either it is absolutely uncommunicative – for example, you want its advice, you go up to it, but the only thing it says is "Feast of the Reformation" – which probably has a deeper significance, but who can discover it? – or, on the contrary, it is nastily ironic.[4]

So in this possible world they will speak of Hume's Disease and of Kafka's Theory of Knowledge. Yet is this possible world so different from that which we inhabit? What leads us to segregate at least some types of mental from ordinary, sane behavior is that they presuppose and embody ways of interpreting the natural and social world which are radically discordant with our customary and, as we take it, justified modes of interpretation. That is, certain types of mental illness seem to presuppose rival theories of knowledge. Conversely every theory of knowledge offers us schemata for accepting some interpretations of the natural and social world rather than others. As Hamlet discovered earlier, the categories of psychiatry and of epistemology must be to some extent interdefinable.

---

4 Letter to his sister Valli, in *I Am a Memory Come Alive*, ed. Nahum N. Glatzer (New York: Schocken Books, 1974), p. 235.

### III

What I have been trying to sketch is a number of conceptual connections, which link such notions as those of an epistemological crisis, a narrative, a tradition, natural science, skepticism, and madness. There is one group of recent controversies in which the connections between these concepts has itself become a central issue. I refer, of course, to the debates which originated from the confrontation between Thomas Kuhn's philosophy of science and the views of those philosophers of science who in one way or another are the heirs of Sir Karl Popper. It is not surprising therefore that the positions which I have taken should imply conclusions about those controversies, conclusions which are not quite the same as those of any of the major participants. Yet it is perhaps because the concepts which I have examined, such as those of an epistemological crisis and of the relationship of conflict to tradition, have provided the largely unexamined background to the recent debates that their classification may in fact help to resolve some of the issues. In particular I shall want to argue that the positions of some of the most heated antagonists – notably Thomas Kuhn and Imre Lakatos – can be seen to converge once they are emended in ways towards which the protagonists themselves have moved in their successive reformulations of their positions.

One very striking new conclusion will however also emerge. For I shall want to reinforce my thesis that dramatic narrative is the crucial form for the understanding of human action and I shall want to argue that natural science can be a rational form of enquiry, if and only if the writing of a true dramatic narrative – that is, of history understood in a particular way – can be a rational activity. Scientific reason turns out to be subordinate to, and intelligible only in terms of, historical reason. And, if this is true of the natural sciences, a fortiori it will be true also of the social sciences.

It is therefore sad that social scientists have all too often treated the work of writers such as Kuhn and Lakatos as sacred texts. Kuhn's writing in particular has been invoked time and again – for a period of ten years or so, a ritual obeisance towards Kuhn seems almost to have been required in presidential addresses to the American Political Science Association – to license the theoretical failures of social science. But while Kuhn's work uncriticized – or for that matter Popper or Lakatos uncriticized – represents a threat to our understanding, Kuhn's work criticized provides an illuminating application for the ideas which I have been defending.

My criticisms of Kuhn will fall into three parts. In the first I shall suggest that his earlier formulations of his position are much more radically flawed than he himself has acknowledged. I shall then argue that it is his failure to recognize the true character of the flaws in his earlier formulations which leads to the weakness of his later revisions. Finally I shall suggest a more adequate form of revision.

What Kuhn originally presented was an account of epistemological crises in natural science which is essentially the same as the Cartesian account of epistemological crises in philosophy. This account was super-imposed on a view of natural science which seems largely indebted to the writings of Michael Polanyi (Kuhn nowhere acknowledges any such debt). What Polanyi had shown is that all justification takes place within a social tradition and that the pressures of such a tradition enforce often unrecognized rules by means of which discrepant pieces of evidence or difficult questions are often put on one side with the tacit assent of the scientific community. Polanyi is the Burke of the philosophy of science and I mean this analogy with political and moral philosophy to be taken with great seriousness. For all my earlier criticisms of Burke now become relevant to the criticism of Polanyi. Polanyi, like Burke, under-stands tradition as essentially conservative and essentially unitary. (Paul Feyerabend – at first sight so different from Polanyi – agrees with Polanyi in his understanding of tradition. It is just because he so understands the scientific tradition that he rejects it and has turned himself into the Emerson of the philosophy of science; not "Every man his own Jesus," but "Every man his own Galileo.") He does not see the omnipresence of conflict – sometimes latent – within living traditions. It is because of this that anyone who took Polanyi's view would find it very difficult to explain how a transition might be made from one tradition to another or how a tradition which had lapsed into incoherence might be reconstructed. Since reason operates only *within* traditions and communities according to Polanyi, such a transition or a reconstruction could not be a work of reason. It would have to be a leap in the dark of some kind.

Polanyi never carried his argument to this point. But what is a major difficulty in Polanyi's position was presented by Kuhn as though it were a discovery. Kuhn did of course recognize very fully how a scientific tradition may lapse into incoherence. And he must have (with Feyerabend) the fullest credit for recognizing in an original way the significance and character of incommensurability. But the conclusions which he draws, namely that "proponents of competing paradigms must fail to make complete contact with each other's viewpoints" and that the transition from one paradigm to another requires a "conversion experience" do not follow from his premises concerning incommensurability. These last are threefold: adherents of rival paradigms during a scientific revolution disagree about what set of problems provides the test for a successful paradigm in that particular scientific situation; their theories embody very different concepts; and they "see different things when they look from the same point in the same direction." Kuhn concludes that "just because it is a transition between incommensurables" the transition cannot be made step by step; and he uses the expression "gestalt switch" as well as "conversion experience." What is important is that Kuhn's account of the transition requires an additional premise. It is not just that the adherents of rival paradigms disagree, but that *every* relevant area of rationality is invaded by that disagreement. It is not just that threefold incommensurability is present, but rationality apparently cannot be present in any other form. Now this additional premise would indeed follow from Polanyi's position and if Kuhn's position is understood as presupposing something like Polanyi's, then Kuhn's earlier formulations of his positions become all too intelligible; and so do the accusations of irrationalism by his critics, accusations which Kuhn professes not to understand.

What follows from the position thus formulated? It is that scientific revolutions are epistemological crises understood in a Cartesian way. Everything is put in question simultaneously. There is no rational continuity between the situation at the time immediately preceding the crisis and any situation following it. To such a crisis the language of evangelical conversion would indeed be appropriate. We might indeed begin to speak with the voice of Pascal, lamenting that the highest achievement of reason is to learn what reason cannot achieve. But of course, as we have already seen, the Cartesian view of epistemological crises is false; it can never be the case that everything is put in question simultaneously. That would indeed lead to large and unintelligible lacunas not only in the history of practices, such as those of the natural sciences, but also in the personal biographies of scientists.

Moreover Kuhn does not distinguish between two kinds of transition experience. The experience which he is describing seems to be that of the person who having been thoroughly educated into practices defined and informed by one paradigm has to make the transition to a form of scientific practice defined and informed by some radically different paradigm. Of this kind of person what Kuhn asserts may well on occasion be true. But such a scientist has been invited to make a transition that must already have been made by others; the very characterization of his situation presupposes that the new paradigm is already operative, even although the old still retains some of its power. But what of the very different type of transition made by those scientists who first invented or discovered the new paradigm? Here Kuhn's divergences from Polanyi ought to have saved him from his original Polanyi-derived conclusion. For Kuhn does recognize very fully and insightfully how traditions lapse into incoherence. What some, at least, of those who have been educated into such a tradition may come to recognize is the gap between its *own* epistemological ideals and its actual practices. Of those who recognize this some may tend towards skepticism and some towards instrumentalism. Just this, as we have already seen, characterized late medieval and sixteenth-century science. What the scientific genius, such as Galileo, achieves in his transition, is by contrast not only a new way of understanding nature, but also and inseparably a new way of understanding the old science's way of understanding nature. It is because only from the standpoint of the new science can the inadequacy of the old science be characterized that the new science is taken to be more adequate than the old. It is from the standpoint of the new science that the continuities of narrative history are reestablished.

Kuhn has of course continuously modified his earlier formulations and to some degree his position. He has in particular pointed out forcefully to certain of his critics that it is they who have imputed to him the thesis that scientific revolutions are nonrational or irrational events, a conclusion which he has never drawn himself. His own position is "that, if history or any other empirical discipline leads us to believe that the development of science depends essentially on behavior that we have previously thought to be irrational, then we should conclude not that science is irrational, but that our notion of rationality needs adjustment here and there."

Feyerabend, however, beginning from the same premises as Kuhn, has drawn on his own behalf the very conclusion which Kuhn so abhors. And surely if scientific revolutions were as Kuhn describes them, if there were nothing more to them than such features as the threefold incommensurability, Feyerabend would be in the right. Thus if Kuhn is to, as he says, "adjust" the notion of rationality, he will have to find the expression of rationality in some feature of scientific revolutions to which he has not yet attended. Are there such features? Certainly, but they belong precisely to the history of these episodes. It is more rational to accept one theory or paradigm and to reject its predecessor when the later theory or paradigm provides a standpoint from which the acceptance, the life-story, and the rejection of the previous theory or paradigm can be recounted in more intelligible historical narrative than previously. An understanding of the concept of the superiority of one physical theory to another requires a prior understanding of the concept of the superiority of one historical narrative to another. The theory of scientific rationality has to be embedded in a philosophy of history.

What is carried over from one paradigm to another are epistemological ideals and a correlative understanding of what constitutes the progress of a single intellectual life. Just as Descartes's account of his own epistemological crisis was only possible by reason of Descartes's ability to recount his own history, indeed to live his life as a narrative about to be cast into a history – an ability which Descartes himself could not recognize without falsifying his own account of epistemological crises – so Kuhn and Feyerabend recount the history of epistemological crises as moments of almost total discontinuity without noticing the historical continuity which makes their own intelligible narratives possible. Something very like this position, which I have approached through a criticism of Kuhn, was reached by Lakatos in the final stages of his journey away from Popper's initial positions.

If Polanyi is the Burke of the philosophy of science and Feyerabend the Emerson, then Popper himself or at least his disciples inherit the role of J. S. Mill, as Feyerabend has already noticed. The truth is to be approached through the free clash of opinion. The logic of the moral sciences is to be replaced by *Logik der Forschung*. Where Burke sees reasoning only within the context of tradition and Feyerabend sees the tradition as merely repressive of the individual, Popper has rightly tried to make something of the notion of rational tradition. What hindered this attempt was the Popperian insistence on replacing the false methodology of induction by a new methodology. The history of Popper's own thought and of that of his most gifted followers was for quite a number of years the history of successive attempts to replace Popper's original falsificationism by some more adequate version, each of which in turn fell prey to counterexamples from the history of science. From one point of view the true heir of these attempts is Feyerabend; for it is he who has formulated the completely general thesis that all such attempts were doomed to failure. There is *no* set of rules as to how science *must* proceed and all attempts to discover such a set founder in their encounter with actual history of science. But when Lakatos had finally accepted this he moved on to new ground.

In 1968, while he was still a relatively conservative Popperian, Lakatos had written: "the appraisal is rather of a *series* of *theories* than of an isolated *theory*." He went on to develop this notion into that of a research program. The notion of a research program is of course oriented to the future and there was therefore a tension between Lakatos's use of this notion and his recognition that it is only retrospectively that a series of theories can be appraised. In other words what is appraised is always a history; for it is not just a series of theories which is appraised, but a series which stand in various complex relationships to each other through time which is appraised. Indeed what we take to be a single theory is always "a growing developing entity, one which cannot be considered as a static structure."[5] Consider for example the kinetic theory of gases. If we read the scientific textbooks for any particular period we shall find presented an entirely ahistorical account of the theory. But if we read all the successive textbooks we shall learn not only that the kinetic theory of 1857 was not quite that of 1845 and that the kinetic theory of 1901 is neither that of 1857 nor that of 1965. Yet at each stage the theory bears the marks of its previous history, of a series of encounters with confirming or anomalous facts, with other theories, with metaphysical points of view, and so on. The kinetic theory not merely has, but is a history, and to evaluate it is to evaluate how it has fared in this large variety of encounters. Which of these have been victories, which defeats, which compounds of victory and defeat, and which are not classifiable under any of these headings? To evaluate a theory, or rather to evaluate a series of theories, one of Lakatos's research programs, is precisely to write that history, that narrative of defeats and victories.

This is what Lakatos recognized in his paper on "History of Science and Its Rational Reconstructions."[6] Methodologies are to be assessed by the extent to which they satisfy historiographical criteria; the best scientific methodology is that which can supply the best rational reconstruction of the history of science and for different episodes different methodologies may be successful. But in talking not about history, but about rational reconstruction Lakatos had still not exorcized the ghosts of the older Popperian belief in methodology; for he was quite prepared to envisage the rational reconstruction as "a caricature" of actual history. Yet it matters enormously that our histories should be true, just as it matters that our scientific theorizing makes truth one of its goals.

5 Richard M. Burian, "More than a Marriage of Convenience: On the Inextricability of History and Philosophy of Science," unpublished paper, p. 38.
6 I. Lakatos, "History of Science and Its Rational Reconstructions," in *Boston Studies in the Philosophy of Science*, vol. VIII, ed. Roger C. Buck and Robert S. Cohen (Dordrecht: D. Reidel, 1971).

Kuhn interestingly and perhaps oddly insists against Lakatos on truth in history (he accuses Lakatos of replacing genuine history by "philosophy fabricating examples"), but yet denies any notion of truth to natural science other than that truth which attaches to solutions to puzzles and to concrete predictions. In particular he wants to deny that a scientific theory can embody a true ontology, that it can provide a true representation of what is "really there." "There is, I think no theory-independent way to reconstruct phrases like 'really there'; the notion of a match between the ontology of a theory and its 'real' counterpart in nature now seems to me illusive in principle."[7]

This is very odd, because science has certainly shown us decisively that some existence-claims are false just because the entities in question are *not* really there – whatever *any* theory may say. Epicurean atomism is not true, there are no humors, nothing with negative weight exists; phlogiston is one with the witches and the dragons. But other existence-claims have survived exceptionally well through a succession of particular theoretical positions: molecules, cells, electrons. Of course our beliefs about molecules, cells, and electrons are by no means what they once were. But Kuhn would be put into a very curious position if he adduced this as a ground for denying that some existence-claims still have excellent warrant and others do not.

What, however, worries Kuhn is something else: "in some important respects, though by no means in all, Einstein's general theory of relativity is closer to Aristotle's mechanics than either of them is to Newton's."[8] He therefore concludes that the superiority of Einstein to Newton is in puzzle-solving and not in an approach to a true ontology. But what an Einsteinian ontology enables us to understand is why *from the standpoint of an approach to truth* Newtonian mechanics is superior to Aristotelian. For Aristotelian mechanics, as it lapsed into incoherence, could never have led us to the special theory; construe them how you will, the Aristotelian problems about time will not yield the questions to which special relativity is the answer. A history which moved from Aristotelianism directly to relativistic physics is not an imaginable history.

What Kuhn's disregard for ontological truth neglects is the way in which the progess toward truth in different sciences is such that they have to converge. The easy reductionism of some positivist programs for

---

7  Thomas S. Kuhn, *The Structure of Scientific Revolutions*, 2nd edn. (Chicago: University of Chicago Press, 1970), p. 206.
8  Ibid., pp. 206–07.

science was misleading here, but the rejection of such a reductionism must not blind us to the necessary convergence of physics, chemistry and biology. Were it not for a concern for ontological truth the nature of our demand for a coherent and convergent relationship between all the sciences would be unintelligible.

Kuhn's view may, of course, seem attractive simply because it seems consistent with a fallibilism which we have every reason to accept. Perhaps Einsteinian physics will one day be overthrown just as Newtonian was; perhaps, as Lakatos in his more colorfully rhetorical moments used to suggest, all our scientific beliefs are, always have been, and always will be false. But it seems to be a presupposition of the way in which we do natural science that fallibilism has to be made consistent with the regulative ideal of an approach to a true account of the fundamental order of things and not vice versa. If this is so, Kant is essentially right; the notion of an underlying order – the kind of order that we would expect if the ingenious, unmalicious god of Newton and Einstein had created the universe – is a regulative ideal of physics. We do not need to understand this notion quite as Kant did, and their antitheological beliefs may make some of our contemporaries uncomfortable in adopting it. But perhaps discomfort at this point is a sign of philosophical progress.

I am suggesting, then, that the best account that can be given of why some scientific theories are superior to others presupposes the possibility of constructing an intelligible dramatic narrative which can claim historical truth and in which such theories are the continuing subjects of successive episodes. It is because and only because we can construct better and worse histories of this kind, histories which can be rationally compared with each other, that we can compare theories rationally too. Physics presupposes history and history of a kind that invokes just those concepts of tradition, intelligibility, and epistemological crisis for which I argued earlier. It is this that enables us to understand why Kuhn's account of scientific revolutions can in fact be rescued from the charges of irrationalism levelled by Lakatos and why Lakatos's final writings can be rescued from the charges of evading history levelled by Kuhn. Without this background, scientific revolutions become unintelligible episodes; indeed Kuhn becomes – what in essence Lakatos accused him of being – the Kafka of the history of science. Small wonder that he in turn felt that Lakatos was not an historian, but an historical novelist.

A final thesis can now be articulated. When the connection between narrative and tradition on the one hand, and theory and method on the other, is lost sight of, the philosophy of science is set insoluble problems.

Any set of finite observations is compatible with anyone out of an infinite set of generalizations. Any attempt to show the rationality of science, once and for all, by providing a rationally justifiable set of rules for linking observations and generalizations breaks down. This holds, as the history of the Popperian school shows, for falsification as much as for any version of positivism. It holds, as the history of Carnap's work shows, no matter how much progress may be made on detailed, particular structures of scientific inference. It is only when theories are located in history, when we view the demands for justification in highly particular contexts of a historical kind, that we are freed from either dogmatism or capitulation to skepticism. It therefore turns out that the program which dominated the philosophy of science from the eighteenth century onwards, that of combining empiricism and natural science, was bound either at worst to break down in irrationalism or at best in a set of successively weakened empiricist programs whose driving force was a deep desire not to be forced into irrationalist conclusions. Hume's Disease is, however, incurable and ultimately fatal and even backgammon (or that type of analytical philosophy which is often the backgammon of the professional philosopher) cannot stave off its progress indefinitely. It is, after all, Vico, and neither Descartes nor Hume, who has turned out to be in the right in approaching the relationship between history and physics.

# CHAPTER 2

# *Colors, cultures, and practices*

I

It is a remarkable fact that the truth or falsity of a judgment about what color some particular object or surface is is and is generally recognized to be independent of how that color happens to look to the particular person who utters that judgment. Someone looking at an object, who suffers from some as yet unrecognized defect of color vision, or who is looking in visually unfavorable circumstances, may have her or his false judgment about its color corrected by someone blind who has been told what color it is by a reliable informant.

Wittgenstein appears to deny this at one point in the *Remarks on Colour*, when he not only asserted "That it seems so *(so scheint)* to human beings is their criterion for its *being* so" (III, 98), but added that only in exceptional cases might *being* and *seeming* be independent of one another (99). If Wittgenstein meant by this no more than that it is a necessary condition of our color judgments being as they are that, for example, "we *call* brown the table which under certain circumstances appears brown to the normal-sighted" (97), then it would be difficult to disagree. But the use of the word "criterion," as I shall suggest later, is misleading. For the recognition of a color is not generally the application of a test. In puzzle cases or deviant cases we may of course consult those with certifiably normal eyesight and perhaps also have been trained in some relevant type of visual discrimination to tell us *how some object looks to them* as a test or criterion of *what color it is*. But this is so only in such exceptional cases. And notice that those who satisfy the required conditions, and therefore are able to provide the needed criterion, had themselves already been tested in respect of their capacity to recognize – without any test or criterion apart from successful recognition – what color the relevant types of objects in fact *are*. They turn out to be, like most of the rest of us, among those for whom in the vast majority of cases the distinction between *what color things or surfaces in fact are* and *what color they seem to be to me here and now* is unproblematic.

This distinction after all is a commonplace. It is unambiguously presupposed in such practical activities as those of painters, interior decorators, sign-makers, and students of the physiology of color vision, as well as by ordinary speakers. That this distinction is so widely presupposed does not of course of itself provide sufficient reason for upholding it. But I shall argue that once we have understood the nature of that distinction, we shall also understand that, although the possibility of abandoning it cannot be logically or conceptually ruled out, that possibility is one which it would be empty to entertain. In so arguing I will be unable to avoid engagement with issues whose present canonical formulation we owe to Wittgenstein, to some degree in his discussions of color, but even more in his examination of the possibility of rule-following in action or judgment by a solitary individual. And because the interpretation of what Wittgenstein says is seriously disputed, questions of interpretation will have to be faced.

My initial aim then is to identify the conditions which enable us to ascribe objectivity to color judgments, so that we can understand how we are able to agree to the extraordinary extent that we do in marking the distinction between *what color objects are* and *what color they seem to be to particular individuals in particular circumstances* and what it is that constrains us in so doing and undermines any tendency by an individual to insist upon making her or his own experience of color the sovereign test of what judgments to make. A first such constraint is provided just by that multiplicity of cooperative types of activity participation in which requires that judgments about color should be understood as true or false, independently of the experience of particular individuals.

We, for example, match the colors in fabrics, we design and interpret signals by the use of colors, we identify flags, flowers, and species of birds partly by colors, physicians use skin color in making diagnoses, weather forecasters refer to colors of clouds and skies, scientific instruments use colors as signs, and painters not only use, but extend the range of and the range of uses of colors in ways that not only require a shared vocabulary, but also shared standards of judgment in the application of that vocabulary. Any but marginal disagreements in the use of that vocabulary would render participation in such activities in anything like their present form impossible. But is this not merely a contingent feature of social life as we know it? Could there perhaps be some alternative form of life in which this constraint upon disagreement had been removed? Consider a passage from the *Philosophical Investigations* (II, xi, p. 226) in which Wittgenstein envisages this possibility:

Does it make sense to say that people generally agree in their judgments of color? What would it be like for them not to? – One man would say a flower was red which another called blue, and so on. – But what right should we have to call these people's words "red" and "blue" *our* "color words"? – How would they learn to use these words? And is the language-game which they learn still such as we call the use of 'names of color'? There are evidently differences of degree here.

What Wittgenstein invites us to imagine seems to be a society in which each person names colors without reference to how they are named by others. The more it is that such persons disagree in their naming of colors, the further they are from resembling us in our uses. But it is important that the difference between them and us is not merely a matter of the *extent* of our agreements and disagreements. For there is a second constraint upon our judgments of color, one embodied in a further set of agreements, agreements upon how to explain and thereby resolve disagreements about color, when they do arise. There are four relevant types of explanation to which appeal may be made.

When one person disagrees with another as to what color a particular object or surface is, we may be able to explain the difference in judgment as a result of inviting them to view that object or surface in the same light from the same angle of vision when placed at the same distance from that object or surface. If under those conditions they come to agree in judgment, we shall reasonably conclude that it was a failure to satisfy one of these three conditions which caused them to perceive the color of that particular object or surface differently and so to judge differently. It may be however that even in the same ideal conditions for the perception of color the two still disagree and a next step is to ask whether one of them has not as yet learned to discriminate adequately, at least so far as the color or colors of this particular object or surface are concerned. A failure of this second type of explanation will lead us then to enquire whether one or both persons suffers from some defective form of color vision, that is, is in some way – whether from physiological or psychological causes – color blind. And, if that too turns out not to be the case, then we shall fourthly and finally ask if the disagreement is not about colors themselves, but only about the names of colors, by confronting the two persons who disagree with some standard set of examples of colors and shades of colors, in which a very large number of shades are discriminated and named, so that they may discover, say, whether a particular shade which one calls "magenta" the other calls "puce," or, as in Wittgenstein's more radical example whether what one calls "red" the other calls "blue."

What we may well discover in searching for such explanations and resolutions of disagreement is evidence of some past failure on the part of one or more of those who now disagree to have learned how to discriminate and to name colors, either because she or he was not adequately exposed to the standard methods of teaching or because, although so exposed, there was some barrier to her or his learning. The standard methods of teaching and learning about colors are of two kinds. There are those involved in acquiring an elementary color vocabulary, the normal property of any child. And there are those involved in the more specialized education required of those apprenticed within particular practices – in learning how to paint ceremonial masks, say, or how to collect medicinal plants – where a wider range of discriminations is required.

So in one and the same process of learning the uses of the color vocabulary are extended and the abilities to recognize and to distinguish are developed. We learn of course not only ostensively, but also at later stages from descriptions and classifications. Having learnt "red" and "yellow," I may have "orange" explained to me not by some further act of ostension, but as a color intermediate between "red" and "yellow," and such a description may enable me to recognize and to name orange. Moreover in learning how to use one and the same vocabulary of colors different individuals often begin the learning process by being introduced to notably different sets of examples. The shade of red which provides my initial paradigm for uses of the word "red" may be very different from that which provides yours. Nonetheless as we and other speakers extend our range of uses beyond these initial examples, we do so in a rule-governed way which gives evidence of common adherence to one and the same set of linguistic rules in terms of which we order our diverse experiences of color.

What can be learned can of course always be mislearned. But what is mislearned is what can be corrected and it is in subjecting our judgments to correction by others, through admitting the force of one or more of the types of explanation invoked to explain and to resolve our disagreements with those others – particularly when those disagreements threaten our cooperative participation in those shared activities which require agreement in judgments concerning color – that we assent to the distinction between *what color objects are* and *what color they seem to me to be in these circumstances,* and so to standards of truth and falsity in judgments concerning what color objects are.

It is important that it is our common conformity to the established and standard rules governing the use and application of color words in the particular shared language in whose uses we participate which makes it possible for us to make true or false judgments concerning color. And if we misuse color words or if we judge falsely, it is our violation of these standards and rules and not the fact that we have deviated from the consensus of an overwhelming majority of speakers of our language which renders us in need of correction. Because the consensus of that majority is an agreement concerning those particular rules and concepts, any failure in respect of the relevant rules and concepts will also of course be a deviation from that consensus. And certainly were that consensus not to be maintained over an extended period of time, a necessary condition for there being established rules and concepts in this area of discourse would no longer hold. Nonetheless it is not the consensus itself which is normative for our use of color or any other words; what is normative is supplied by the rules and concepts in assenting to which the majority brings that consensus into existence.

To suppose otherwise would be a mistake. For it would make of the customary uses of the majority a particular kind of *criterion* for correct use, a criterion to which appeal could be made to determine correct use and application, independently of an ability to recognize correct uses and applications by oneself or by others. Were there such a criterion, knowing what it is would be one thing and being able to apply it would be quite another. But there is no such criterion and none is needed (compare what Wittgenstein says in *Remarks on the Foundations of Mathematics*, VII, 40 about identity: "For of course I don't make use of the agreement of human beings to affirm identity. What criterion do you use, then? None at all." See also VII, 39). When someone knows how to apply and use color words correctly, and how to recognize correctness and incorrectness in others, there is nothing else remaining for him or her to know, something that would, as it were, provide an extrinsic guarantee. True judgment requires no more than recognition. Yet this claim may be thought to encounter the following difficulty.

If there are rules governing the use and application of color words, then, as Wittgenstein insists, there must be a difference between merely thinking that you have used such words in conformity to those rules, while not having actually done so, and actually having done so (*Philosophical Investigations* 202). But if there is no extrinsic criterion, how is this difference to be established in particular cases? It is established in the same way that disagreement is resolved, that is, by appealing to one or more of the four types of explanation which I sketched earlier. One defends the correctness of one's own judgments first by explaining how one had viewed the relevant object of vision in terms of distance, angle of vision, and light, secondly by establishing that one had learned to make the relevant set of discriminations between, say, this shade of purple and that of magenta, thirdly by providing the evidence that one has no form of psychological or physiological color blindness or distortion, and fourthly by establishing one's grasp of the relevant set of names of colors. There is nothing further to be done to show that one has reported correctly what color something is rather than having been deceived by how it looks or looked to oneself.

This reply however may generate another objection. For it is obvious that as a matter of historical fact the use of color vocabularies predates an ability to formulate and make any systematic use of some of our commonest explanations of disagreement. Knowledge of the range and types of color blindness and distortion, for example, requires a certain kind of scientific sophistication, not available in all times and places. And true judgments about color antedate catalogues of colors and shades by millennia. Perhaps some aspects of these types of explanatory procedure will have been invoked from some very early stage when disagreements arose over color, but anything like appeal to them in a fully fledged form must occur at a late stage in the history of the rule-governed use of color language.

What this objection brings out is that agreement in the rule-governed use of color language requires the *possibility* of explanations of these general types being given in more or less fully fledged form. It does not require that any particular competent user of such language should be able to give them in such form. What is necessary is both that such users should be able to distinguish implicitly, if not explicitly, between the question of what color that particular object or surface or light *is* and the question of what color it *seems to me to be* and that in so doing they should recognize implicitly, if not explicitly, that true judgments about color are independent of the point of view of any particular person. In so doing they will be acknowledging that on any particular occasion the standpoint of some other person may be superior to their own in respect of the truth as to some particular judgment concerning color. It is this reference to and regard for the standpoint of other persons which renders our ordinary and normal language of colors inescapably social, one the rules for whose correct use are independent of the standpoint of any particular individual and in this way impose a certain kind of impersonality in judgments concerning color.

The corrigibility and impersonality of our judgments as to what color objects or surfaces are both arise then from the same set of established social agreements which constrain our applications of the color vocabulary. But this is not the only aspect of judgment of color which seems to be inseparable from the social dimensions of the language of colors. Judgments about colors are uttered as speech acts and the intelligibility of a speech act is a matter of socially shared understandings of what additional information about the speaker has to be supplied or presupposed if a given speech act is to be construed as an intelligible performance.

Consider the actions of someone who moves around a room judging truly of each object what color it is: "That is magenta," she or he says, and then "That is ultramarine" and "That is emerald green." We can without difficulty imagine acquiring additional information about such a performance which renders it fully intelligible. This is, for example, a child or a foreigner trying out newly acquired English color words to make sure that she or he has got them right. Or perhaps she or he has been suffering from some type of loss of memory and is testing the extent of her or his recovery of memory by naming colors. In each of these types of case the point and purpose of making such color judgments can be discovered, so that the agent's actions can be understood as intelligible in the light afforded by that point and purpose. But suppose instead that when asked what he or she is doing, the person engaged in such a performance has no true reply to offer, except "Judging truly about color." "Judging truly about color" does not by itself without any further point and purpose name an intelligible type of speech act or indeed an intelligible action of any kind. In what does the unintelligibility of such a performance consist?

Intelligibility of actions in general and of speech acts in particular has two aspects.[1] An action is intelligible firstly if and insofar as others – socially versed others, that is – know how to respond to it. When such others are baffled by what someone else has just done, because there is no appropriate way of acting in response, it is because they are unable to bring what has been done under some description of a kind which in turn makes it understandable for them – by the standards of everyday life – to act in some particular way. A second feature of intelligible action is that in performing it not only can the agent reasonably expect to elicit a certain

---

1 See my "The Intelligibility of Action" and Arnelie O. Rorty's "How to Interpret Actions" in *Rationality, Relativism, and the Human Sciences*, edited by J. Margolis, M. Krausz, and R. M. Burian (Dordrecht: Reidel, 1986).

range of types of response from others, but she or he can find some point or purpose in doing whatever it is, within the wider range of activities and projects which that agent can recognize as her or his own. To act unintelligibly is not merely to puzzle others; it is oneself to be at a loss about what one is doing in doing this.

These two aspects of intelligibility are closely related. When someone performs an action which she or he finds unintelligible to be doing in that context – walking round the room naming colors, for example – she or he would be unable to say either to others or to herself or himself what the point of doing *that then* and *there* was. When someone finds someone else's action unintelligible, that unintelligibility can only be removed by that person's being able to explain what the point and purpose of doing *that then* and *there* was. To say "I am just doing it for its own sake" or "for no particular reason" is not sufficient to remove the unintelligibility. What has to be added is some description which makes doing *that kind of thing* on *appropriate occasions,* whether for its own sake or for the sake of something further, intelligible. If neither of these can be specified, the action will remain unintelligible. If both are successfully specified, the action will have been made intelligible by being assigned a place in the sequence of the agent's actions, so that it can be understood as standing in some specific type of relationship to what precedes it (sometimes not what immediately precedes it) and to what may follow it.

Intelligibility is thus a property of actions in their relationship to the sequences in which they occur, both those sequences of interaction in which agents respond in turn to each other and those sequences of actions which some particular agent makes. For an action to be unintelligible is for it to be uninterpretable, given the context in which it has occurred, in terms of those types of reason, motive, purpose, and intention for which the norms of the shared culture specify certain types of response, either immediately or later, as appropriate or inappropriate. Of course an action may seem unintelligible on occasion to those who observe it only because they lack the necessary information about some particular agent's reasons, matters, purposes, and intentions or about the context in which he is acting. Were that information to be supplied, the action would then be understood as intelligible. But, when all relevant information has been made available, it may turn out that certain actions just are unintelligible. So, for example, if in the course of a conversation between physician and patient, in a darkened room, the physician, between giving a prognosis for the patient's eye ailments and offering nutritional advice, was to interject "The red of the poppies stands out against the cornflowers," his utterance would be at least *prima facie* unintelligible, whereas were the same person commenting on the landscape, while looking out of the window together with someone else, the same utterance would be perfectly intelligible.

What I have suggested so far is that our uses and understandings of judgments concerning color are informed by socially established standards of corrigibility, of impersonality, and of intelligibility. And, if this is so, it might seem to follow that participation in and mastery of some socially established language are necessary conditions for any unproblematic use and application of a vocabulary of colors.

Suppose, for example, as some have done, that somewhere there is or was a solitary human language-user, deprived from earliest infancy of the society of other language-users, but herself or himself the inventor somehow or other of something that is or approximates to a language. If such a person is to make genuine judgments concerning colors, then it would seem from what has been said so far that they must be corrigible. Yet how could such a solitary and isolated person correct herself or himself in respect of judgments of color on the basis of nothing more than her or his own experiences? And if such a person is to make *correct* reports of her or his experiences of color, then it would seem that those reports must be such that any honest reporter would make the same reports of those same experiences, that is, that certain requirements of impersonality would still have to be satisfied. But how could someone restricted to her or his own experiences, and unable to refer to others for any sort of corroboration or correction, achieve such impersonality? And again, since such a person could only be talking to and for her or himself, how could we discriminate in her or his case between the intelligible utterance of a judgment of color from the mere repetition of certain strings of sounds elicited by certain repeated experiences? What would enable us to regard her or his speech acts as intelligible? How then would it be possible for such a solitary and isolated person to satisfy these three conditions conjointly, conditions of corrigibility, and of impersonality of judgment, and of intelligibility of utterance?

These are not mere rhetorical questions. To answer them we need to be able to supply a philosophically adequate account of what kind of language use might be possible for just such an isolated and solitary individual with adequately rich and repeated color experiences. Happily for us, this is an area already explored by Wittgenstein and, even if his account has turned out to be open to rival and incompatible interpretations, it remains nonetheless the best account that we possess so far.

II

Wittgenstein in the *Philosophical Investigations* clearly and unambiguously argued for the conclusion that there cannot be such a thing as a private language, if by that is meant a language not only used by only one person, but composed of expressions referring only to such private objects as her or his sensations. Colors, as we have seen, are not such private objects and so this conclusion has no bearing on my question. What does bear on it is the further conclusion, which some interpreters have ascribed to Wittgenstein, that a single, solitary individual is incapable of rule-following of the kind required for the use of anything worth calling a language.

Wittgenstein wrote:

Is what we call "obeying" a rule something that it would be possible for only *one* man to do, and to do only *once* in his life? . . . It is not possible that there should have been only one occasion on which someone obeyed a rule. It is not possible that there should have been only one occasion on which a report was made, an order given or understood; and so on. To obey a rule, to make a report, to give an order, to play a game of chess, are *customs* (uses, institutions). . .

(*Philosophical Investigations* 199).

He also wrote that it means nothing to say: in the history of mankind just once was a game invented, and that game was never played by anyone . . . Only in a quite definite surrounding do the words 'invent a game' 'play a game' make sense . . . In the same way it cannot be said either that just once in the history of mankind did someone follow a signpost. . ."

(*Remarks on the Foundations of Mathematics* VI, 43).

Everyone agrees that in these and cognate passages Wittgenstein is denying that it could ever be the case that on only one occasion a rule was followed, an expression meaningfully used, a concept given application. The sharpest of disagreements arises over what answer Wittgenstein is taken to have given *to* the question of whether it could ever be the case that only one person followed a particular rule, used a particular expression meaningfully, or gave application to a particular concept.

Colin McGinn interprets Wittgenstein in *Philosophical Investigations* 199 to be asserting "that if there is just one man then he must follow his rules more than once, but if there are many men it can be enough that *each* follows" the rules just once, or possibly not at all, since what are required, on Wittgenstein's view thus interpreted, are many occasions of rule-following, but not necessarily many rule-followers.[2] So when

---

2 Colin McGinn, *Wittgenstein on Meaning* (Oxford: Basil Blackwell, 1984), p. 81.

Wittgenstein speaks of "customs," "uses," "institutions," and elsewhere of "practices," McGinn points out that such words "are never qualified with 'social' or 'community'" and that so to qualify them "is not pleonastic."[3] So his conclusion is that Wittgenstein held that "a sign has meaning only in virtue of being (repeatedly) used in a certain way. *This thesis does not in itself carry any suggestion that meaning is inconceivable in social isolation.*"[4]

McGinn himself goes even further: "Wittgenstein is right to describe rule-following as a practice or custom only in the sense that necessarily rules are things that *can* be followed on repeated occasions, not that necessarily they are repeatedly followed. . ."[5] So neither McGinn's Wittgenstein nor McGinn would presumably see anything conceptually impossible in the notion of an isolated person inventing and using in speech only with herself or himself a vocabulary of colors. McGinn imagines someone who, surviving in conditions of complete solitariness from infancy onwards, later, while still isolated, invents sign-posts and keeps records of the weather,[6] tasks of just the kind for which color discriminations are often employed.

Norman Malcolm has retorted that in constructing his imaginary account of such a person McGinn has failed to recognize that such activities as those involved in inventing sign-posts cannot be carried through except by those who already possess a language, who are already rule-followers.[7] So the notion of an isolated rule-follower does not make sense, "because the idea of a rule is embedded in an environment of teaching, testing, correcting – within a community where there is agreement in acting in the way that is called 'following the rule'. To withdraw that environment is to withdraw the concept of following a rule."[8]

Malcolm goes on to argue that the example of an isolated rule-follower constructed by McGinn[9] presupposes that such a rule-follower already possesses a language, which presumably she or he had had to learn from someone else, so that the example is not after all one of a person inventing a rule-following use in isolation from others.[10] A problem with Malcolm's reply to McGinn is that, if sound and if generalized, it proves too much. For if no one could ever innovate by producing a new rule-following use

---

3 Ibid., p. 78.        4 Ibid., p. 79.        5 Ibid., p. 133.        6 Ibid., pp. 196–97.
7 Norman Malcolm, *Wittgenstein: Nothing is Hidden* (Oxford: Basil Blackwell, 1986), pp. 176–78.
8 Ibid., p. 178.
9 McGinn, *Wittgenstein on Meaning*, pp. 194–97.
10 Malcolm, *Nothing Is Hidden*, pp. 176–78.

of language, unless he or she already possessed language, how could language ever begin? If Malcolm's argument is sound, it raises difficult questions about the possibility of a first introduction of language. It is indeed likely that at the very first beginning of language use, whenever and wherever that was, there were behaviors which approximated to language use before there was genuine rule-following; but there clearly was a time before *any* language and a time when genuine language use had already begun. And how such a transition could have taken place seems puzzling on Malcolm's view. Is McGinn then right on the point of philosophical substance? (Whether it is Malcolm or McGinn who is right as to the interpretation of Wittgenstein is a question which for the moment I leave open.)

The difficulties which McGinn's view confronts can best be brought out by returning to the question of whether or not the three conditions which would have to be satisfied, if a solitary and isolated person were to be held to possess and to be able to use a genuine language of colors, can be jointly satisfied. It will however illuminate what is at stake in McGinn's position if we begin by considering only the first two of these, the requirement that genuine uses of a color vocabulary must be corrigible and that therefore the isolated and solitary person must possess the resources necessary for correcting both her or his misuses of language and own false judgments, and the requirement that judgments about color should be impersonal.

Earlier I connected the need for judgments about color to be corrigible with their impersonality as instances of rule-following. What assures us both in such judgments and more generally that something is a case of actual rather than merely apparent rule-following ("to *believe* one is following a rule is not following the rule," *Philosophical Investigations* 202, as translated by Malcolm) in the making of a particular judgment is, as I noted, that it would be judged to be so by *anyone* with the requisite competence and integrity, no matter what their standpoint. An impartial and impersonal spectator would so judge concerning it. It is only insofar as we accord this impersonal character and a correspondingly impersonal authority to rules that we treat them as *rules*.

In the case of judgments about color the distorting partialities to be overcome are those of perceptual standpoint and the incompetences to be remedied those derived from deficiencies of color vision or vocabulary. With other types of judgment it is other types of partiality and incompetence which have to be identified and overcome from some similarly impersonal point of view. The question therefore is: how is it possible for us to assume a properly impersonal standpoint with regard to our own judgments, both generally and in respect of judgments concerning colors?

If an impersonal standpoint is one that is neutral between the claims and interest of different actual persons, it cannot be the standpoint of McGinn's socially isolated person. But McGinn could of course reply that the impersonality of rule-following only requires always being open to the *possibility* of correction by others and that these others need be no more than *possible* others. McGinn's solitary individual might therefore be able to provide for these possibilities, even in isolation from all actual others. She or he would be open to the possibility of self-correction by imagined, possible others, that is in fact by her or himself, in the imagined role of a possible other. A set of counterfactuals, specifying how she or he would react, were he or she to be challenged by others, would be true of her or him. But they could remain counterfactual without damaging her or his status as a rule-follower.

What this brings out is the way in which the development of McGinn's position places continually increasing demands on the conceptual imagination. McGinn says on an allied point: "I am merely reporting my intuitions of logical possibility," acknowledges that other philosophers do not share his intuitions, but asserts that "they are all one has to go on in deciding modal questions."[11] His position thus formulated seems to entail that between the contingent impossibilities disclosed by empirical enquiry and purely logical possibility there is no stopping-place in conceptual investigations concerned with determining possibilities. That this is false is suggested by reopening the question of the joint satisfiability by a solitary and isolated language-user of the three conditions for the use of a language of colors.

Consider first one further aspect of the first, the corrigibility condition. David Pears in arguing that Wittgenstein may not have rejected the possibility of a solitary language-user has pointed out that, in actual linguistic communities, not only do language-users correct their judgments by reference to two "stabilizing resources" – "standard objects and reassuring interlocutors" – but their use of these resources is such that appeal to one is not independent of appeal to the other.[12] It is only because and insofar as we suppose that other members of our community have continued to use the same words of the same objects that we are able to appeal to their use to confirm or correct our own. And of course it is

11 McGinn, *Wittgenstein on Meaning*, p. 197.
12 David Pears, *The False Prison*, vol. II (Oxford: Clarendon Press, 1988), pp. 368–69.

also only because and insofar as we are assured that those objects have continued to possess the properties which make it correct to use those same words of them that we are able so to appeal. In our normal procedures the appeal to reassuring interlocutors and the appeal to standard objects stand or fall together.

With our imagined solitary, isolated person it is quite otherwise. For in her or his case there are no reassuring interlocutors. So it is not only that the appeal to standard objects is detached from that to interlocutors, but that by being made independent it is itself weakened. In this weaker form can it still provide the required degree and kind of corrigibility? Before I propose an answer to this question, there is another type of difficulty to be considered.

Any use of a color vocabulary which is more than minimal involves, as I noticed earlier, the rule-governed extension of the use and application of color words beyond the situations and the types of situation in which they were first used; any use of a color vocabulary which achieves intelligible utterance requires the performance of a certain *range* of intelligible speech acts in giving expression to judgments about colors. What degree of extension and what precise range I leave open. There is even so a tension between the satisfaction of these two requirements and the satisfaction of the corrigibility condition. For the larger the degree of such extensions of use, and the wider the range of intelligible speech-acts, the greater the need to show and the greater the difficulty in showing that the corrigibility condition is sufficiently strong and adequately satisfied. So an isolated, solitary, speaker capable of only the most limited judgments expressed in a very narrow range of speech acts would need far less in the way of resources of corrigibility than does a normal speaker in an ordinary linguistic community.

Does this rescue McGinn's thesis from its difficulties? I think not and for a crucial reason. In trying to envisage McGinn's isolated, solitary speaker, whether as a speaker of the language of colors or more generally, we have moved too far away from the actualities of language use, as we know them, to be able to say with any precision or confidence what is possible and what is not. In so contending I am relying upon a very different conception of possibility from McGinn's.

The paradigmatic example of the possible is the actual. As we in any particular type of case move away from the actual in thought, carefully stripping it of its properties one by one we move from imagined cases in which we can clearly say "Although never actual this type of person, thing or state of affairs is clearly possible," for we can specify with some precision and confidence what would have to be the case for the otherwise merely possible to become actual, through intermediate cases to those in which so much has been stripped away that, although we have not arrived at the limiting case of the logically impossible, we no longer know what to say. And this, I want to suggest, is how we ought to respond to the case of an imagined solitary and isolated user of a language of colors.

Moreover there is some reason to believe that this position on possibility may be closer to that presupposed by Wittgenstein than that of either McGinn or Malcolm. McGinn notes that Wittgenstein asks, but does not answer the question: "Is what we call 'obeying a rule' something that it would be possible for only *one* man to do?" (*Philosophical Investigations* 199), yet goes on to impute an answer to Wittgenstein.[13] Malcolm interprets Wittgenstein's question: "Could there be only one human being that calculated? Could there be only one that followed a rule? Are these questions somewhat similar to this one 'Can one man alone engage in commerce?'" (*Remarks on the Philosophy of Mathematics* VI, 45) by asserting that "just as carrying on a trade presupposes a community, so too does arithmetic and following a rule."[14] So each converts a question into a thesis. But perhaps all that we are capable of when the conceptual imagination has been stretched to this point by this type of case are questions, unanswerable questions. We have no a priori resources for going beyond questions to answers and in acknowledging this our original question finds its answer. The concept of a solitary, isolated speaker of language, whether concerning colors or more generally, is neither that of an evidently possible type of person or of an evidently impossible type of person. It is instead a concept whose nature and status is essentially problematic.

Does it follow that all claims which assert or presuppose the possibility or actuality of someone initially isolated from or later somehow disengaged from the shared agreements of a common language, who has or fabricates in its place some language of her or his own, must be rejected? Are stories of infants reared by wolves who come to speak in a language of their own or of philosophical inventors of egocentrically defined phenomenalist languages fables always to be rejected? Nothing so radical follows. What does follow is that the onus is upon those who make such claims to show how and why in these particular detailed circumstances possibilities of which we can make so little when they are articulated only in general

---

13 McGinn, *Wittgenstein on Meaning*, p. 80.    14 Malcolm, *Nothing Is Hidden*, p. 382.

terms can be acknowledged. For until the detail has been spelled out, we do not know precisely what it is which we are being invited to declare possible or impossible. Until then we have been provided with insufficient material for our modal intuitions to address. "An infant reared by wolves who invents a language" does not as yet either succeed or fail in specifying a concept with possible application. Notice that on this view of possibility, to assert that something is possible goes further than to assert that it has not yet been shown to be impossible. To make the former assertion we need to know a good deal more than is required in the case of the latter, in McGinn's example a good deal more about how the presuppositions of individual and solitary language use are to be supplied. The agreements of shared languages give expression, just as Wittgenstein says, to shared customs, uses, and institutions. An individual who separates her or himself from or is separated from those agreements would have, as McGinn recognizes, to invent her or his own customs, uses, and institutions. But in such invention much more has to be involved than McGinn's fables recognize. My claim is not at all Malcolm's, that such invention can be shown to be impossible. It is that everything that we know about customs, uses, and institutions tells us that in different types of case different and often enough quite complex conditions would have to be satisfied; and that whether they *could* be satisfied in any particular instance needs to be shown for that particular instance. And what holds more generally also holds of questions about solitary and isolated users of a language of colors.

It is at this point that someone may protest impatiently that the examination of these Wittgensteinian arguments has been an irrelevant excursus, a misleading distraction from very different considerations towards which the arguments of the first part of this essay ought to have directed us. In that first part I identified the nature of the social agreements embodied in or presupposed by our uses of language concerning colors. In this second part I have tried to show that those agreements exemplify the constraints of shared social uses, customs, and institutions in just the way that Wittgenstein claimed that they did, that what is true in these respects of the language of colors is what is true of language in general. But, so the objector whom I am imagining will complain, the agreement in use and application of a vocabulary of colors needs to be explained quite differently, in a way that is specific to that vocabulary, namely by an appeal to the scientific facts about color and its perception.

Jonathan Westphal has argued compellingly that "there is a 'general formula' of a certain kind under which the same colours, correlated with different frequencies, fall," a formula according to which what makes yellow objects yellow is "the small amount of blue light *relative to light of the other colours* which they reflect" and "a green object . . . is an object which *refuses* to reflect a significant proportion of red light relative to lights of the other colors, including green."[15] The wavelengths of light, the facts of reflection and of lightening and darkening thus provide a way of defining color. But, so our imagined objector might proceed, the physical facts are invariant, so that what is presented by way of color for perception must be one and the same for all perceivers. The neurophysiology of color perception is also generally uniform. There is of course a small minority of defective perceivers. But given the invariant facts of color perception for the vast majority of persons and the invariant facts of the physics of color, agreement in color discrimination is physically and neurophysiologically determined.[16] And these facts are what underpin and explain agreement in color vocabulary and agreement in color judgment. The social features of such agreement are at best secondary.

Yet if this final conclusion were justified, we would expect to find something approaching complete agreement in color vocabulary not only within particular cultural and social orders, but between different and heterogeneous cultural and social orders. So that our next question has to be: do we in fact find such agreement?

III

Nothing is more striking, so it turns out, than the range of variations and disagreements which are embodied in the different schemes of color identification and classification which are deployed in different languages. So that if we were to conclude from Wittgenstein's or any other arguments – such as the argument from the facts of physics and neurophysiology – that in respect of colors we must speak as all, or almost all other human beings do, we should be mistaken. Indeed my use of the pronoun "we" up to this point has now to be put in question. Like Wittgenstein, like many other philosophers, I have used this pronoun recurrently without ever asking who "we" are. But the "we" of one social and cultural order turns out to speak very differently from the "we" of certain others.

15 Jonathan Westphal, *Colour* (Oxford: Basil Blackwell, 1987), pp. 80–81.
16 For how far this is so see not only Westphal, *Colour*, but also C. L. Hardin, *Color for Philosophers* (Indianapolis: Hackett, 1988), esp. pp. 155–86.

Consider then the range of differences between the languages spoken in different cultural and social orders in respect of the vocabulary of colors. The Dani of New Guinea have only two color words "*mili*" which is used of blacks, greens, and blues and "*mota*" which is used of whites, reds, oranges, yellow, and some kindred colors.[17] In Irish, Dinneen's *Dictionary* says of the adjective "*gorm*" that it means "blue; rich green, as grass; negro tint," as well incidentally as "noble." In Tarahumara, an Uto-Aztecan language, "*siyóname*" is used both of what we call "blue" and what we call "green."[18] In the Berber language, Kabyle, "*azegzaw*" is used of blue, green and grey.[19] Berlin and Kay have indeed been able to distinguish eight stages in the development of color vocabularies, ranging from languages, such as that of the Dani, with only two terms, to the eleven terms of contemporary everyday American English or the eleven terms of Zuni and the twelve terms of Hungarian and Russian.

Difference however extends beyond vocabulary. We noticed earlier that, when the learners of some particular color vocabulary are initiated into its use by means of paradigmatic examples, they also, insofar as they are successful learners, acquire a capacity to extend the use and application of the expressions which they have learned to an indefinite range of further examples. To this we must now add that characteristically and generally this extended set of uses includes a variety of metaphorical applications and that agreement in metaphor within any one social and cultural order is as striking as agreement in the use of color words in general. This is obvious and indeed unimpressive when the metaphors are dead metaphors, as when in current English we speak of feeling blue or seeing red. But those metaphors which are alive in a particular language-in-use give expression to a variety of beliefs about identity, resemblance, and relationship which are thus articulated in a way that makes them available for the categorization of objects and properties and happenings. And indeed in such cases the distinction between literal and metaphorical uses is characteristically drawn only from the standpoint of some external observer, in terms of what would be accounted a literal use or a meta-phorical use in that observer's language rather than in the language of the observed. So it would be if we as observers, speaking French or English,

17 Brent Berlin and Paul Kay, *Basic Color Terms* (Berkeley: California University Press, 1969), pp. 46–47.
18 Paul Kay and Willett Kempton, "What is the Sapir-Whorf Hypothesis?", *American Anthropologist* 86 (1984): 65–79.
19 Pierre Bourdieu, *Outline of a Theory of Practice*, translated by R. Nice (Cambridge: Cambridge University Press, 1977), p. 226.

were so to classify the uses of "*azegzaw*" in Kabyle. And living and powerful metaphors vary, of course, from language to language and from culture to culture, both generally and in the metaphorical uses of color terms.

A third aspect of difference is that of how color words enter into the conceptual organization of experience in combination with other types of expression, so that realities as encountered within a particular culture are categorized in one way rather than another. In consequence colors act as signs of other realities and both the nature of the color vocabulary and the place of colors in the conceptual and categorical organization of experience set constraints upon what kinds of signs they can be. So in the Kabyle language "*azegzaw*," being used of vegetables and herbs which are eaten green and raw in the spring and of the fodder which feeds the cattle, is associated with spring and with morning and is a sign of good fortune, so that to make a gift of something green, especially in the morning, is to contribute to the good fortune of the recipient.[20] But in other societies green will function quite differently or not at all in their culture's semiotic code.

So here we have a third kind of difference – albeit one closely related to the second kind – distinguishing the ways in which the language of colors is used in some social and cultural orders from that in which it is used in others. It thus seems that we have to relativize the Wittgensteinian thesis about agreement in the use and application of a vocabulary of colors to the languages-in-use of different social and cultural orders. Within each such order agreement in judgments concerning colors is just what that thesis said that it was, an inescapable feature of the use of the language of colors. But differences in color vocabulary, metaphorical extension, and categorical organization between different languages-in-use make it the case that the inescapable agreements of one social and cultural order are not the same as the inescapable agreements of certain other such orders. There is not just one language of colors which *we* speak; there are multifarious *we's*, each of whom has its own language.[21]

One response to the discovery of the extent of the differences between the color vocabularies and idioms of different languages has been to attempt to minimize the significance of those differences by suggesting that they have a superficial character. And this would presumably be the

20 Ibid.
21 My argument follows closely that of George Lakoff in *Women, Fire, and Dangerous Things* (Chicago: Chicago University Press, 1987).

response of the objector whom I imagined earlier. The physics and neurophysiology of color vision do indeed, so it is claimed by such an objector, ensure that all, or almost all human beings perceive and discriminate the same spectrum of colors and shades. It is just that in different languages that spectrum is segmented at different points, so that in some languages, for example, there is a single name for the range that includes both blue and green, while in others, as in English, there are two names, one for blue and one for green. But there is an answer to this response. For the facts about differences in color perception and discrimination turn out to be somewhat more complex than this claim is able to allow.

There are, of course, important invariances in color perception and discrimination, due to the uniformities discovered by physics and neurophysiology, and also correspondingly important uniformities in color vocabularies. A range of focal colors, primary and nonprimary, can be identified, which speakers with very different color vocabularies from different social and cultural orders can agree in identifying without much difficulty in a variety of ways; but note at once that even nonprimary focal colors, such as purple, orange, and brown, are assimilated in different cultures with different color vocabularies to different primary focal colors, so that brown will be in one instance assimilated to yellow and in another to black (consider how in neither type of language for very different reasons would we ask Wittgenstein's question: "What does it mean to say 'Brown is akin to yellow'?" *Remarks on Colour* III, 47). And in cases where two primary focal colors are given a single name, as is sometimes the case with blue and green, there are some cultures in which the paradigmatic example of the color so named, offered by native speakers, will be focal blue and others in which it will be focal green, so that in this type of case difference is not just a matter of the segmentation of a spectrum. The neurophysiology of color vision thus to some significant extent underdetermines the discrimination of color and its attentive perception, and the different color vocabularies of different cultures do seem genuinely to give expression to differences in discrimination and attention which have been embodied in socially established practices.[22]

---

22 See for a summary of the relevant empirical findings Lakoff, *Women, Fire, and Dangerous Things*, 26–30; for the most important items in the literature summarized see Paul Kay and Chad McDaniel, "The Linguistic Significance of the Meaning of Color Terms," *Language* 54, no. 3 (1978): 610–46, and Robert MacLaury, "Color Categories in Mesoamerica: A Cross-Linguistic Study," Ph.D. dissertation, University of California at Berkeley.

Moreover in experiments in which speakers of Tarahumara, a language in which, as I noted earlier, "*siyóname*" names a color which includes both what English speakers name "blue" and what English speakers name "green," were matched with speakers of English, there were significant differences between the two groups in the performance of a certain type of discriminatory task to which the Tarahumara speakers had been introduced for the first time, differences which the evidence warrants us in ascribing to the difference in color vocabulary. So language itself does at least to some degree determine attention and discrimination and, when in some at least of the languages to which I have referred – *not* including contemporary English or for that matter contemporary Zuni – the particular organization of the experience of color is integrated in some highly specific way into both those metaphorical uses of language which link color to other aspects of experience and that categorical scheme through which, for the speakers of that language, experience in general is organized, the "we" who speak that particular language will in some cases find themselves separated from the speakers of some other alternative languages with their own idiosyncratic integrative schemes by the mutual untranslatability of their languages. For in such cases there will be in their particular language sentences and sets of sentences for which there are no equivalents in some of the others. And the speakers of one of any two such mutually untranslatable languages will use such sentences to make often true, and occasionally false, judgments which cannot be made in the other.

To speak of the partial underdetermination of language by neurophysiological stimulation and of a consequent partial untranslatability may suggest that something like Quine's position is being advanced. But the differences from Quine are crucial. Quine's theses are conceptual. The theses propounded by Lakoff and others are empirical. And the same type of evidence which shows that some judgments about color are underdetermined by the neurophysiological facts also shows that other judgments about color, those concerning the primary focal colors for instance, are sufficiently determined by those facts. So that the relevant issues of untranslatability are not at all those raised by Quine.

What such untranslatability may well seem to warrant is some kind of empirically grounded relativism. If there are alternative schemes of identification and classification embodied in different, sometimes untranslatable languages of color, each with its own standards of correct use and of truth and falsity internal to it, then it may well seem that no question of judging one scheme superior to another can even arise. For the only relevant standards of judgment are those embodied in each scheme. Someone living on the boundary between two radically different cultures with distinctively different languages of color may have to choose which of the two languages to speak, but this will be a choice of standards, not a choice guided by standards. Just this kind of relativistic conclusion is reached by George Lakoff,[23] yet it is the work which Lakoff and such predecessors as Berlin and Kay have done which perhaps undermines a relativist position.

For there is at least one language of colors which seems to receive insufficient attention from Lakoff: his own, that is, contemporary English. And his own language is distinctive, although not unique, in that he is able to translate into it – or, when necessary, to provide explanations which substitute for the work of translation – every language which provides him with his evidence for relativism. Lakoff may perhaps hold that this is irrelevant, since he asserts that the "translatability preserving truth conditions" of two or more languages does nothing to show that the "conceptual systems" to which they give expression are genuinely commensurable, if on any of four other criteria – especially perhaps that provided by the ability or inability of speakers of one language genuinely to understand those of another – those conceptual systems are incommensurable.[24] But this reply would miss the point, which is that what Lakoff through his combination of translation and explanation provides is not only a high degree of translatability, but also of understanding. That is to say, we can as users of the same language as Lakoff understand the uses and applications of the color vocabularies of certain languages the speakers of which lack resources necessary to understand our uses and applications of color words. The relationship of understanding is asymmetrical. Does this in itself show that our language and, to use Lakoff's terminology, our conceptual scheme is superior to theirs? Not at all; for that to be the case we would also have to show that such understanding serves some good, which we can achieve, but of which those with certain types of limited color vocabulary are inevitably deprived.

Yet if this has to be shown might we not simply find ourselves recommitted to relativism, since on Lakoff's criteria it might well appear that different conceptual systems exhibit incommensurable difference and diversity in respect of goods as well as in respect of colors and that by the standards of one such system, for example, that shared by Lakoff and

23 Lakoff, *Women, Fire, and Dangerous Things,* pp. 334–37.
24 Ibid., p. 336.

his intended readers, this kind of superior understanding is accounted a good, while by the standards of some other such systems it is not so accounted (Lakoff himself of course says nothing about goods)?

It may well be that nothing can prevent the vindication of this conclusion if the facts of incommensurable difference and diversity are conceded *and* it is also allowed that the only standards to which anyone can appeal in judging what is a good and what is not are the standards embodied in the ordinary language of each particular group, the standards embodied in what Lakoff calls a conceptual system and I have called the language-in-use of a cultural and social order. But it is this latter contention which I now wish to deny.

IV

To what standards may we appeal against those of the particular cultural and social order which we happen to inhabit and whose language we happen to speak? To those of some practice or practices which have grown up within that order and developed to some significant degree its or their independent evaluative standards. The concept of a practice upon which I am relying is that which I introduced in *After Virtue*.[25] practices are forms of systematic human activity, each with its own goods internal to it. Practices develop through time in directions dictated by the conceptions of achievement internal to each, the achievement both of the goods specific to each particular type of practice and of excellence in the pursuit of those goods. Examples of practices are the activities of games, arts, and scientific enquiries, as well as such productive activities as farming, fishing, and architecture. Practices which use, need, and extend vocabularies of color include a variety of natural scientific enquiries, the enquiries of comparative linguistics exemplified in Lakoff's work, and, almost unnoticed in the argument so far, painting. Practices often innovate linguistically and could not progress towards their goals without so doing. How in respect of colors do these innovations relate to the established language-in-use of whatever cultural and social order within which a particular practice is being carried on?

Established languages-in-use are not themselves static. I have so far followed Brent and Kay in speaking of "the" color terms or "the" color vocabulary used in some particular language. But their work is meant to

25 *After Virtue,* 2nd edn. (Notre Dame, Ind.: University of Notre Dame Press, 1984), pp. 187–91.

teach us lessons about the historical development as well as about the diversity of such vocabularies. And it is clear from their accounts that within many languages-in-use color vocabularies have developed in remarkably uniform and systematic patterns, patterns which reflect the social use of discriminations made possible by the physics and neurophysiology of color vision. Doubtless changes in and the multiplication of discriminatory tasks promote such development in numerous ways. Brent and Kay note that "there appears to be a positive correlation between general cultural complexity (and/or level of technological development) and complexity of color vocabulary,"[26] although they are appropriately cautious about the imprecision of such notions as cultural complexity. One area – and Brent and Kay do not note this – in which such growing complexity is evidenced is in the relationship between the culture in general of some particular order and the development of a variety of practices, as the linguistic innovations required by those practices enrich or displace or otherwise transform the prior vocabularies of the general language-in-use. Consider the relationship of vocabularies of color to examples of the innovative needs of the practice of painting.

The examples to which I am going to appeal are drawn from the history of European painting, but this does not make it improper to speak of "the" practice of painting. I could as easily have drawn upon the history of, say, Japanese painting. The criteria for the identity of practices are in important respects transcultural. Initially, of course, it is within each practice, as it is situated within some particular culture and as it is developed from the resources afforded by that particular culture, that criteria are developed for what is to be accounted an example of the practice or an extension of it, rather than a corruption or a violation. It was in the light afforded by such criteria that painters in Renaissance Flanders and painters in Renaissance Italy accorded each other mutual recognition, learned from each other's innovations, and discovered in each other's achievements new standards to be surpassed. It was no different, even if more complex, when a good deal later Japanese painters discovered Western painting, and some time after that Western painters discovered Japanese art, each according to the other the same kind of recognition. It is from *within* the practice of painting in each case that shared standards are discovered, standards which enable transcultural judgments of sameness and difference to be made, both about works of

26 Brent and Kay, *Basic Color Terms*, p. 16.

art and about the standards governing artistic practice and aesthetic evaluation. Identity of standards rooted in large similarities of practice provides on occasion common ground for those otherwise at home in very different cultures and societies. They thereby acquire a certain real, if limited, independence of their own social and cultural order. This does not mean that how a practice develops within a particular social and cultural order is not characteristically affected by other features of that order. Nonetheless insofar as a practice flourishes it always acquires a certain autonomy and has its own specific history upon which it draws in developing an institutionalized tradition into which its practitioners are initiated. What those practitioners have to learn are the standards of judgment specific to that particular form of enquiry, including the standards to which appeal is made in reformulating those standards. It is through this learning that abilities to discover, and to justify claims in respect of, new truths and to correct our understanding of what has been hitherto accepted as true are acquired. The acquisition of such abilities and of criteria which enable us to distinguish those who possess them and those who do not is a precondition for according the status of objectivity to the judgments of a practice and the possession of such abilities in painting is characteristically expressed in part in powers of color discrimination.

Wittgenstein asked "Mightn't shiny black and matt black have different colour-names?" (*Remarks on Colour* III, 152). Van Gogh wrote to his brother: "Frans Hals has no less than twenty-seven blacks." Only someone who needed to learn from Hals how to see what Hals saw, by discrimination and attention of the same order, and how to represent as Hals represented, either so as herself or himself to paint or so as to look at paintings with the painter's eye, would so need to distinguish. And if there were a sufficient number of such people engaged in communicating their visual observations, so as to educate themselves further, then they would need an enlarged color vocabulary, with perhaps twenty-seven names for different blacks.

What type of color vocabulary painters need and the range of uses to which they put that vocabulary depends in part upon the tasks specific to different periods of painting. Wittgenstein doubted "that Goethe's remarks about the character of the colours could be of any use to a painter" (*Remarks on Colour* III, 90). But Turner not only towards the end of his life developed the theoretical conceptions of color, which he had both expounded in his Royal Academy Lectures and put to work in his own paintings, into a critique of Goethe's account, but also produced a visual critique of Goethe's theory in his paintings exhibited in 1843,

*Shade and Darkness: The Evening of the Deluge* and *Light and Colour (Goethe's Theory): The Morning after the Deluge Moses Writing the Book of Genesis.* Turner had read Eastlake's translation of Goethe in 1840, but he had moved in circles in which Goethe's theory was familiar much earlier, and we can see in the paintings how thinking and talking about colors informed Turner's practice.

Turner's most basic quarrel with Goethe was with the latter's treatment of darkness as nothing but the absence of light (*Farbentheorie* 744). Goethe's thesis that colors are shadows evoked a comment on the margins of Turner's copy of Eastlake: "nothing about shadow or Shade as Shade and Shadow Pictorially or optically."[27] What matters for my present argument is neither the detail of Turner's productive disagreements with Goethe nor who was right, but only that, in developing his reflections both on the merits and demerits of various paintings and on the natural world represented in his paintings, as an integral part of his practice of painting, Turner had to develop an understanding of colors in relation to light and darkness, which required the identification of a range of colors and hues, which could not have been achieved without an extended color vocabulary. Not all the discriminations required that there be names for every distinct shade; Turner's range of yellows, for example, outran the then vocabulary of color. But the use of names played an essential part in Turner's reflections. As they did, too, with such later reflective painters as Signac and Mondrian.

There are cultures which are not, as they stand or stood, open to the possibilities disclosed by excellence of achievement in painting, whether that painting is European, Japanese, or whatever. And what debars the inhabitants of such cultures from openness to those possibilities is in part the standards of discrimination embodied in too meagre a vocabulary of colors. Of course the achievement of an enriched and sophisticated vocabulary of colors as part, although only part, of the resources needed for the color discrimination of great painting is always partly the effect of the impact of a practice such as painting upon the language-in-use of a particular social and cultural order, rather than its cause. Nonetheless too impoverished a set of practices of discrimination, expressed in a severely limited vocabulary, are signs of a lack of possibility. So the inhabitants of a culture may have to come to recognize that from the standpoint of the

---

27 John Gage, *Color in Turner* (London: Studio Vista, 1969), p. 178; for a cogent contemporary development of Goethe's thesis which resolves the puzzles about particular colors posed by Wittgenstein in the *Remarks of Colour*, see Westphal, *Colour.*

goods and excellences achievable only in and through some particular type of practice their culture as it has existed hitherto has to be judged as inadequate relative to certain others. Or they may be unable to recognize this, because their culture cannot for some reason accommodate that particular type of practice. Or again acquaintance with the practice might lead them to deny, from their external point of view, that the goods of the practice can be genuine goods and to exclude the practice from their culture, as representational art has been deliberately and altogether ex-cluded from some cultures.[28] Yet from the standpoint afforded by the practice such a culture will be impoverished. It is perhaps in the capacity to recognize the poverties and defects of one's own culture and to move, so far as is possible, towards remedying it, without in the process discard-ing that culture in its integrity, that the greatness of a social and cultural order is shown.

Relativism about social and cultural orders thus fails, insofar as the standards provided by practices, such as the practice of painting, can be brought to bear upon their evaluation. The languages-in-use of some social and cultural orders *are* more adequate than those of some others in this or that respect; the vocabularies of color of some social and cultural orders are more adequate than those of some others in respect of the tasks of color discrimination set by the practice of painting. It is not that the color judgments made by the inhabitants of such orders fail in respect of truth, but that the conceptual scheme informing those judgments is inadequate to the realities of color disclosed by the practice of painting and also perhaps to those disclosed by scientific and philosophical enquiries into the nature of color.

There is thus after all a possibility of dissenting from the established linguistic consensus regarding color in our own social and cultural order and the constraints which it imposes upon our judgments of color, not through the kind of idiosyncrasies of linguistic use involved in an indi-vidual's using her or his own color words in her or his own way, but through resort to the standards of adequacy and inadequacy provided by the institutionalized norms of some practice. We can of course become aware of the contingency of any particular color vocabulary and of the variety of ways in which it might have been other than it is merely by becoming aware of the range of diversity to be found in different social and cultural orders. But that awareness in itself provides no good reason

---

28 I owe this point to Philip Quinn.

for judging either one vocabulary or one conceptual scheme partially expressed through a vocabulary superior to another. It is from the standpoint and only from the standpoint afforded by and internal to practices, such as the practice of painting, that questions about the adequacy or inadequacy of such vocabularies and conceptual schemes can be intelligibly posed, let alone answered. And of course what those who participate in the relevant practice characteristically seek to produce, if they radically put in question the vocabulary and conceptual scheme of their own culture, is the achievement of some new consensus with its own new set of constraints upon linguistic use and upon judgment.

I wish to express my indebtedness to Wilson P. Mendonça and to Philip L. Quinn for criticisms of an earlier draft of this essay.

# CHAPTER 3

# *Moral relativism, truth and justification*

## TO WHAT ARE THE MOST PLAUSIBLE VERSIONS OF MORAL RELATIVISM A RESPONSE?

Often, if not always, moral relativism is a response to the discovery of systematic and apparently ineliminable disagreement between the protagonists of rival moral points of view, each of whom claims rational justification for their own standpoint and none of whom seems able, except by their own standards, to rebut the claims of their rivals. Examples of such systematic moral conflict are not difficult to find.

Consider for example a certain kind of disagreement about marriage and divorce. Kaibara Ekken, an influential seventeenth-century Japanese NeoConfucian, followed Confucian tradition in arguing that sufficient grounds for a husband to divorce a wife include not only that she is sexually unfaithful, but also that she is disobedient to parents-in-law, or barren, or jealous, or has a serious illness, or engages in frequent gossip and slander, or is a thief. What these grounds provide is evidence of an inability to sustain the social role of a wife, as understood by NeoConfucians.[1] Further justification of these claims would be provided by considering the place of the role of wife and mother within the family, the relationship of the structure of the family to that of the social and political order and the way in which both of these give expression to a cosmic order, recognized in that practice of the virtues in which an understanding of what is appropriate for each role is embodied.

Yet to hold that a woman's being barren or jealous or a gossip provides sufficient grounds for a husband to divorce her is from some other points of view a gross error. So it is notably from the standpoint of that natural law tradition which developed out of Stoicism and Roman law through a

---

1 See Mary Evelyn Tucker, "*Moral and Spiritual Cultivation*" in *Japanese NeoConfucianism* (Albany: SUNY Press, 1989), pp. 116–18.

series of definitive medieval statements, most notably by Aquinas (on marriage and divorce see the *Commentary on the Sentences* IV 26, 1 and 39, 6), into the arguments and theses about natural law advanced by modern Thomists.[2] Had a follower of Ekken debated with someone whose conception of natural law was derived from Aquinas, disagreements about practical conclusions would have turned out to be reinforced by disagreements about practical premises, and yet further theoretical disagreements about the nature and status of the relevant practical premises.

Certainly some standards of justificatory reasoning and some premises would be, and could not but be, shared by both rival traditions. But the extent of the differences in fundamental theses and concepts in the schemes of rational justification internal to each of these two great traditions is such that no resolution of their basic disagreements seems possible. For it is to a significant extent the standards by which disagreements are to be evaluated and resolved which are themselves the subject of disagreement. The relationship of conscience to reason, as understood by the natural law tradition, provides what is taken to be a knowledge of primary practical precepts of a kind for which the Confucian scheme affords no place. And the Confucian appeal to what are taken to be shared insights into the nature of cosmic order fails to justify what the Confucian takes it to justify, when evaluated from a natural law perspective. So, neither standpoint seems to possess the resources for constructing a rational justification of its own position in terms which would make that justification rationally compelling to the adherents of its rival. There are, so it appears, no standards of justification, neutral between both traditions, available to any person simply *qua* rational person, and sufficient to provide good reasons to decide the questions disputed between the two moral standpoints. And it is not only the disputes between Confucians and natural law theorists which seem to be irresolvable in this way.

Disagreements over marriage and divorce after all extend beyond the quarrel between Confucians and natural law theorists. The utilitarianism elaborated in Britain from the eighteenth to the twentieth century warrants conclusions on these and other matters radically at variance with those of both the Confucian and the natural law theorist. And the justificatory appeal by the utilitarian to an impersonal, consequentialist measurement of costs and benefits involves quite as radical a disagreement with the practical and theoretical premises from which Confucians and

2 See M. B. Crowe, *The Changing Profile of the Natural Law* (The Hague: Nijhoff, 1977).

natural law theorists argue. The utilitarian shares this with her or his opponents, that the principles which each invokes to resolve fundamental disagreements turn out to be among those principles about which there is fundamental disagreement. Such disagreements therefore appear to be intractable and not susceptible of rational resolution.

It is perhaps then unsurprising that some should have concluded that, where such rival moral standpoints are concerned, all fundamental rational justification can only be internal to, and relative to the standards of, each particular standpoint. From this it is sometimes further and at first sight plausibly inferred that this is an area of judgment in which no claims to truth can be sustained and that a rational person therefore could, at least *qua* rational person, be equally at home within the modes of life informed by the moral schemes of each of these standpoints. But this is a mistake. In fact a relativist who so concluded could be at home in no such standpoint. Why not?

### WHAT PUTS THE RELATIVIST AT ODDS WITH THOSE ABOUT WHOM SHE OR HE WRITES?

The protagonists of those standpoints which generate large and systematic disagreements, like the members of the moral communities of humankind in general, are never themselves relativists. And consequently they could not consistently allow that the rational justification of their own positions is merely relative to some local scheme of justification. Their claims are of a kind which require unqualified justification. Aristotle articulates their claim in speaking of fourth-century Greeks who "consider themselves of good breeding and free not only among themselves, but everywhere, but the barbarians of good breeding only where they are at home, taking it that being unqualifiedly of good breeding and free is one thing, being qualifiedly so another" (*Politics* 1255a33–36). And in twentieth-century Java, according to Clifford Geertz, people quite flatly say, "To be human is to be Javanese."[3] Ancient Greeks and modern Javanese are in this respect typical human beings. What then is it about these claims to unqualified moral hegemony, so nearly universal among human cultures, which has escaped the attention of moral relativists? It is the fact that they are claims to *truth*. What is being claimed on behalf of each particular moral standpoint in its conflicts with its rivals is that its distinctive

---

3 'The Impact of the Concept of Culture on the Concept of Man' in *New Views of the Nature of Man*, ed. John R. Platt (Chicago: University of Chicago Press, 1965), p. 116.

account, whether fully explicit or partially implicit, of the nature, status, and content of morality, both of how the concepts of a good, a virtue, a duty, and right action are to be correctly understood, and of what in fact are goods or the good, virtues, duties, and types of right action, is *true*.

Two aspects of this claim to truth are important to note at the outset. The first is that those who claim truth for the central theses of their own moral standpoint are thereby also committed to a set of theses about rational justification. For they are bound to hold that the arguments advanced in support of rival and incompatible sets of theses are unsound, not that they merely fail relative to this or that set of standards, but that either their premises are false or their inferences invalid. But insofar as the claim to truth also involves this further claim, it commits those who uphold it to a non-relativist conception of rational justification, to a belief that there must be somehow or other adequate standards of rational justification, which are not the standards internal to this or that standpoint, but are the standards of rational justification as such.

Secondly, just because this is so, making a claim to truth opens up the possibility that the claim may fail and that the outcome of an enquiry initially designed to vindicate that claim may result instead in a conclusion that the central moral theses of those who initiated the enquiry are false. One might have concluded from the account of the fundamental disagreements between rival standpoints which relativists have taken to warrant their conclusion that, just because the standards to which the partisans of each appeal are to a significant degree internal to each standpoint, any possibility of something that could be recognized as a refutation of one's own standpoint by that of another was precluded. Since each contending party recognizes only judgments by its own standards, each seemed to be assured of judgments only in its favour, at least on central issues. But when one notices that the claim made by each contending party is a claim to truth, this inference is put in question.

Notice that what I am questioning here is not the initial description of the relationships between the contending parties and their modes of rational justification which misled the relativist. It may be that this description will have to be modified or corrected at certain points. But in substance it does seem to capture crucial features of fundamental moral disagreement, including the extent to which the standards to which the adherents of each standpoint make their ultimate appeal are indeed internal to each standpoint, something that explains the *de facto* ineliminability of fundamental disagreement between persons of different standpoints, often from different cultures, all of whom appear equally capable of rational judgment.

Yet if what impressed itself upon the relativist's attention is important, so equally is what escaped the relativist's notice, the claim to truth. It is these two taken together which constitute the problem with which I shall be concerned in this paper. Is it possible to bring into coherent relationship, and, if so, how, a recognition that all rational justification of particular moral standpoints is, to the extent that I have suggested, internal to those standpoints, and an elucidation of the claim to truth universally or almost universally advanced – implicitly or explicitly – by the protagonists of each of those standpoints, a claim which involves appeal to rational justification *as such*, that is, to some mode of justification which transcends the limitations of particular standpoints? To answer this question we have to begin by enquiring what conception of truth it is with which we have to be concerned.

### HOW DOES THE CONCEPTION OF TRUTH PRESUPPOSED IN FUNDAMENTAL MORAL DEBATES RELATE TO RATIONAL JUSTIFICATION?

It is already obvious that the understanding of truth involved cannot be one which equates truth with what is rationally justified in terms of the scheme of each particular standpoint. For it is precisely and only because the claim to truth involves more and other than the claim to such justification that a problem is posed. It is perhaps less obvious, but as important, that the understanding of truth involved cannot be one which equates truth with rational justification in any way. No one of course has ever claimed that "true" means the same as "rationally justified" – but a succession of pragmatist thinkers have held "that truth comes to no more than idealized rational acceptability" or that "truth is to be identified with idealized justification."[4] (Putnam has since reformulated his view in *Representation and Reality*,[5] saying that his intention was to suggest only "that truth and rational justification are *interdependent* notions.") There are three reasons for rejecting any such identification.

The first is that the notion of idealization invoked has never been given adequate content. Actual rational justifications are characteristically advanced by particular persons at particular stages of particular enquiries, while truth is timeless. And the later discovery that an assertion made by

---

4 See for these formulations Hilary Putnam in *Realism with a Human Face*, ed. James Conant (Cambridge, Mass.: Harvard University Press, 1990), pp. 41 and 115.
5 Cambridge, Mass.: MIT Press, 1988, p. 115.

someone at some earlier stage of enquiry is false is not at all the discovery that that person was not justified in making it. So that the conceptual distance between ascriptions of truth and actual justificatory practice, whether in the natural sciences or elsewhere, is very great. And those who, like Putnam in his earlier writings, have equated truth with idealized rational justification have always recognized this. But what they have not done is to supply an account of idealization which will provide what their thesis needs. For the only type of rational justification which could be equated with the relevant conception of truth would be one whereby the ideal rational justifications in question were such that we could not say of anyone, real or imagined, that her or his assertions were in this ideal way rationally justified, but not true. That could hold only of some type of rational justification, claims to which were claims that it would and could never be displaced by some superior mode of rational justification, affording different and incompatible conclusions. It would involve a notion of some type of rational justification whose properties guaranteed its status as the ultimate terminus of enquiry in the relevant area. But how this could be no one has ever explained.

Suppose however that this problem did not arise. A second kind of difficulty would remain. For where fundamental moral disagreements of the type which I have described are in question, each contending stand-point has internal to it its own scheme and mode of rational justification, one which of course shares some important features with its rivals, but at key points appeals to principles and to modes of grounding principles which are specific to it and inadmissible from the standpoints of some at least of its rivals. And to the degree that this is so, what constitutes an idealization of rational justification will also be specific and idiosyncratic to the standpoint of that particular tradition. Thus an idealization of a NeoConfucian appeal to those principles of natural order which structure the cosmos, the social order more generally, and the familial order in particular would be very different from an ideally satisfactory account in Thomistic Aristotelian terms of the epistemology of natural law, con-science, and practical reasoning and both will differ from what any utilitarian would take to be ideal rationality.

If the response to this is that ideal rational justification must be con-ceived as standpoint-independent, then once again the conceptual distance between the actualities of rational justification and the proposed idealiza-tion is too great for us to be able to understand what kind of idealization could be constructed that would be adequate. And a third consideration suggests that perhaps we should not be surprised by this. For the project of assimilating truth to rational justification, let alone that of liquidating truth into warranted acceptability, has the unfortunate effect of distorting our understanding not only of truth, but also of rational justification. Rational justifications are characteristically advanced in the context of what are or could become systematic enquiries. It is when and only when the truth about some subject matter is at issue that there is point or purpose in advancing and evaluating them. And it is when the truth about that subject-matter has been achieved that the relevant set of rational justification has served its purpose.

Practices of rational justification are thus devised and are only fully intelligible as parts of all those human activities which aim at truth: questioning, doubting, formulating hypotheses, confirming, disconfirming, and so on. This is why attempts to give an account of truth as no more than rational acceptability or rational justification, idealized or otherwise, are bound to fail. And when the activities, in the course of which rational justifications of one sort or another are invoked, disallowed, amended, and the like, are systematically organized in the form of extended and long-term enquiry, as they are in the practices of the sciences, their goal-directedness towards what is more and other than any particular form of rational justification is all the more evident.

Aristotle said that "Truth is the *telos* of a theoretical enquiry" *(Metaphysics* II 993b20–I) and the activities which afford rational justification are incomplete until truth is attained. What is it to attain truth? The perfected understanding in which enquiry terminates, when some mind is finally adequate to that subject matter about which it has been enquiring, consists in key part in being able to say how things are, rather than how they seem to be from the particular, partial, and limited standpoint of some particular set of perceivers or observers or enquirers. Progress in enquiry consists in transcending the limitations of such particular and partial standpoints in a movement towards truth, so that when we have acquired the ability of judging how in fact it seems or seemed from each limited and partial standpoint, our judgments are no longer distorted by the limitations of those standpoints. And where there is no possibility of thus transcending such limitations, there is no application for the notion of truth.

Successful enquiry terminates then in truth. If we assert that a particular statement is true, we are of course committed to a corresponding claim about its rational justification, namely that any type of rational justification which provides logical support for a denial of that statement must somehow or other be defective. But to explain truth in terms of rational justification will be, if some version of this type of Aristotelian account can be adequately defended, to invert their relationship. What importance does this have for the discussion of moral relativism?

It enables us to identify more precisely what is at issue between on the one hand the protagonists of a variety of fundamental moral standpoints and on the other the proponents of moral relativism. For if it is correct to ascribe to those protagonists a claim, sometimes explicit, sometimes implicit, to the *truth* of the account of goods, rules, virtues, duties, and the right which is embodied in each particular type of moral practice, and if moreover it is a claim which presupposes just that kind of understanding of truth which I have sketched, then such protagonists are committed, whether they recognize it or not, to defending three theses.

First they are committed to holding that the account of morality which they give does not itself, at least in its central contentions, suffer from the limitations, partialities, and one-sidedness of a merely local point of view, while any rival and incompatible account must suffer to some significant extent from such limitations, partialities and one-sidedness. Only if this is the case are they entitled to assert that their account is one of how things are, rather than merely of how they appear to be from some particular standpoint or in one particular perspective. And this assertion is what gives content to the claim that this particular account is true and its rivals false.

Secondly, such protagonists are thereby also committed to holding that, if the scheme and mode of rational justification of some rival moral standpoint supports a conclusion incompatible with any central thesis of their account, then that scheme and mode must be defective in some important way and capable of being replaced by some rationally superior scheme and mode of justification, which would not support any such conclusion.

Thirdly and correspondingly, they are committed to holding that if the scheme and mode of justification to which they at present appeal to support the conclusions which constitute their own account of the moral life were to turn out to be, as a result of further enquiry, incapable of providing the resources for exhibiting its argumentative superiority to such a rival, then it must be capable of being replaced by some scheme and mode of justification which does possess the resources *both* for providing adequate rational support for their account and for exhibiting its rational superiority to any scheme and mode of justification which supports conclusions incompatible with central theses of that account. For otherwise no claim to truth could be sustained.

So there is from the standpoint of every major moral tradition a need to resist any relativist characterization of that standpoint as no more than a local standpoint. What any claim to *truth* presupposes is, as Nietzsche well understood, a denial of any version of perspectivism. Conversely the abandonment of claims to truth, even if in the guise of a revision of our conception of truth, so that truth is to be understood as no more than an idealization of rational acceptability or justification, makes it difficult and perhaps impossible to resist perspectivist conclusions, and obviously so in the type of case in which fundamental moral standpoints are in contention. For how any particular moral issue or situation is to be character-ized, understood, and rationally evaluated – indeed whether any particular situation is to be regarded as posing significant moral issues – will depend, it must seem, upon which particular conceptual scheme it is in terms of which our own moral idiom is framed. Yet if the claims made from the rival and contending points of view are not claims to *truth*, the adherents of the different standpoints in contention will not be able to understand the central claims of their own particular standpoint as logically incompatible with the claims of those rivals.

Consider the nature of the fundamental claim made from within each rival standpoint, if it is formulated only in terms of rational justification and acceptability and not in terms of some substantive conception of truth. That claim will be of the form: "Given that rational justification is what this particular tradition takes it to be, then the nature and status of goods, rules, duties, virtues, and rights are such and such, and therefore we ought to live the moral life accordingly." But a claim of this form advanced from within, say, the Confucian tradition would not contradict a claim of the same form advanced from within either the natural law standpoint or some version of utilitarianism. It is only insofar as the claims of any one such tradition are framed in terms of a conception of truth which is more and other than that of some conception of rational acceptability or justification that rival moral standpoints can be understood as logically incompatible.

If therefore someone who rejected such a conception of truth were to reinterpret the claims made by each of the rival standpoints, so that those claims were no longer to be accounted, in the sense afforded by such a conception, true or false, then that person would indeed be entitled to draw not only perspectivist, but also and in consequence relativist conclu-sions. So long as the protagonists of such rival standpoints were each understood as claiming truth for their distinctive contentions, the possi-bility that each or all of them would in the end be rationally defeated remained open. But when that possibility no longer exists, because the rival protagonists are no longer understood as advancing logically incompatible claims, the issues between them can no longer turn on the question of which, if any, is rationally superior to its rivals. And to say this would be to have conceded the substance of relativism.

Whether or not an inference from premises concerning the facts about fundamental disagreements between moral standpoints to a relativist conclusion can or cannot be drawn therefore depends first upon whether it is in fact correct, as I have asserted, to ascribe to the adherents of those traditions an implicit, if not an explicit, claim to substantive truth for their accounts of the nature, status, and grounds of moral practices and judgment, and secondly upon whether the conception of truth to which appeal is thus made can be rationally sustained.

## HOW ARE ACTS OF ASSERTION, INCLUDING THE ASSERTION OF FUNDAMENTAL MORAL THESES, RELATED TO TRUTH?

In the case of some well-developed moral standpoints the question of whether the adherents of those standpoints are or are not making a claim to *truth* is easily and uncontroversially answered. For just such a claim has at some stage been made explicit in the course of articulating the systematic structure of the beliefs which inform those standpoints. Both the natural law tradition and utilitarianism provide examples. But how are we to judge in those cases in which, if there is a claim to truth, it is implicit in the accounts advanced by the protagonists of those particular standpoints, but not spelled out or philosophically elucidated or defended? The answer to this question is a matter of how we are to construe the acts of assertion of such protagonists, in advancing their own distinctive answers to evaluative and practical questions, and – a closely related matter – the nature of the arguments by which they support their assertions.

It is a commonplace that truth and assertion are intimately connected. But there are of course ways of understanding that connection which involve an attempt to discredit any substantive conception of truth by interpreting ascriptions of truth as nothing more than expressive endorsements of acts of assertion. Such attempts must, if they are to succeed, construe assertion in some way which makes it expressive of the attitude of whoever utters the assertion, so that truth is not a property of what is asserted, let alone a property of a relationship between what is understood by whoever utters the assertion and that which makes what is asserted true. This is not, of course, on the face of it a plausible account of how assertion and the use of truth-predicates are actually understood and employed in any natural language. And some of the most cogent of such attempts therefore are those which are presented not as analyses of how truth-predicates have hitherto been used and understood, but instead as proposals for a radical revision and reinterpretation of some of the uses and presuppositions of expressions in natural languages.

An excellent example of such proposals is Robert Brandom's "Pragmatism, Phenomenalism, and Truth Talk,"[6] which treats pragmatist accounts of truth as an "innovative rethinking" of how truth and belief are to be understood. At the core of that rethinking are the theses that "Taking some claim to be true is endorsing it or committing oneself to it" and that "Endorsing a claim is understood as adopting it as a guide to action . . ." (p. 77). What is it in the discourse of natural languages which resists such rethinking and which therefore for its proponents requires either elimination or reinterpretation? The answer is surely: just those properties of assertion and of the relationship of acts of assertion to the propositions asserted by those acts to which Peter Geach drew our attention in his definitive account of how a variety of misunderstandings of the nature of assertion are to be avoided.[7] What this and subsequent discussions by Geach have made clear is that the notion of assertion cannot be explicated independently of that of truth. It must therefore be the case – this is my inference from Geach's conclusions and he should not of course be held responsible for the use to which I am putting his arguments – that any attempt to give an account of assertion prior to and independent of an account of truth is in the end bound to fail. But without such an account the explanation of truth in terms of assertion is empty. The contemporary neopragmatist reply will presumably be some further expansion of what Brandom says in expounding his thesis that "Endorsing a claim is understood as adopting it as a guide to action, where this, in turn, is understood in terms of the role the endorsed claim plays in practical inference" (pp. 77–79). But the onus here – and one not yet discharged – is upon the neopragmatist to show that what has hitherto been understood as assertion has not been replaced by mere expressions of assertiveness.

What such a replacement could have no genuine counterpart for, I suggest, are those features which connect assertion with valid and sound inference, features already identified in "Assertion" but whose significance

---

6 *Midwest Studies in Philosophy* XII, ed. P. A. French, T. E. Uchling, Jr., and H. K. Wettstein (Minneapolis: University of Minnesota Press, 1988).
7 "Assertion," *Philosophical Review* 74 (1965): 449–65.

has been further clarified in the later development of examples, by appeal to which Geach has shown[8] that the interpretation of types of sentences involving local connectives, in particular disjunctions and conditionals, requires a notion of meaning only to be explained in terms of truth-conditions, an interpretation without which we should not be able to elucidate the difference between unqualified assertion of indicative sentences on the one hand and disjunctive and conditional uses of the same sentences on the other. In showing this Geach has reiterated the importance of what in "Assertion" he first called "the" Frege point: "que uno y el mismo pensamiento puede ser expresado tanto en una sentencia asertórica, como en una mera clausula dentro en una sentencia mas larga" ("that one and the same thought can be expressed both in an assertoric sentence and in a mere clause in a longer sentence", p. 84) adding to Frege's point Aristotle's, that one and the same premise may be asserted or used without assertive commitment in a dialectical argument (*Posterior Analytics* 72a 8–11). It is because in those different types of context the meaning of sentences put to dialectical, disjunctive, and conditional uses must be the same as when they are put to assertive uses, while the thought is treated as in one type of context assertible, but in another not, that meaning cannot be understood in terms of assertibility, warranted or otherwise. And it is because it is precisely truth which is transmitted through valid inference from true premises, that the relationship between the meaning of premises and the meaning of conclusions in such arguments, depending as it does on the truth-functional meaning of the logical operators, cannot be understood apart from the truth-conditions of both.

Simon Blackburn has argued against Geach from the standpoint of his own projectivist version of emotivism[9] that assertive form may in the case of moral and some other types of judgment be interpreted as presenting merely expressive content in a way that takes full account of "the Frege point." But this challenge to Geach's thesis is one to which it is both difficult and unnecessary to respond, until a compelling explanation has been provided of what remains so far obscure, namely how on an emotivist or projectivist view the attitudes allegedly evinced or expressed in moral judgments are related to the assertion of sentences of the relevant type. Are those attitudes to be understood as psychological states which can be adequately identified and characterized prior to and independently of such assertions? If so, then the projectivist claim turns out to be an

8 See '¿Verdad o Assercion Justificada?' *Anuario filosofico* 15 (1982): 2.
9 *Spreading the Word* (Oxford: Clarendon Press, 1984), pp. 189–96.

empirical psychological one and is, I believe, false; if not, then such assertions must be characterizable independently of any expressive function, as Geach indeed characterizes them. I have argued elsewhere[10] that emotivism may on occasion seem to have become plausible, because in a certain kind of social situation types of sentences previously used to express true or false moral judgments may have come to be used for purely expressive purposes. But when they are so used to give expression to sentiments which can only be understood as psychological residues, the meaning of such sentences cannot be explained in terms of their expressive use. Geach's thesis remains the best account of assertion that we possess.

What is the relevance of this to my own overall argument? What Geach's conclusions supply are reasons for holding that we are entitled to ascribe claims to truth to the protagonists of rival moral standpoints, even when such claims have not been explicitly articulated, just because their assertions of their various and incompatible points of view are assertions, and indeed unqualified assertions, and just because the inferences to which they appeal for support are inferences formulated by standard uses of sentences in natural languages. For claims to truth are already present in such acts of assertion and in reliance upon such inferences. *Some* of Geach's arguments in support of this conclusion have been accepted even by some of those who take a radically different view of the present state of debate about truth and justifiability, most notably by Michael Dummett in "The Source of the Concept of Truth."[11] For, although Dummett there denies what Geach has urged about disjunctions – and even entertains the possibility that Geach's account is vulnerable to emotivist criticisms – he agrees with Geach about conditionals that "Although there is indeed a way of understanding conditionals that can be explained in terms of justifiability, rather than of truth, it does not yield even a plausible approximation to the actual use of conditionals in natural language; and that is why it is their use that forces us to form an implicit notion of truth" (p. 9).

A realistic notion of truth and a conception of meaning in terms of truth-conditions are thus "deeply embedded" in our use of language, but that this is so is nonetheless "no *defence* of the concept of truth, realistically conceived" (p. 14). For this concept of truth is such that, so Dummett

---

10  *After Virtue* (2nd edn., Notre Dame: University of Notre Dame Press, 1984), chapters 2 and 3.
11  *Meaning and Method: Essays in Honor of Hilary Putnam*, ed. by George Boolos (Cambridge: Cambridge University Press, 1990).

claims, to move beyond the concept of justifiability in the requisite way, in order to acquire it, would require "a conceptual leap", for which, he says, no justification has ever been made available. The realist about truth has still to show, on Dummett's view, that such a conception of truth does not involve inescapable incoherence, the incoherence involved in holding that over and above satisfying those conditions which specify how justification can be afforded to the use of a sentence by a speaker's exercise of her or his cognitive abilities, an asserted sentence can satisfy a condition which relates to "some state of affairs obtaining independently of our knowledge" (p. 12).

What Dummett concedes to Geach's arguments – and an adequate statement, let alone critique, of Dummett's positions[12] is far, far beyond the scope of this paper – is perhaps however at least as important as what he denies about realist conceptions of truth. To what Dummett denies one might initially respond by putting in question the metaphor of a conceptual leap with its implications of cognitive inaccessibility. Certainly, as I have already argued, the concept of truth, "realistically conceived," or at least conceived so that an antirealist interpretation is excluded, cannot be reduced to or constructed out of that of justifiability, any more than the concept of a physical object can be reduced to or constructed out of that of sense-data or the concept of pain reduced to or constructed out of that of bodily expressions of pain. In each such case there have been philosophers prepared to make a reductionist objection, parallel to that advanced by Dummett. But the reductionist appears to her or himself to face the problem of a conceptual leap, only because she or he has matters the wrong way round. Bodily expressions of pain have to be already understood in terms of pain, if they are to be understood as expressions of pain and not as something else, and not vice versa, and sense-data equally have to be already understood in terms of physical objects and not vice versa. So too justifiability has to be already understood in terms of truth and not vice versa. There is no conceptual gap waiting to be crossed.

Why this is so I suggested earlier, when I characterized truth as a property of that type of understanding which is the goal and the terminus of systematic rational enquiry concerning any particular subject matter. We provide rational justifications for the assertion of this or that sentence in the course of moving towards that goal, and the evaluation and

---

12 See especially *The Logical Basis of Metaphysics* (Cambridge, Mass.: Harvard University Press, 1991).

reevaluation of such justifications is in terms of their contribution to the achievement of that goal. It is for this reason, and not at all because truth is definable or needs to be redefined in terms of justifiability, that all claims to truth have implications for justification. For if I assert that "p" is true, I am thereby committed to holding that, through the history of any set of enquiries concerned to discover whether it is "p" or "~p" that is true, either "~p" will never be supported by any scheme and mode of rational justification or, if it is so supported, that scheme and mode of rational justification which at some particular stage of enquiry appears to provide support for the conclusion that "~p" will in the longer run be rationally discredited. And in asserting that "p" is true I am also committed to holding that anyone whose intellect is adequate to the subject matter about which enquiry is being made would have to acknowledge that p.

Even a preliminary development of this kind of response, whether to Dummett's position or to neopragmatist proponents of antirealist positions, such as Brandom's, would require an account of truth as *adaequatio intellectus ad rem* which would bring together the issues concerning truth raised in recent philosophical debate and what has now been better understood about Aquinas's discussions.[13] What would such a development be designed to achieve? Its primary goal would be to exhibit the relationship between truth as the adequacy of an intellect to its *res* and the truth-conditions of those sentences which express the judgments characteristic of such an intellect. When and insofar as, on Aquinas's type of account, a particular person's intellect is adequate to some particular subject matter with which it is engaged in its thinking, it is what the objects of that thinking in fact are which makes it the case that that person's thoughts about those objects are what they are – and, in respect of the content of that thought, nothing else. So the activity of the mind in respect of that particular subject matter is informed by and conformed to what its objects are; the mind has become formally what the object is. This adequacy of the intellect to its objects – and its primary objects are, for example, the actual specimens of sodium or chlorine about which the chemist enquires, or the actual strata about which the geologist enquires, not, as in so many later accounts of mind, ideas or presentations of those specimens or strata – is expressed in the making of true judgments about those objects. And true judgments are uses of sentences which satisfy the truth-conditions for those sentences.

13 See most recently John F. Wippel, "Truth in Thomas Aquinas" I and II, in *Review of Metaphysics* XLIII, 2 and 3l, December 1989 and March 1990.

It is towards this condition of enquiry that the mind moves in its enquiries, its *telos* provided by its conception of the achievement of just such a relationship of adequacy to *what is*. A mind which has achieved such a relationship will have overcome those limitations of perspective and of cognitive resource which previously restricted it to judgments as to *what seems to be the case* here and now under the limitations of some particular local set of circumstances. And whether and how far those limitations were distorting will only have been recognized when they have been overcome. So, as I remarked earlier, claims to truth, thus conceived, are claims to have transcended the limitations of *any* merely local standpoint. Dummett in a 1972 "Postscript" to his 1959 "Truth"[14] characterized the agreements and the disagreements which ought to be recognized between realists and antirealists about truth, by saying that both ought to agree "that a statement cannot be true unless it is in principle capable of being known to be true" but that 'the antirealist interprets "capable of being known" to mean "capable of being known *by us*" whereas the realist interprets it to mean "capable of being known by some hypothetical being whose intellectual capacities and powers of observation may exceed our own"' (pp. 23–24). A Thomistic realist would by contrast characterize this difference in terms of an actual or possible progress from a condition in which the mind has not yet freed itself from the limitations of one-sidedness and partiality, towards or to adequacy of understanding. The intellectual capacities and powers of observation of Dummett's hypothetical being have to be understood, on a Thomistic view, as the capacities and powers exercised by an adequate intellect.

How then ought we to envisage the relationship between unqualified claims to truth, on the one hand, which commit those who make them to asserting that this is how things in fact are and, on the other, those qualified claims which through some explicit or implicit parenthetical reservation say no more than this is how things appear to be from some particular local point of view? (On how we are able to move from saying how things seem to be from some particular point of view to saying how they are, see Aristotle, *Eudemian Ethics* VII 1235b 13–18; on the consequences of not moving beyond saying how they seem to be from some particular point of view see *Metaphysics* XI 1062b 12–1063a 10.) Insofar as we recognize that a claim as to how things seem to be is no more than that, we are already making a claim about what is unqualifiedly the case,

---

14 Both reprinted in *Truth and Other Enigmas* (Cambridge, Mass.: Harvard University Press, 1978).

namely that this *is* how things seem to be and that from *any* point of view it ought to be recognized that this is how they seem to be from this point of view. And part of knowing how things *are* is being able to say how in consequence they must appear to be from a range of different, limited, local points of view. That is to say, if and when we know how things are, we must be able to explain how things appear to be from such local and partial points of view, in key part by appealing to how they in fact are, and it is only insofar as we have already transcended the limitations of local and partial points of view that we will be entitled to make unqualified assertions about how things must appear to be from such points of view. So it is in part at least by the extent to which they are able to provide such explanations that claims to truth are to be vindicated.

I have argued then that the refutation of moral relativism turns on the further development and rational justification of a conception of truth which is at odds with two major contemporary sets of philosophical theses about truth, both of them involving, but in very different ways, radical revisions of the commitments involved in the standard linguistic uses of the speakers of natural languages. So that for those engaged in these as yet unsettled philosophical controversies there is both much constructive and much critical work to be undertaken. But the adherents of the moral standpoints embodied in the lives of a variety of ongoing moral communities, speaking a variety of natural languages, do not have to wait on the outcome of those controversies in order to decide whether or not to persist in those affirmations and commitments which are bound up with their conception of the truth of what they assert. All that they have to ask is whether any kind of conclusive reason for not so continuing has as yet been offered to them by the adherents of those theories of truth which would, if vindicated, undermine the claims that they make on behalf of their various and contending traditions. And here the force of what has already been said on behalf of the conception of truth to which they are committed, both by writers in the Thomistic tradition in one mode and by Geach in another, suffice to make it evident that nothing remotely like a conclusive reason for not so continuing has yet been advanced.

## HOW THEN CAN A MORAL STANDPOINT BE RATIONALLY VINDICATED AGAINST ITS RIVALS?

Yet it may appear that this view of the relationship between truth and rational justification itself raises an insuperable difficulty. I have followed Aristotle in taking truth to be the *telos* of rational enquiry; and rational enquiry so conceived must involve progress towards that *telos* through the replacement of less adequate by more adequate forms of rational justification. So that progress in rational enquiry concerning the nature and status of human goods, duties, virtues, and rights would have to exhibit a movement from initial local, partial, and one-sided points of view towards a type of understanding – and in the case of the moral life a type of practice – freed in some significant way from the limitations of such partiality and one-sidedness and possessed of the resources which would enable it to explain, in the light of the comprehension thus achieved, just why it is that they appear to be otherwise from the limited perspectives of those local, partial, and one-sided standpoints whose limitations have now been transcended. Yet it must seem that, on the account which I initially advanced of the apparently unresolvable fundamental disagreements between major moral standpoints, such progress in rational enquiry concerning the nature of the moral life cannot occur. Why not?

On that account those contending standpoints each have internal to them their own standards of rational justification, and so each, it must seem, is locked into its own mode of rational justification and into the conceptual scheme to which that mode gives expression. But if that is indeed so, then there can surely be no way in which the adherents of each rival standpoint can transcend the limitations of their own local point of view, for the only standards of judgment available to them are the standards of each local standpoint. Yet central to progress in rational enquiry, as I have characterized it, is an ability to transcend such limitations and in so doing to identify and to explain the partiality and the one-sidedness which they impose upon those whose perspective is defined by them. If progress in rational enquiry, so understood, is impossible, then the conception of truth which blocks the inference from the facts about fundamental moral disagreement to the moral relativist's conclusions loses its application, for truth cannot be the *telos* of any type of enquiry condemned for ever to remain locally limited and constrained.

The line of argument which leads to this conclusion is however mistaken. For even in those cases where the facts about fundamental disagreement between moral standpoints are as I have described them, and each of the contending traditions has internal to it its own standards of rational justification, the possibility of transcending the limitations of those standards, as hitherto formulated and understood, through the progress of rational enquiry into the nature of the moral life is not in fact ruled out. One approach to understanding how and why this is so would be to re-examine the history of, for example, the natural law tradition,[15] in which at more than one stage in the development of its own internal enquiries, and of its critical relationships to other traditions, the challenge of transcending the limitations hitherto imposed upon it by its own standards of rational justification has been successfully met. But to understand how this has been possible in such particular cases a more general account of how such limitations can be overcome is needed. There are distinctive characteristics necessary for the development of any enquiry whose starting-point is from within this type of moral position, if it is to have any prospect of success in such overcoming.

The first is an acceptance by those engaged in it of the justificatory burden imposed upon anyone who is committed, as they are, to a substantive conception of truth. What burden is that? It is the onus upon the adherents of each particular rival tradition of showing, so far as they can, that, if and only if the truth is indeed what they assert that it is, and if and only if it is appropriated rationally in the way that they say that it must be appropriated, can we adequately understand how, in the case of each rival moral standpoint, given the historical, social, psychological and intellectual circumstances in which that standpoint has been theoretically elaborated and embodied in practice, it is intelligible that this is how things should seem to be to the adherents of those other standpoints. How things seem to them from their merely local and therefore limited point of view is to be explained in the light of how things are. But since this onus is equally on the adherents of every standpoint for whose account of morality truth is claimed, different standpoints can be compared in respect of their success in the provision of such explanations, even if to some extent different standards of explanation and intelligibility are invoked from within each contending moral tradition. For the type of understanding yielded by such explanations must, if it is to discharge the justificatory burden, and therefore permit the claim to truth to be sustained, be specific and detailed enough to be open to falsification at a wide variety of points. And that detail and specificity must enable us to understand how the different types of moral disagreement with which we are confronted are generated under different conditions and circumstances. What form would such explanations take?

To answer this question we need to remind ourselves of a central feature of every important moral standpoint. Every standpoint of any theoretical depth that purports to provide an overall account of the moral

15 See Crowe, *Changing Profile.*

situation of human beings and of the standards of moral success and failure has internal to it not only its own distinctive theses and arguments, but also its own distinctive problems and difficulties, theoretical or practical or both. And another characteristic necessary for any enquiry which is designed to transcend the limitations of its own standpoint-dependent starting-point is a systematic investigation and elaboration of what is most problematic and poses most difficulty for that particular moral standpoint. It is of course by the degree of ability of its adherents to make progress in solving or partially solving or at least reformulating such problems, first by identifying areas in which either incoherence or re-sourcelessness threatens, and then by furnishing remedies for these, that a particular standpoint is or is not vindicated by and for those adherents. For we are speaking here of what is or at least ought to be problematic by the standards of that standpoint for whose adherents these issues arise.

So for example within utilitarianism the problem of how the happiness of any particular individual is related to the general happiness, a question at once theoretical and practical, was answered initially in one way by Bentham, then in another by Mill, in a formulation designed to supply the defects evident by utilitarianism's own standards in Bentham's re-sponse, and then again by Sidgwick in an attempt to correct Mill. And in Japanese Confucianism of the seventeenth and eighteenth centuries we find a continuing and unresolved tension between an evident need to adapt and revise older prescriptions for familial relationships to new familial and household arrangements and a continuing requirement that one and the same set of principles should inform both new and older prescriptions. But at a certain point in the history of such attempts to deal with such problems it can become plain that they are not only persistent, but intractable, and irremediably so.

When we find that the adherents of a particular moral standpoint, confronted by this type of persistent and intractable problem, can only avoid resourcelessness at the cost of incoherence, that if enough is said to be practically useful, too much has to be said to remain practically or theoretically consistent, a question is always thereby posed to the adher-ents of that particular standpoint, whether they recognize it or not, as to the extent to which it is the limitations imposed by their own conceptual and argumentative framework which both generate such incoherences and prevent their resolution. Insofar as it can be established that this is so, by explaining why and how precisely these particular problems must inescap-ably arise within that particular framework and the obstacles to resolving them be just those obstacles which our diagnosis has enabled us to identify, to that extent the local limitations of that particular standpoint and of its particular established scheme and mode of rational justification will have been transcended. But how could this be achieved?

It would require an ability to put in question the conceptual framework of that particular standpoint from within the framework itself by the use of argumentative resources not so far available within that framework, but now made so available. It will in the first instance have been only from the standpoint of some other rival moral position that such limitations can have been identified. But how is it possible that someone whose moral beliefs and practice are both informed and limited by the concepts and standards of her or his own particular point of view could have acquired the ability to understand her or his own standpoint from some external and rival vantage point? The answer is that through the exercise of philosophical and moral imagination someone may on occasion be able to learn what it would be to think, feel, and act from the standpoint of some alternative and rival standpoint, acquiring in so doing an ability to understand her or his own tradition in the perspective afforded by that rival. The analogy here is with the ability of an anthropologist to learn not only how to inhabit an alternative and very different culture, but also how to view her or his own culture from that alien perspective.

The exercise of this imaginative ability to understand one's own fundamental moral positions from some external and alien point of view is then yet another characteristic necessary for those engaged in enquiry who, beginning within some one particular moral standpoint, aspire first to identify and then to overcome its limitations. What this ability can on occasion achieve is a discovery that problems and difficulties, incoherences and resourcelessnesses, in dealing with which over some extended period one's own standpoint has proved sterile, can in fact be understood and explained from some other rival point of view as precisely the types of difficulty and problem which would be engendered by the particular local partialities and one-sidednesses of one's own tradition. If that alternative rival point of view has not proved similarly sterile in relation to its own difficulties and problems, then the enquirer has excellent reasons for treating the alternative rival point of view as more powerful in providing resources for moving rationally from a statement of how things seem to be from a particular local point of view to how they in fact are, by revealing what it was that was hitherto limiting in that standpoint which had up till now been her or his own.

So even although all such reasoning has to begin from and initially accept the limitations and constraints of some particular moral standpoint, the resources provided by an adequate conception of truth, by logic, and by the exercise of philosophical and moral imagination are on occasion sufficient to enable enquiry to identify and to transcend what in those limitations and constraints hinders enquiry or renders it sterile. But in this progress of rational debate, in which one standpoint may defeat another by providing the resources for understanding and explaining what is or was intractably problematic for that other, some at least of the adherents of a defeated set of positions may remain unable to recognize that defeat. For such adherents will still have all the reasons that they had previously had for invoking the standards of their own particular established scheme and mode of rational justification in support of a denial of rival conclusions. And they may never acquire the ability to understand their own positions from an external standpoint, so that nothing that *they* would have to recognize as a refutation of their own standpoint need have been offered. At most they may only be compelled to acknowledge the intractability of some continuing long-term problems. Insofar as this is the case, the relationship between the two standpoints in conflict will thus have become asymmetrical, and this in two ways. First, one of these two rival moral standpoints will have acquired through the exercise of philosophical and moral imagination the conceptual resources to provide not merely an accurate representation of its rival, but one which captures what by the standards of that rival is intractably problematic, while the continuing adherents of that rival will lack just that type of resource. And secondly it will have provided in its own terms a compelling explanation of why what is thus intractably problematic is so. But the terms in which that explanation is framed may well remain inaccessible to most and perhaps all continuing adherents of that rival standpoint. So on fundamental matters, moral or philosophical, the existence of continuing disagreement, even between highly intelligent people, should not lead us to suppose that there are not adequate resources available for the rational resolution of such disagreement.[16]

---

16 I am greatly indebted for criticisms of an earlier version of this essay to Marian David, Paul Roth, and David Solomon.

# CHAPTER 4

# Hegel on faces and skulls

I

*The Phenomenology of Spirit* was written hastily. It is notorious that *one* outcome of this is that arguments are compressed, that the relation of one argument to another is often unclear, and that paragraphs of almost impenetrable obscurity recur. The commentator is therefore liable to feel a certain liberty in reconstructing Hegel's intentions; and the exercise of this liberty may always be a source of misrepresentation, perhaps especially when Hegel's arguments are relevant to present-day controversies. Nonetheless, the risk is sometimes worth taking, for although it is true that to be ignorant of the history of philosophy is to be doomed to repeat it, the joke is that we are doomed to repeat it in some measure anyway, if only because the sources of so many philosophical problems lie so close to permanent characteristics of human nature and human language. It is in this light that I want to consider Hegel's arguments about two bad sciences – physiognomy and phrenology – and their claims to lay bare and to explain human character and behavior, and the relevance of those arguments to certain contemporary issues.

Physiognomy was an ancient science that in the eighteenth century enjoyed a mild revival, especially in the writings of Johann Kaspar Lavater (1741–1801). The central claim of physiognomy was that character was systematically revealed in the features of the face. Character consists of a set of determinate traits, and the face of a set of determinate features. In some cases the cause of the face's being as it is is the character's being as it is, but in other cases certain experiences, such as the experiences incurred in certain occupations, may leave their marks both on the character and the face. In this latter type of case the features of the face are not effects of the traits of character, but remain revelatory of character.

In his discussion of physiognomy, Hegel begins by noting that its adherents assert that their science makes a different type of claim from that made, for example, by the adherents of astrology. Astrologers assert that types of planetary movement and types of human action are correlated in certain regular ways; the connection is purely contingent and external. But the face is an *expression* of human character; what a man is, appears in his face. Hegel next notes the difference between this claim as it is made by the physiognomist and this claim as it is made in everyday life. Part of our ordinary human relationships is to read off from each other's faces thoughts, moods, and reactions. But we do not treat the facial expression simply as a sign of something else, the outer as a sign of something inner, any more than we treat the movement of the hand in a human action as a sign of something else, the inner meaning of what is done, the intention. We treat the expression of the face and the movement of the hand as themselves actions, or parts or aspects of actions. In this connection Hegel makes four points.

It is not what the face is, its bone structure or the way the eyes are set, that is the expression of character or action; it is what the face does that is such an expression. We are therefore not concerned with mere physical shapes, but with movements that are already interpreted. This leads on to Hegel's second point. A man's character is not something independent of his actions and accessible independently of his actions. There is nothing more to his character than the sum-total of what he does. Hegel here sides with Ryle in *The Concept of Mind* in his enmity to the notion of dispositions as causes of the actions that manifest them. The conjoint force of these two points is as follows.

When we see someone with a sad expression on his face, we do not infer to an inner sadness he feels on the basis of an observed correlation between such a physical arrangement of the facial features and inner states of sadness. We read or interpret the expression as one of sadness in the light of the conventions in our culture for interpreting facial expressions. Notice that we have to learn how to do this in alien cultures, and that no amount of correlating one observable characteristic with another in the search for regularities would assist us in the task of such learning. There is thus a difference between seeing a set of physical features and seeing that set as a face and as a face with a particular expression, just as there is a difference between seeing a string of physical shapes and seeing that string as an English sentence and as a sentence with a particular meaning. To learn how to read a face or a sentence is not to follow rules justified by observation that embody a correlation between two sets of items, one of which is the physical features or shapes.

What Hegel's argument has done so far is to show that the physiognomist's treatment of the face as expressive of character, and the physiognomist's treatment of the face as (at least sometimes) the effect of character, cannot be combined without damaging inconsistency. Hegel's two next points are still more damaging to the claim of physiognomy to go beyond the prescientific understanding of facial expression to a scientific knowledge of the causal relations allegedly underlying that expression. He points out sharply how the rules that we use in everyday life in interpreting facial expression are highly fallible. We can express Hegel's point in this way: if someone is apparently glaring at me and I accuse him of being angry with me, he has only to retort that he was thinking of something quite different and I shall have no way to rebut him by appeal to some set of rules for interpreting facial expression. Hegel quotes Lichtenberg: "If anyone said, 'Certainly you behave like an honest man, but I can see from your face that you are compelling yourself to do so and are a villain underneath,' there is no doubt that every brave fellow so greeted will reply with a box on the ear."

Finally – although Hegel makes this point earlier in the discussion – our dispositions of character, as expressed in our actions, speech, and facial expressions, are not simply given as physical features are given. My bone structure can be altered by surgery or violence, but at any given moment it is simply what it is. But my character is not determinate in the same way as my bone structure, and this in two respects. First, a disposition to behave in a particular way always has to be actualized in some particular context, and the nature and meaning of the action that manifests the disposition is in many cases unspecifiable apart from that context. If I strike a man dead when he attacks me murderously, my action does not have the same nature and meaning as when I strike a man dead in a fit of bad-tempered gratuitous aggression. Dispositions that are actualized independently of context are like tendencies to sneeze or to produce compulsive movements. Their manifestations will be happenings that in virtue of their independence of context cannot be viewed as intelligible behavior, except perhaps as nervous habits. But about my action produced in a context, we can ask if it is appropriate or inappropriate in the light of the norms defining intelligible behavior in such a context; indeed this is a question that any agent can ask about his own actions. In asking this, he has to characterize his actions in such a way that he becomes self-conscious about what he is doing.

An agent, for example (my example, not Hegel's), may find himself performing a set of multifarious individual actions. Becoming conscious of the character of these, he becomes aware that his over-all conduct is jealous, let us say, or cowardly. But now he is able to place, indeed cannot but place, his conduct *qua* jealous or *qua* cowardly in relation to what Hegel calls "the given circumstances, situations, habits, customs, religion, and so forth," i.e., in relation to the relevant norms and responses of his culture. But to do this is to provide himself with reasons, perhaps decisive reasons, for altering his conduct in the light of those norms and responses and of his own goals. It is of the nature of the character traits of a rational agent that they are never simply fixed and determinate, but that for the agent to discover what they are in relation to his unity as a self-conscious agent – that is, what they are in his personal and social context – is to open up to the agent the possibility of exchanging what he is for what he is not.

Moreover, the agent who does not change his traits may change their manifestations. Indeed, for him to become conscious that he manifests certain traits and so appears in a certain light, is to invite him to do just this. The relation of external appearance, including facial appearance, to character is such that the discovery that any external appearance is taken to be a sign of a certain type of character is a discovery that an agent may then exploit to conceal his character. Hence, another saying of Lichtenberg, in *Über Physiognomik*, which Hegel also quotes: "Suppose the physiognomist ever did have a man in his grasp; it would merely require a courageous resolution on the man's part to make himself again incomprehensible for centuries."

II

Yet who now is likely to be impressed by the claims of physiognomy? Reading Lavater's *Physiognomische Fragmente zur Beförderung der Menschenkenntniss und Menschenliebe*, with all its romantic whimsy – Lavater on the basis of a youthful acquaintance associated piercing eyes with power of memory, for instance – one might well ask, ought anyone ever to have been impressed by such claims? Part of the answer is that we should be interested in bad sciences, if only in order to illuminate the contrast with good ones. The study of astrology, physiognomy, or phrenology is justified insofar as it helps us to understand the character of chemistry and physiology. But another part of the answer concerns the way in which certain issues may be raised in just the same way by bad sciences, such as phrenology and physiognomy, as by good ones, such as genetics or neurophysiology.

In the case of phrenology some of the central theses actually survive through the history of physiology into the present day. It was, for instance, a central thesis of phrenology that different types of activity were localized in different areas of the brain. This thesis survives in a somewhat different form, although our contemporary understanding of localization is very different from that of the phrenologists. There is secondly the thesis, distinctively phrenological, that the different areas of the brain correspond to different areas of the cranial bone, and that the shapes of these areas, the famous bumps of the phrenologists, reveal the different degrees of development of each area of the brain. It is scarcely necessary to remark that this empirical contention is false. There is finally the thesis that the local activity of the brain is the sufficient cause and explanation of behavior, and that therefore the shape of the cranium allows us to predict behavior.

Buried in these dubious contentions is one that is less obviously dubious, that is indeed familiar and widely accepted. I mean of course the thesis that there are biochemical or neural states of affairs, processes, and events, the occurrence and the nature of which are the sufficient causes of human actions. This thesis wore phrenological clothing in 1807; today its clothing is as fashionable as it was then, only the fashions are not what they were. Moreover, when Hegel attempted to rebut the claims of physiognomy and phrenology, he did so in such a way that, if his rebuttal is successful, it would hold against the thesis that I have just stated, whatever its scientific clothing.

At this point, someone may object to my metaphor. The thesis, so it may be protested, does not merely wear scientific clothing, it is itself part of science and, because it is a scientific thesis, it is an empirical question, and purely an empirical question, whether it is true or false. My reply to this point, and what I take to be Hegel's reply to this point, occupies a large part of the rest of the essay. But it is worth noting initially that the thesis *has* survived the most remarkable changes in our empirically founded beliefs about the anatomy, physiology, and chemistry of the human body, and that, if it is a thesis in natural science, it is certainly not a thesis at the same level as the contention that the shape of the brain is partly the same as that of the cranium or that the nucleic acids play a specific part in reproduction.

In the debate about phrenology in the early nineteenth century, the attempt to challenge the thesis was undertaken by a number of writers very different from Hegel, and his project deserves to be sharply distinguished from theirs. The standard statement of the phrenological position was taken from the writings and lectures of Franz Joseph Gall (1758–1828) and his pupil J. C. Spurzheim, who developed Gall's doctrine, later claiming both that he had in fact originated some of the basic ideas and also that his doctrine was very different from that of Gall. Gall and Spurzheim drew maps of the cranium locating not only character traits but abilities in different parts of the brain, and their manifestations in what they took to be the corresponding parts of the skull. Examples of traits are secretiveness, combativeness, and acquisitiveness; examples of abilities are the power of speech and the power of imagination. Gall was charged by his critics with determinism, materialism, and consequently atheism. Both Gall and Spurzheim denied these charges, Spurzheim seeking to show that they held of Gall's version of phrenology but not of his. The critics in question, notably Francis Jeffrey, the editor, and Brougham, the lawyer, fastened all their attention on the alleged causes, seeking to show that the mental cannot have a physical, or more specifically a physiological cause. To show this, they rely on a simple dualism of matter and mind, and the vapid naivete of Gall's and Spurzheim's science is matched only by the vapid naivete of Jeffrey's and Brougham's philosophy.

The spirit of their attack on phrenology is as alien to the spirit of Hegel's attack as any could be. Hegel's opposition to Cartesian dualism is of so thorough-going a kind that he would have had to reject all the premises of Jeffrey's and Brougham's attacks. Nor is Hegel interested in showing that there cannot be physiological causes of the type cited by the phrenologists. His whole attention is focused not on the existence or non-existence of the alleged causes, but on the character of their alleged effects.

Hegel deploys a number of arguments that are closely allied to his arguments against physiognomy in the interests of his conclusion that "it must be regarded as a thoroughgoing denial of reason to treat a skull bone as the actuality of conscious life . . ." What Hegel means by this is indicated by his further contention that "It is no use to say we merely draw an inference from the outer as to the inner, which is something different . . ." Hegel wants to say that if we regard the traits of a rational agent as belonging to the type of item that can stand in a genuinely causal relation to anatomical or physiological or chemical states, then we are misconceiving the traits of a rational agent. Why does Hegel think this? We can usefully begin from a point that Hegel did not make in his discussion of physiognomy.

Traits are neither determinate nor fixed. What does it mean to say that they are not determinate? "Just as, e.g., many people complain of feeling a painful tension in the head when thinking intensely, or even when thinking at all, so it might be that stealing, committing murder, writing poetry, and so on, could each be accompanied with its own proper feeling, which would over and above be bound to have its peculiar localization." Hegel's discussion in terms of the localization of feeling has of course a specific reference to contemporary phrenology; but what he goes on to say about local feelings can easily be translated into a thesis about particular dispositions.

Feeling in general is something indeterminate, and that feeling in the head as the center might well be the general feeling that accompanies all suffering; so that mixed up with the thief's, murderer's, poet's tickling or pain in the head there would be other feelings, too, and they would permit of being distinguished from one another, or from those we may call mere bodily feelings, as little as an illness can be determined from the symptom of headache if we restrict its meaning merely to the bodily element.

What would the corresponding theses about dispositions be? Let us consider points from two of Hegel's examples – those of the murderer and of the poet. A given murderer, for instance, commits his crime because he fears his own humiliation by losing his beloved. If we are to look at the traits and other qualities manifested in his action, they do not include a disposition to commit murder, but such things perhaps as a general intolerance of suffering, a disposition to avoid specific kinds of humili- ation, his love for the young woman, and so on. The same dispositions might explain to precisely the same extent the same person's outbidding others in giving to a deserving cause in order to impress the same young woman. But just this fact puts in question the use of the word "explain." Hegel makes this point in relation to phrenology: "And again his mur- derous propensity can be referred to any bump or hollow, and this in turn to any mental quality; for the murderer is not the abstraction of a murderer . . ."

Suppose that to this the reply is made that the same given set of dispositions may well produce quite different actions, but that this is because the agent is responding to quite different situations (although in some sense, in my example, the situations are certainly the same). So that we explain the particular action by reference to a conjunction of a set of dispositions and some feature of the situation, we then explain the action in an entirely familiar and unproblematic way by appealing to a general- ization of the form "Whenever such and such a set of dispositions and such and such a type of situation are conjoined, such and such an action will occur." To cite human traits in such an explanation would be precisely parallel to citing the dispositional properties of physical objects in explaining physical events.

But this is to suppose that what the agent is responding to is some conjunction of properties and not a highly specific and particular historical situation. No empiricist would be prepared to draw this contrast; for him, there is nothing to any specific historical situation but a set of properties, the conjunction of which may as a matter of contingent fact be unrepeated, but which is in fact repeatable. Why, then, does Hegel insist on the contrast and deny this characteristic empiricist contention?

A particular historical situation cannot on Hegel's view be dissolved into a set of properties. One reason for this is that such a situation has to be characterized in terms of relations to earlier particular events and situations. There is an internal reference to the events and situations that constitute its history. So the English revolt against Charles I not only has as key properties reactions to particular acts of Charles I, but responses to events and situations in the past as recent as acts of Elizabeth and as far off as Magna Carta and the Norman Conquest. To respond to a particular situation, event, or state of affairs is not to respond to any situation, event, or state of affairs with the same or similar properties; it is to respond to *that* situation conceived by both the agents who respond to it and those whose actions constitute it as the particular that it is.

Suppose that to this position some empiricist were to respond as follows: that the agents treat the situation as particular and that the situation is partially constituted and defined by reference to the particular events and situations, does not show that everything relevant to explanation cannot be expressed in terms of repeatable properties. But this reply fails to notice one key point. Hegel would be the last to assert the ultimacy of unanalyzed and unanalyzable particulars (such as Russell's logical atoms). But he does assert what we may call the ultimacy of concreteness. What the ultimacy of concreteness amounts to is this: just as there are good conceptual reasons for holding that existence is not a property, so there are good conceptual reasons for holding that occurrence at some specific time and place is not a property.

By a property I mean that kind of attribute which a subject of the appropriate type (appropriate for that type of attribute) may or may not possess, which a given subject may possess at one time but not at another, and which may (although it need not) be possessed by more than one subject. On such an account of properties, existence fails to count as a property, because the appropriate type of subject cannot either possess it or fail to possess it and because the appropriate type of subject cannot possess it at one time but not at another. On the same account of properties, occurrence at some specific time and place (e.g., at 3 p.m. in the year 1776 at the point where the Greenwich meridian crosses the south bank of the Thames) fails to count as a property, because any subject of the appropriate type (events, situations, states of affairs) cannot possess any particular example of this attribute at one time but not at another and because any particular example of this type of attribute cannot be possessed by more than one subject.

It is properties about which we construct genuine empirical generalizations of such forms as $(C\Phi x\psi x)$ and $(C\Phi x\psi y)$, in which the values of variables of the type of $\Phi$ and $\psi$ are property-ascribing predicates. But it is on Hegel's view universals particularized in their concrete occurrence to which we respond in our actions – particulars which we encounter in the actual world as the intentional objects of our beliefs, attitudes, and emotions. A poet does not take pride in his having written some poem that has properties of such and such a kind, but in his having written *this* poem. A murderer did not strike out at anyone who happened to have such and such properties but at *this* person. Just because this concreteness is not constituted by a mere collection of properties, it evades causal generalizations and so makes causal explanation, whether phrenological or neurophysiological, inapplicable.

Note what Hegel is *not* saying. Hegel is not asserting that the movements of the murderer's hand or the poet's hand do not have causal explanations. Nor is he asserting that it is impossible that there should be agents with responses only to the abstract universal and not to the concrete. It is just that insofar as someone did respond to presentations of properties with the degree of uniformity that would warrant the construction of causal generalizations, he would not be at all like characteristic human agents as we actually know them and as they actually exist. It is a contingent empirical fact about human beings that they are as they are and not otherwise, but in Hegel's philosophy there is no objection to taking notice of such contingent empirical facts. Nonetheless, Hegel is not denying that it is logically possible for some human actions to have causes, and he is not denying that some human actions do or may have physiological causes. Let me draw a parallel with another type of case.

Some Africans who believe in witchcraft point out that to explain the onset of a disease by referring to bacterial or virus infection leaves unexplained such facts as that Jones should have been afflicted by such an infection immediately after quarreling with Smith. "What is the cause of that conjunction?" they enquire, pointing out that Western science gives no answer. Now, if indeed it were true that every event had a cause, that event which is Jones-going-down-with-measles-on-the-day-after-he-quarreled-with-Smith would presumably have a cause. But no champion of the explanatory powers of natural science feels affronted by the assertion that this is not an event with a cause or an explanation, although the event that is Jones-going-down-with-measles certainly has a cause and an explanation. So also, when Hegel allows that a certain kind of causal explanation will not give us the understanding that we require of self-conscious rational activity, his argument does not require him to deny that many properties of the agents engaged in such activities will have such explanations.

I now return to Hegel's point that traits are not determinate or fixed. I have argued that the indeterminacy of traits is an indeterminacy vis-à-vis any action or given set of actions. From the fact that an agent has a given trait, we cannot *deduce* what he will do in any given situation, and the trait cannot itself be specified in terms of some determinate set of actions that it will produce. What does it mean to say that traits are not fixed? Let me reiterate the crucial fact about self-consciousness, already brought out in Hegel's discussion of physiognomy; that is, its self-negating quality: being aware of what I am is conceptually inseparable from confronting what I am not, but could become. Hence, for a self-conscious agent to have a trait is for that agent to be confronted by an indefinitely large set of possibilities of developing, modifying, or abolishing that trait. Action springs not from fixed and determinate dispositions, but from the confrontation in consciousness of what I am by what I am not.

It is a failure to notice this that on Hegel's view most of all underlies those would-be sciences that aspire to give to observation the same role in the study of human beings that it has in enquiries into nature. For what we can observe in nature is, so to speak, all that there is to discover; but what we can observe in human beings is the expression of rational activity, which cannot be understood as merely the sum of the movements that we observe. (For a Hegelian, Hume's failure to discover the character of personal identity is the result of his fidelity to the methods and criteria of observation.) From Hegel's position, a radical thesis about experimental psychology would follow.

For a large class of psychological experiments, a necessary condition for experimental success is that the stimulus that is administered or the situation with which the agent is confronted shall have its effect independently of the agent's reflection on the situation. The situation or the stimulus must be the same for all experimental subjects; so one subject's envisaging the situation in a particular way must not constitute that situation a different one from that which it is for a subject who envisages that situation in some quite different way. Now, there is a real question as to whether this requirement can ever in fact be satisfied except in experiments in which the stimulus is purely physical (for example, a variation in intensity of light) and the response purely physiological (for example, a constriction of the pupil). But this question I shall put on one side. What Hegel would assert is that even if such experiments are possible, they are so different from the key situations in which rational agents operate, that any inferences from the behavior of such experimental subjects to behavior outside the experimental situation will be liable to lead us into error.

III

Whatever else the arguments in this essay may or may not establish, they do seem to show that between the Hegelian mode of understanding human action and the mode that has dominated characteristic modern thinking about the relevance of such sciences as neurophysiology and genetics, there is a basic incompatibility. Hence, the refutation of Hegelianism in the relevant respects would be a prerequisite for that mode of thought and not merely that kind of positivistic refutation to which Hegel has so often been subjected. Whether a more adequate refutation is possible, I shall not discuss here. What I do want to do, in conclusion, is to try to characterize Hegel's alternative mode of understanding enquiry into human action.

Three features of Hegel's account stand out: the first is the way in which each stage in the progress of rational agents is seen as a movement towards goals that are only articulated in the course of the movement itself. Human action is characteristically neither blind and goalless nor the mere implementation of means to an already decided end. Acting that is the bringing about of such an end by a calculated means certainly has a place, but a subordinate place, in human activity. That it is only in the course of the movement that the goals of the movement are articulated is the reason why we can understand human affairs only after the event. The owl of Minerva, as Hegel was later to put it, flies only at dusk. The understanding of human beings is not predictive in the way that natural science is.

The second feature of Hegel's account is the role of rational criticism of the present in the emergence of the future. Hegel did not believe that the future followed from the present simply as its rational sequel; this he denies as strongly as Voltaire does. But it is in the working out of the failure of the present to satisfy the canons of reason that the future is made. It is this which involves Hegel in seeing history as composed of sequences in which the actions that constitute later stages of sequences involve reference to, and thus presuppose the occurrence of, actions that constituted earlier stages of the same sequences. The sequences that constitute history are themselves discrete and can stand in the same logical relation to each other as can the stages of a single sequence. The doctrine that all the sequences of history constitute a single movement towards the goal of a consciousness of the whole that is absolute spirit is a thesis certainly held by Hegel himself to be the key to his whole doctrine. Yet some of Hegel's other theses as to human history, including those that I have discussed, do not seem in any way to entail his doctrine about the Absolute, and to be unwilling to admit the truth of that doctrine ought not to be a source of prejudice against Hegel's other claims.

A third feature of Hegel's account relates closely to his criticism of physiognomy and phrenology. Historical narratives are for Hegel not a source of data to be cast into theoretical form by such would-be sciences. Instead Hegel sees our understanding of contingent regularities as being always contributory to the construction of a certain kind of historical narrative. History, informed by philosophical understanding, provides a more ultimate kind of knowledge of human beings than enquiries whose theoretical structure is modeled on that of the natural sciences. It is outside the scope of this essay to develop or to assess Hegel's view on this matter, but a concluding remark may be in place.

It concerns the question: if history is not a matter of general laws and of theories, in what sense does it give us understanding at all? The Hegelian reply is that the self-knowledge of a self-conscious rational agent has always to be cast in a historical form. The past is present in the self in so many and so important ways that, lacking historical knowledge, our self-knowledge will be fatally limited. Moreover, this type of self-knowledge could never be yielded by theoretical sciences that aspire to explain behavior in terms of physiological structures and processes. It is in fact just because our history constitutes us as what we are to so great an extent, that any explanation that omits reference to that history, as did and do the explanations of phrenology and neurophysiology, may explain the aptitudes and conditions of the human body, but not those of the human spirit.

# CHAPTER 5

# *What is a human body?*

To the question "What is a human body?" I intend to propose seven preliminary answers: that it is an animal body with various powers of movement, some voluntary and directed; that it is a body whose movements afford expression to intentions and purposes that thereby possesses a certain directedness; that, as an expressive body, it is interpretable by others and responsive to others; that, as an interpretable body, a variety of its characteristics are signs whose meaning others can understand; that its directedness has the unity of agency; that it cannot be adequately understood except in terms of the social contexts in which it engages with others and others with it; and that it is in certain respects enigmatic, a source of puzzlement, since alone among animal bodies it occasionally emits the question "What is a human body?" and directs its powers towards giving an answer to that question.

An incautious reader may suppose that in giving these answers I am making philosophical claims. And it is true that they will provide what I take to be grounds for rejecting certain standard types of philosophical theory which give or entail certain kinds of account of the body, namely, those types of theory that are committed to some version of dualism, whether Platonic or Cartesian, and those types of theory that are committed to some version of materialism or physicalism. It is also true that in characterizing the powers, movements, and signs of the human body I have drawn upon distinctions and idioms elaborated by various philosophers, to whom I am indebted. But I do not advance my answers to the question "What is a human body?" as a set of philosophical propositions, to be defended by argument as philosophical propositions are customarily defended. For what I invite is not argumentative assent or dissent, but recognition. My claim is that anyone who has or rather – given my answers – *is* a human body and who reflects upon what it is that she or he is will recognize the truth of these answers. My claims, that is, are prephilosophical rather than philosophical. It is only when we have recognized the truths to which they afford expression that we will have matter for philosophical enquiry.

About the truth of some of these answers I may of course be mistaken. And I will be shown to be mistaken, if plain unphilosophical or not yet philosophical persons prove unable to recognize the truth of what I assert, even after adequate reflection. My aim is to provide a starting-point for peculiarly philosophical enquiry by drawing attention to the enigmatic character of the human body. How such enquiry should proceed is a question only to be posed subsequently.

What then is a human body? A first answer is that it is one kind of animal body and as such liable to injury and to disease, either of which may to varying degrees incapacitate it. What then are the capacities and powers specific to a human body? They are in the first instance capacities for exercising movement, movements of arms and hands in reaching and picking, movement of legs in walking, kneeling, and kicking, movement of the whole body or of large parts of it in standing or sitting up, lying or sitting down, movements of the head, and facial movements. Such movements fall into three classes, but I begin from a twofold division: some are voluntary and intentional, some not. Voluntary and intentional movements constitute voluntary and intentional actions. They are performed on those occasions when it is appropriate to ask the agent whose body it is, "For what reason did you do that?" (The agent's answer may well be: "For no particular reason.") That is, we understand some movements of the arm and the hand as constituting the action "Picking up the bag," and insofar as we do so understand them, it is appropriate to ask "For what reason did you pick up the bag?" And we contrast such movements with those that do not constitute actions, including among these: reflexive responses to stimuli, such as blinking at a sudden light or sneezing uncontrollably, movements when someone is asleep, and movements when a body falls down or is propelled forward as a result of being struck forcibly.

The class of voluntary and intentional bodily movements is however wider than the class of movements that constitute voluntary and intentional actions. For when someone does something unintentionally, intending to do one thing, but in fact doing another, as when someone mistakenly taking sugar for salt unintentionally sweetens the soup. Her action was unintentional, but her bodily movements are intentional. Not only was it in the agent's power to move or not move the relevant parts of the body, but the relevant bodily powers were exercised as embodiments of an intended action. Notice that "as." It would have been a mistake to write instead: "so as to bring about the intended action." The action is not one thing, the bodily movements another, so that the production of the one is a means to the production of the other. The action just is the bodily movements, or rather, it is the bodily movements as informed by the agent's intention. And to characterize the bodily movements apart from that intention would be to mischaracterize them. For it would omit a crucial dimension of those movements, their directedness towards that which is the object of the action, the object specified by the agent's intention.

Consider three instances of what appear from the standpoint of an external observer, watching from behind a screen, to be the very same movements of an arm and a hand. The same muscles are at work. The same extending and clenching take place. The first of these three instances occurs accidentally, a movement that this body just happens to make. The second occurs in obedience to the injunction of a physiologist who is studying voluntary movement and who has said to his experimental subject: "At precisely 2.53 extend your arm and clench your hand." The third occurs as the movement through which the agent, without thinking about it, picks up his pen in order to write an article about his experience as an experimental subject.

The first of those movements is wholly undirected, the second is directed towards being just that movement, and the third is directed beyond the movement to the completion of an act constituted by the directedness of the movement. It is the nature of this directedness of many, although not of all its movements, that differentiates a human body that is exercising its specific powers from, say, a severely incapacitated body in a state of coma, moving as it breathes, as it digests, as its blood circulates, but not in any way exhibiting directed movement.

An incapacitated human body is still of course a human body. But the corpse of a human being is no longer a human body. What distinction do I mark by saying this? A corpse is not a human body, just because it no longer has the unity of a human body. The unity of a human body is evidenced on the one hand in the coordination of its voluntary and directed movements, in the way in which different series of movements by eye and hand are directed to one and the same end and in the ways in which movement towards a range of different ends is directed, and on the other in the coordination of its nonvoluntary and nonintentional movements. No such teleology, no such directedness, and certainly no voluntariness characterizes the movements of a corpse.

We may put this by saying that a human body is an embodied mind and that a corpse is a mindless body. A body, that is, is the expression of a mind, even although not all its movements are thus expressive. It is not however that the body stands to the mind as their means of expression stand to artists, as though the mind could view the body as external to it, as a mere instrument of the mind's independent purposes. The primary expressions, although not the only expressions, of mind are bodily expressions and human minds exist only as the minds of this or that particular body. The particularity of mind is initially the particularity of the mind's body.

To say that the human body is expressive is to say that such bodies are what they are in virtue of their social relationships to other bodies. All expression is potential or actual communication. What someone expresses by smiling or gesturing or spitting or yawning, by approaching slowly or suddenly turning away, by sitting or kneeling, let alone by the sounds that he or she utters, communicates to others the meaning expressed by such bodily movements. So each interprets what others communicate by expressive movements and we are able to do so because of shared, socially established conventions of interpretation. I do not mean to deny that there are some expressive movements that are universal or near universal among human beings: cries of pain, laughter, flight. But even the significance attached to these varies from culture to culture, from one set of conventions of interpretation to another. Four features of such interpretation invite attention.

First, it presupposes that the other who is the object of interpretation has the same kinds of perceptual and intellectual powers as those possessed by the interpreter and that those powers are exercised in the same kinds of intentional acts as those of the interpreter. You take me to be expressing amusement by my smile, because you take me to have seen such and such that just occurred and you understand why and how someone such as me would find that occurrence amusing.

Secondly, it presupposes that the interpreted other is an interpreting other, not only that while I am interpreting your bodily movements as expressive of particular intentions and responses, you are interpreting my bodily movements as similarly expressive, but also that each of us is interpreting the other as an interpreter of the other. So I may understand you as exhibiting indignation that I have not fully appreciated the generosity of your attitude towards what you take to be my disapproval of . . . And in such cases the action that is my response to you may well be adequately intelligible only as a sequel to my interpretation of what is expressed by your bodily movements. If so, the directedness of my action and therefore of those bodily movements that are the embodiment of my action is correctly identifiable only insofar as my interpretation of the directedness that is expressed by your bodily movements has been understood.

It turns out therefore that an external observer, unaware of that attitude or action of yours to which I am responding, and therefore unable to understand the intention embodied in my bodily movements, will not be able to identify the directedness of those movements. For example, my eye moves. The everyday observer is able to note the eye movement; the anatomically and physiologically informed observer with suitable instruments is able to observe muscular and neural changes. But the directedness of the movement will disclose itself only to those able to answer some such sequence of questions as this: was this movement a wink or a blink? If a wink, was it initiating an exchange with another or was it a response to a smile or a remark or a wink by someone else? Or was it perhaps a signal conveying a message only to those provided with the code that gives one meaning to one wink, another to two winks, and a third to no winks at all?

Without answers to these and other such questions we cannot determine to what end, if any, that particular eye movement was directed. And without knowing whether or not it is directed to an end and, if so, to what end it was directed, we cannot identify what the antecedents are by reference to which its occurrence could be made intelligible. Note that we cannot dispense with the notion of directedness even in characterizing movements that do not posses it, such as the blink of an eye or an involuntary sneeze. In identifying a blink as such, I identify it as not-a-wink. The movements of the human body that are undirected to any end, that are neither voluntary nor intentional, have to be understood as just that. And, when we interpret some particular set of movements of some body as thus undirected, they provide very different objects for others to respond to than do directed movements. I do not mean by this that involuntary, unintended movements may not on occasion be an appropriate target for such attitudes as resentment or indignation. For it may be that the involuntary and unintended sneeze could have been controlled, or that I could have turned my head away from the light that caused me to blink. So that resentment or indignation may in some circumstances be intelligible and justified, when directed to mere happenings, happenings that express no intention of the agent, but that it was in the agent's power to prevent.

Thirdly, the other or others to whom I may respond in the ways that I have characterized need not be and often are not present. They may indeed be at any distance, whether in space or in time. I may be remembering some event from some years ago and still feel anger at or gratitude for what someone did. And these emotions may find expression in my present bodily movements, in a frown or a gesture. Or I may think about a friend who has gone abroad and express my feelings towards that friend by smiling. And in such cases the directedness of my bodily movements can be known only to myself and to those to whom I disclose the feelings expressed in the movements.

What both these and my earlier examples are intended to bring out is that, when some bodily movement is the expression of some thought, feeling, attitude, or decision, we may distinguish the bodily movement from what it expresses for certain analytical purposes, but there are not two distinct occurrences or states of affairs. It is certainly possible, for example, for a physiologist to study the muscular contractions involved in a smile without having regard to the fact that those contractions are a smile and not a frown. And it is equally possible for someone, a cartoonist, say, to have regard to the smile, without paying any attention to the muscles. But there are not two things, the muscular contraction *and* the smile, or rather, there are not three things, the muscular contraction *and* the smile *and* the pleasure expressed in the smile. The pleasure does not exist apart from its expressions (of which the smile may be only one) and the smile just *is* the muscular contractions. So that if I try to understand these particular muscular contractions independently of their constituting a smile or the smile independently of its constituting an expression of pleasure, I shall fail to understand it. That is to say, physiological explanations may contribute to, but cannot by themselves supply an account either of what it was that I did in expressing my pleasure by smiling or why I smiled as I did. On this of course many have been tempted to think otherwise, supposing that what can be analytically distinguished is in fact distinct. And this supposition, for reasons with which we will have to be concerned a little later, is one that is genuinely tempting to make. But I put on one side for the moment a consideration of this temptation, in order to remark on a fourth characteristic of the interpretation of bodily movements as expressive.

Whatever can be interpreted can be misinterpreted. We may always be mistaken and we sometimes are mistaken in the thoughts and feelings that we ascribe to others on the basis of our interpretation of their bodily movements as expressive. What we take to be anger may be no more than impatience. What we take to be friendliness may be no more than courtesy. And the source of such mistakes is commonly in the limitations on our ability to discriminate one emotion or attitude from another. Some of us are better at such discrimination than others, but we are all fallible. Yet it is a shared presupposition in all our everyday transactions and social relationships that we are in the vast majority of cases able to interpret one another correctly, so that we know how to respond appropriately. And it is this confidence in our powers of interpretation that sometimes renders us vulnerable to intentional deception by others. For what others express may be not grief, but instead a simulation of grief, not cordiality, but pretence of cordiality. The bodily movements in such cases are indeed expressive of the agent's intention, but part of that intention is an intention that her intention should be misinterpreted by others.

Misinterpretation, however, is not always the result of intentional deception. And I shall want to suggest that we have not yet adequately understood what human bodies are and how they behave, until we have understood some sources of certain kinds of systematic misinterpretation. But a necessary prologue to identifying those sources is to take note of three further sets of salient bodily characteristics: those to do with age, those to do with health, and those to do with clothing. For in all these three cases there is the possibility of differences between how my body appears to me and how it is presented to others. And when such differences occur, there are consequent possibilities of misinterpretation and misunderstanding. Consider first age and aging.

At this or that moment of time every human body has existed for just so many years, days, and hours, and this length of time is its age, its chronological age. But bodies age at very different rates and so human bodies that have the same chronological age may differ considerably in respect of the effects and signs of aging. You at thirty-five may seem to be, and may commonly be, taken to be much younger than other 35-year-old women. I at forty-five may seem to be, and may commonly be, taken to be much older than other 45-year-old men. And you at age thirty-five may still think of yourself as "young," while someone else of the same chronological age thinks of themselves as "middle-aged," while I at forty-five may think of myself as "already beginning to leave middle age behind," while someone else of the same chronological age thinks of themselves as still "on the threshold of middle age." (How we use such expressions varies of course from culture to culture, but in some cultures at least, including our own, there is also variation from individual to individual.) What age we are taken to be by others partially, but importantly, determines how those others respond to us. What age we take ourselves to be partially determines whether we find those responses appropriate or inappropriate and this in turn partially, but importantly determines our responses to those responses.

Human bodies not only age, but, like other animal bodies, they suffer from a range of ailments and injuries. An ailment or an injury is accounted such because it interferes with or prevents normal functioning and, since both what is and what is accounted normal functioning vary with age, the kind of response that is judged appropriate to different types of ailment or injury varies with the age of the sufferer. But human bodies are of course vulnerable to types of ailment and injury which are and cannot but be recognized as seriously disabling at *any* age. Such manifest ailments and injuries, which obtrude themselves on the attention of others, necessarily elicit a response. For to ignore them altogether is itself a response and, in most circumstances, a very striking one. Different cultures will of course have different conventions governing how it is appropriate for different kinds of individual to respond in different kinds of situations. But the response-engendering character of manifest seriously disabling ailments and injuries belongs to human bodies as such, whatever the culture.

Human bodies, that is, present themselves to others as of a certain age and as in this or that state of health. A corpse has an age and may have wounds. But it does not present itself to others as aging or wounded. A living body does. And these are not the only characteristics that are important for the body's self-presentation and self-awareness. Human bodies are not only young or old and healthy or diseased, they are also clothed or unclothed. And to be unclothed is not merely to lack clothing; it is to present oneself as lacking clothing so that one's nakedness is a sign. The infant found lying unclothed at midday in squalid conditions presents itself as uncared for. The adult taking off her or his clothes during a medical examination presents her or himself as naked in a very different way from the same adult preparing to go to bed with husband or wife.

Moreover the body presents itself to others through the kind of clothing that it wears: in a uniform or other formal dress or in informal clothing; in light colors and striking forms or in drab and dull dress; in clothes that conform to fashion or in clothes that defy it. Once again conventions will vary from culture to culture and also within cultures, but in all, or perhaps almost all cultures clothing signifies, just as the appearances of age and health signify. A body both in its movements and in these other types of characteristics presents itself as a set of signs. Of these signs and of how they are construed by others the agent may be aware or unaware. And, while some of those signs of which the agent is aware may express her or his intentions, and be intended to be construed as expressive of intention, others may not be under the agent's control. Notice too that, although what is signified depends in key part on local cultural conventions, that the human body in its movements and appearances is a set of signifiers is a truth about the human species as such.

Consider now the catalogue of types of bodily characteristic, as it has been rehearsed so far. We began with bodily powers of movement and types of movement, discriminating the voluntary from the nonvoluntary and the intentional from the nonintentional. We then noticed that, insofar as they are voluntary and intentional, they invite responses and that they themselves may be such responses. They are able to be and to elicit responses, because they are expressive, that is to say, because they are open to interpretation, and therefore also to misinterpretation by others. But such interpretation extends beyond bodily movements to characteristics of the body that derive from its aging, its health, and its clothing. They too are interpretable, that is, they can be – and are – treated as signs.

The items in this catalogue stand in two kinds of relationship. First, items later in time sometimes presuppose items earlier in time and in such cases the later could not occur as they do, unless the earlier occurred as *they* do. Clothing and outward signs of health and of aging have the kind of significance that they do, only because they provide a context for the construal of movements expressive of intentions, including movements expressive of responses. Movements expressive of intentions are able to function as they do, only because some of our movements are voluntary and because we are able to distinguish movements by others that are voluntary from movements that are not. So in forming my intentions I may and often will take account of how their expression will be construed and in so doing the significance of how my body presents itself in terms of age, health, and clothing will have to be considered. What is expressed and what is conveyed by someone old and infirm frowning, standing, and picking up his stick at a certain point in a conversation will be very different from what is expressed and conveyed by someone young and vigorous making more or less the same set of movements. And both the young and the old cannot but know this.

Of sequences of bodily movements, that is to say, it always makes sense to ask not only "To what end is this sequence of movements directed?" but also "What is expressed or communicated by this sequence of movements?" And just as the answer to the first question may always be "To no end; it is a sequence of movements without directedness," so the answer to the second question may always be "Nothing is expressed or communicated by this sequence." But that a bodily movement or a sequence of such movements lacks directedness or expresses nothing is a salient fact about it in a way in which the lack of direction or expression in the movements of the branch of a tree is not.

I have from the outset emphasized the social character of expressive movement. To present one's movements as interpretable by others is to presuppose the existence of those others. To present one's movements so that, by being interpreted in this way rather than that, they will elicit this kind of response rather than that is to presuppose that those others have certain types of belief and attitude. But what is true of the expressive holds also of the directed. How I frame my intentions, and so what intentions it is that are expressed in the directedness of my bodily movements, depends upon the nature of the responses by others that I need to take into account. To move as though mine were the only human body in the world would be to move in a way well designed to implement few, if any intentions and this is something of which no human agent could fail to become aware. But to recognize this is to recognize that we cannot intelligently describe, let alone explain, the movements of one human body in isolation from those of others, except in those rare cases where a salient fact about some particular body is that it is abnormally isolated.

Just as with ants or wasps or dolphins, the minimum unit for description cannot be the individual human body, but rather some social network, some set of bodies in physical and social relationship. Human bodies, that is, are partially constituted by their social relationships, just because their movements can only be intelligently characterized and represented in terms of social interaction. This has important implications for how we think about our bodies, but we will only be able to spell out those implications if we first consider two closely related characteristics of human bodies that have been recurrently alluded to in what has been said so far: self-reference and self-awareness. At once it becomes impossible to avoid voicing an objection, even an indignant protest, that will already have been elicited from many readers. How can you possibly assert, such readers will ask, that self-reference and self-awareness are characteristics of *bodies*? It is not, they will insist, my body that is aware of itself, it is I who am aware of my body, I who am self-aware. Such readers will add that I have sometimes used the expression "the agent" in speaking of the body, but that agents cannot be identified with their bodies and that in other locutions too – my use of "one" for example – I seem to have presupposed a conception of the self as more than and in some respects other than the body, while at the same time speaking of the body as if it just were the self.

How should I respond to this complaint? First of all by making it my own, by recognizing that I cannot but appear to have been damagingly inconsistent. For on the one hand I have spoken as if I am my body – and in the sense in which I intended that assertion to be taken I do indeed affirm this – and yet on the other hand I have used expressions which, construed as they are usually construed, do indeed seem to imply otherwise. And it would have been difficult to escape from either of these modes of speech. Consider the relationship between the use of "I" and the use of "my body." The latter can rarely, if ever, be substituted for the former without change of sense. If, instead of saying "I did it," I say "My body did it," I will be taken to be making a joke. If, when you say "I saw you there," I retort "You saw my body there," you will be puzzled. We often use "my body," that is, in ways that distinguish what is true of me from what is true of my body.

It is true of me that I am accountable for my actions and my omissions, that I am aware of the objects that I perceive, that I am able to reflect not only on my actions and my experiences, but also on my reflections on my reflections on my actions and my experiences. And none of these are true of my body. Yet interestingly what is true of my body is (generally) true of me. If my body is six foot tall, I am six foot tall. If my body aches, I ache. It is all too easy to conclude that there is something referred to by "I" that is other than, although intimately related to, what is referred to by "my body." But to conclude this would involve at least two kinds of error.

The first is that of supposing that there is something which I am over and above my body, namely, a disembodied human mind. But prior to death, in our present human condition, there is no such thing as a disembodied *human mind.* If a human body is an embodied mind, a human mind correspondingly is a set of powers that express themselves through a body. And, when they are so expressed, what philosophers have thought of as "mental" and what philosophers have thought of as "physical" are fused in one and the same set of directed movements. When I pick up some object and hand it to you, there are not two things going on, the one to be characterized as the intentional act of giving something to somebody, the other as a set of changes in the muscles and nerves of the arm and the hand. There is one act or sequence of acts, one change or sequence of changes. The giving *is* the movements of arm and hand.

Were we to think otherwise, were we to suppose the mind to exist apart from its bodily expressions, we would be confronted by a set of insoluble problems about the relationship of the mind to the body, for we would be compelled to conceive of the body as an external instrument, contingently related to the mind. I shall not here say anything further about the problems thus generated, but will only remark that one important motive for regarding mind and body in this misleading way has been provided by reflection on the phenomenology of the inner life and more particularly by thinking about what thinking appears to be. When thought is expressed in speech or in writing, we seem to have just one more example of powers of the mind exercised through their bodily expression, but certainly episodes of thought occur, when there is no such expression, when the mind presents itself to itself as an inner theatre of reflections, images, and feelings. And these episodes do suggest that the powers of the mind can be exercised independently of their bodily expression.

One mistaken response to this suggestion is to suppose that in such episodes the bodily expression of thought is through a series of happenings in the brain. Of course it is true that, whenever we think, neurons fire in particular areas of the brain. But when our thinking is expressed in speech or writing, neurons fire. And, when we pick up objects with our hands, neurons fire. Thinking unexpressed in speech or writing is of course accompanied by neuronal events, but it does not stand in the same relationship to occurrences in the brain that thinking expressed in speech or writing stands to the movements of the vocal chords or of the hands. Thinking that proceeds without outward bodily expression is not localizable within the body in the way that thinking expressed in particular sets of bodily movements is, something that our habit of thinking of thinking as occurring in the head – as when we say to a child learning mental arithmetic "Try to do the sum in your head" – is apt to obscure. How then should we respond?

It is an equally inept response to ignore or deny the relevant phenomenological facts about our inner life, those facts disclosed by focused attention to those inner thoughts, images, and feelings that receive no outward expression. What we need to do instead is to attend more carefully to the character of the happenings in the inner theatre and to ask what it is that makes each happening the particular happening that it is. What makes this perhaps inchoate thought of Cleopatra a thought of Cleopatra rather than of Claudia? What makes this image an image of a schooner rather than of a frigate? What makes this feeling a feeling of anger rather than excitement? In each case the only answer is in terms of what this thought or image or feeling would be, if it were to receive bodily expression. It is because my thought about Cleopatra, if expressed in speech or writing, could only be expressed by uttering the name "Cleopatra" that it is a thought about Cleopatra. It is because my image, if it received verbal or pictorial expression, would be expressed as a description of or as a picture of a schooner that it is an image of a schooner. What goes unexpressed is always expressible and the characteristics that we ascribe to it are ascribed in virtue of the characteristics that it would have if expressed.

In characterizing our inner unexpressed thoughts, images, and feelings we also make use of metaphor and are bound to do so. I wrote a moment ago about the theatre of our inner life, making use of one familiar metaphor; and, when we speak of what is stored in the memory or of pursuing a line of thought, we use other metaphors so familiar that we have to remind ourselves that they *are* metaphors, metaphors through which we situate our thoughts, images and feelings by analogy with what occurs in the public social world. The terms, that is to say, which we employ in identifying and characterizing the inner life of the mind take their sense from their prior uses either to characterize acts in which thoughts, images, or feelings are expressed in bodily form or to name or describe other features of the public world. The uses of those linguistic expressions without which we would be unable to identify and reflect upon the inner life of the mind are secondary to and dependent upon this prior set of uses.

Nonetheless, although thinking always begins from and relies upon materials drawn from the external public world, it does acquire a genuine autonomy. It sets its own goals, it finds itself entangled in a variety of problems and unclarities, it identifies the constraints imposed by logical and conceptual necessities, and, as it moves towards and beyond its goals, it is always distinctively *my* thought, the thought of this particular thinker. To say that it is my thought is initially to say that it is thought beginning from and relying upon materials drawn from the experiences afforded by my particular body. But my thought acquires an identity as mine that is derived from, but becomes in a significant way independent of the identity of my body. This autonomous existence of thought is something of which some become more aware then others, able to withdraw into the life of their own mind and so less disabled in their thinking, when their physical powers fail.

Thought differs from perception, whose objects belong to the body's immediate spatial environment. By contrast thought can find its objects anywhere in space and time. It is, unlike the body, undetermined by physical location. So it cannot but understand itself as simultaneously *my* thought, the embodied thought of this particular thinker with this particular body, and yet also thought that transcends the limitations that the spatiotemporal location of my body imposes on perception. It is this that gives us our sense of what it would be like to be a thinker without a body. Could we actually become such a thinker? There are those who would deny trenchantly that this is a conceivable possibility. But the onus is on them to provide sufficient grounds for their denial and they have not as yet done so.

A realistic phenomenological account of the inner life of thought does then raise important questions. But a willingness to recognize this must not blind us to the fact that in our present condition we know ourselves only as thinkers whose locus is this particular body and whose thought is expressed in and through the media afforded by this body. And we should resist any temptation to capitulate to dualist modes of thought, whether Platonic or Cartesian. The price to be paid for yielding to that temptation is not only to misconceive the autonomy of mind and thereby to generate insoluble problems concerning the mind-body relationship, it is also to obscure the single most important set of facts about the human body, those that concern the nature of its unity, a unity that has two aspects, the coordination of the body's various movements at any one time and the narrative unity of the body's various movements through time. Consider each of these in turn.

We took note earlier of the variety of types of movements exhibited by the human body: the undirected movements of the heart, lungs, and digestive organs, involuntary reflex responses to stimuli, and directed voluntary and intentional movements, including those that are expressive of intentions or of states of mind. But the activity of the body has a unity, so that, as I walk across the room, respond to the visual attractiveness of the food on the table, inhibit a sneeze, and pick up a sandwich, each of these types of movement is involved in a pattern of intentional activity, directed towards a single end. And the beating of my heart, my breathing, my glandular secretions, will also be coordinated so as to facilitate the achievement of the end, so long, that is, as the body is in good order.

For a body to be in good order is for it to exhibit the kind of unity and coordination that it needs if it is to achieve its goods. For a body not to be in good order is commonly for it to lack that kind of unity, so that defects of heart or lungs or glandular irregularities or erratic or ill-designed purposes disrupt the unity necessary for achievement. Think of the degree of physical and mental coordination necessary for someone to win or to aim seriously at winning the *Tour de France* or think of the degree of physical and mental coordination necessary for someone to prove or to aim seriously at proving some conjecture in mathematics and you have two very different exemplifications of that single-mindedness that is an excellence of human agency and of the human body, or rather of the human body as agent. For the unity and the excellence of the human body are the unity and excellence of agency.

Agency is exercised through time. To be an agent is not to engage in a series of discrete, unconnected actions. It is to pursue ends, some closer at hand in time, some more remote, some to be achieved for their own sake, some for the sake of furthering some further end, and some for both. And to pass from youth through middle age towards death characteristically involves changes in and revisions of one's ends. Furthermore the ends that one pursues through sometimes extended periods of time are often not only one's own, but are ends shared with others, ends to be achieved only through the continuing cooperation of others or ends that are constituted by the ongoing participation of others. And so the exercise of the powers of the body through time in the exercise of agency requires a variety of types of engagement with others.

To have understood this is a key to understanding better the relationship between our use of the first person pronoun "I" and our use of the expression "my body." When I use "I," I speak as agent and patient, as one who acts, suffers, and responds. I refer to and present myself to others as responsible and responsive. When I use "my body," I refer to and present myself to others in quite another way. For I can be said to be answerable for my actions and to be able or unable to control this or that bodily movement, but my body cannot be said to be so answerable. I am aware or unaware of this or that bodily movement; my body is neither aware nor unaware. My body presents itself to others; it does not present itself to me. It is because we are specifically human bodies, that is, embodied minds, that we need two modes of self-reference and that we do need both modes is itself a salient fact about the kind of body that we are.

I have spoken hitherto of how I use "I" and "my body." But I do not understand these expressions unless I understand that you too use "I" and "my body" in the same senses as, but with quite other references than, I do. So you present yourself as responsible and responsive in presenting your body to me and I understand that you are aware – or unaware – of yourself, as I am aware or unaware of myself. It is this shared understanding that is presupposed in those exchanges that can occur only between those who are both interpreters and interpretable. And that is to say, or rather to reiterate, that human bodies are intelligible only as potentially and actually in relationship with others, others who are recognized as possessing the same kinds of powers. Human bodies are essentially, not accidentally social. Yet the materials out of which they are constructed are not social. The movements of muscles and nerves, the circulation of the blood, the changes in the digestive system can all be adequately characterized without reference to social interaction, even if they are in fact involved in or elicited by responses to others. Someone's anger at an affront may cause their blood pressure to rise, but the phenomena of blood pressure can be adequately characterized in physiological and biochemical terms.

Even more obviously the movements of those particles of which every human body is composed can be both characterized and explained without reference to anything but physical items and physical laws. It follows that any attempt to give an account of the body exclusively in terms of the particulars of which it is composed is bound to fail, for all those features of the body that belong to it in virtue of its social character will have been omitted. (I take this also to be true of other complex animal bodies, such as those of dolphins and apes.) It also follows that any attempt to give a reductive account of the human body, in the hope of deriving and explaining its social properties and relationships by appeal to its physical composition confronts obstacles that, if not insuperable, show no sign of being superable in any terms that have so far been suggested by those who, having understood what is wrong with a dualist account of mind and body, suppose that the only alternative left to them is some version of a materialist monism. The relationship between what we understand about the body in terms of its expressive intentionality, its interpretability, and its social dimensions and what we understand about the physical materials of which it is composed stands in urgent need of characterization. But neither of the two classical philosophical attempts to supply such a characterization retain plausibility.

To the question "What is a human body?" we therefore need to respond that, when we have provided the most adequate account that we now can, it seems to remain an enigma, a source of puzzlement to all those of us who are human bodies. And that what it is to be a human body has this puzzling character may itself be among the more interesting properties of human bodies. For what we are puzzled about is how it is possible to be a human body and to be puzzled about what it is to be a human body. To be puzzled and to attempt to solve or dissolve some puzzle or set of puzzles is to be directed towards an end, the end of understanding at some point in the future what we cannot now understand. The powers that we set to work to achieve this end are those physical and mental powers whose integration exhibits the unity of

agency. Moreover we attempt to recruit others to this project of understanding by communicating to them the nature of our puzzlement and by
drawing upon resources that they are able to provide by the exercise of
their physical and natural powers. And, that is to say, a set of
human bodies recurrently exhibits in their activity a teleological organization of their structures and powers, a common end towards the
achievement of this kind of which each is directed. Projects aimed at
the achievement of understanding are of course not the only projects that
give such teleological form to the body's activity, but they are
paradigmatic examples of such projects.

Yet we should now remind ourselves that a human body is a physical
object, a set of law-governed particles, and that teleological concepts find
no application to physical particles as such. And we should also remind
ourselves that, although the human body as physiologically structured is a
set of systems – cardiovascular, digestive, and the like – that generally tend
towards some state of equilibrium, the teleology involved in the self-
maintenance of such systems is very different from the teleology of an
organism that moves towards some new end, an end set for it by itself
for the first time, perhaps in the company of others similarly directed.
The teleological directedness of the human body as a complex whole
engaged in understanding itself is not something derivable from or to be
understood in terms of either its physical or its physiological composition.

Yet how then are these related? We have at last arrived at a philosophical question or rather we have discovered what it is about the question
"What is a human body?" that renders it philosophical. One way to put
that question so as to exhibit the kind of philosophical question that it is
is to say that it is a question about how Aristotle's four types of cause find
application to the activity, structures, unity, and directedness of the
human body. It seems relatively easy to provide initial answers to
the questions about material and final causality. We are able to say
what the body is made of and this in reasonable detail. And we are able
to identify the ends to which the activity of bodies are directed. But what
we do not know how to answer is the question of how something of this
kind of material composition could have this kind of finality.

Medieval philosophers were not sufficiently puzzled by this question,
because they knew too little about the materials of which the human body
is composed. Modern philosophers have not been sufficiently puzzled by
this question, because, from La Mettrie to AI programs to the theorizing
of philosophers recently engrossed by the findings of neurophysiology and
biochemistry, they have tended to suppose that, if only we knew enough

about the materials of which the body is composed, the problem of how we find application for teleological concepts would somehow be solved or disappear. But perhaps the time has now come when we should recognize that progress in understanding the material composition of human bodies has brought us no nearer and shows no sign of bringing us any nearer to an answer to this question. So where do we go from here? The point of this essay is to identify just where it is that we now are and by doing so to suggest that we need to begin all over again.

# CHAPTER 6

# Moral philosophy and contemporary social practice: what holds them apart?

Contemporary academic analytic moral philosophy is a relatively flourishing sub-discipline. Its internal debates are conducted at more than one level: some concern the semantics or the epistemology of moral claims; in others rival standpoints on substantive normative and evaluative issues are matched against each other; and in a third type of discussion issues arising in other philosophical areas – concerning, for example, personal identity, the nature of rule-following or of agency – are brought to bear on normative and evaluative problems. But at all three levels the focus is provided by a limited set of central conceptions, the status of and relationships between which provide the theorizing of the moral philosopher with her or his subject matter: the right and the good, and more particularly justice and rights, utility and the virtues. Yet of course academic moral philosophy is not the only or the most important place where we encounter such conceptions. For they inform the idioms and the modes of practice of a great deal of everyday social life.

Within those small- and large-scale organized corporate spheres, in which most working days are spent, as well as in the family and in a range of voluntary organizations, complaints are framed in terms of invasions of rights, colleagues, subordinates, and superiors are evaluated by ascribing virtues and vices, and policies are advocated or impugned in cost-benefit terms which involve some measure of utility. But more than this, many of the established procedures, formal and informal, of life in a variety of such milieus presuppose some kind of practical agreement on some tolerably detailed conception of justice and rights, and/or of the virtues, and/or of utility, conceptions articulated at the level of practice, but not necessarily to any great extent or at all at that of theory. We thus encounter conceptions of justice and rights, of the virtues and of utility in two very different ways: in one form as providing a subject matter for academic theorists within moral philosophy and in quite another as socially embodied realities defining a variety of social relationships, norms, and goods.

An external observer might therefore have expected moral philosophers to be professionally concerned not only with the different types of theoretical enquiry in which they are engaged, but also with the nature of the relationships between those conceptions which provide them with a subject matter for theorizing and their socially embodied counterparts. Consider two sets of issues that concern those relationships. Moral philosophers of more than one standpoint have argued that the rules of morality are those rules which could not but be acknowledged by any rational person whatsoever. They are, on one such view, the rules required for the intelligent practical pursuit of self-interest, on another the rules required for genuinely impersonal practical judgment. On both views they are of course rules of practice. But they are always characterized by moral philosophers in high abstraction from the realities of actual practice. By contrast theorists of military tactics and strategy know that what it is for a precept or maxim to be applied can be understood only through the study of its actual applications or failures of application in real campaign or battle situations and that a necessary condition of knowing how a particular precept can be extended to new, perhaps as yet unforeseen situations requires a grasp of the concrete detail of, and if possible experience of, past applications or failures of application of that same precept or maxim. Why should it be any different with moral rules, maxims, and precepts? The interesting issue is raised not by any answers given to this question, but by a general failure to ask it. The moral theory of philosophers is almost always pursued at a level of abstraction from the concreteness of everyday life which is exhibited only by the strategy and tactics of those general staffs whose armies are about to be defeated.

A second point at which reference to the detail of practice might have been expected to occur is in the writings of those moral philosophers for whom an appeal to moral intuitions is central. Perhaps impressed by the failure among those moral philosophers, whose project it was and is to identify those moral rules about which any rational person whatsoever would have to agree, to agree on what those rules are and indeed on what rationality requires – a type of disagreement which if sufficiently far-reaching and irremediable itself provides the strongest of reasons for abandoning that project – such philosophers have instead appealed to what they sometimes speak of as our moral intuitions, that is, to a set of our ostensibly prephilosophical moral judgments which they aspire both to elucidate and to render coherent. So their task becomes not that of providing an account of the morality and practical evaluations of rational agents as such, but rather of the morality and practical judgment of the members of whatever social group it is whose intuitions provide them with their subject-matter. Given that this is their self-defined task, an external observer might have expected that they would immediately confront two related issues.

The first of these is how to characterize the relevant social group. But what moral philosophers in fact attempt in this regard is minimal. They are apt to speak of "our" intuitions without ever making it clear who is included and who excluded from this particular "we." And when they do go beyond this, characteristically it is only to specify the group to which they are relativizing their project in the abstract and general political and legal terms of high-level principle. Why does this matter? The answer to this question raises a second issue. What are too easily taken to be the same rules, maxims, and precepts always may and sometimes do vary considerably both in how they are construed and in what their application in practice amounts to in different social contexts and in the lives of different groups. Consider for example the different functions of lying – or rather of intentionally asserting what is believed by the speaker to be false – within different networks of social relationships. Where the norms of conversation are such that crucial areas of privacy in the lives of individuals or of small groups are generally protected at least from casual invasion, and perhaps from all or almost all invasion, by conversational enquiry, conversation will be such that everyone may reasonably expect to be told what the speaker believes to be true and a lie will be a gratuitous violation of such expectations. In social situations where by contrast some crucial areas or even all are treated as open to invasion without violating the accepted norms of conversation, some types of falsehood may afford the only available minimal protection to such invasion, and may be understood as justified, precisely because they do so.

Suppose that those who inhabit the former type of network of social relationships express their moral judgment by asserting that all lying is wrong, while those who inhabit the latter express their apparently incompatible moral judgment by asserting that some lying is permissible or even obligatory: would we, if we overheard an inhabitant of the former type of network judge that all lying is wrong, without knowing anything of her or his social relationships, and in similar ignorance overheard an inhabitant of the latter type of network judge that some lying is permissible, know as yet that they are in moral disagreement? Surely not, for we do not as yet know whether in each case their social circumstances merely happen to provide those speakers with a social context in which they affirm a judgment which they would be prepared to affirm of any person in any circumstances whatsoever, or whether instead some features of their particular social circumstances are presupposed in their judgments and would be cited in the reasons which they would adduce in support of those judgments, if they were fully spelled out, or indeed whether the judgment of either or both speakers is indeterminate between these two possibilities.

Dugald Stewart believed that, if we asked and answered this type of question correctly, by spelling out everything relevant in adequate detail, we would discover that all appearance of fundamental moral disagreement is illusory[1] and his survey of the evidence designed to support this conclusion, while it does not in fact settle the question in the way that he supposes, is a remarkable opening up of such an enquiry. But among contemporary academic philosophers who appeal to intuitions – as Stewart also in effect did – he has had almost no followers. The importance of this, as I have already suggested, is not only that of identifying from which group and what kind of social relationships a particular moral judgment emerges. It is also that of recognizing that utterances of one and the same form of words, apparently serving one and the same purpose of moral judgment, may in different contexts yield a very different meaning and use, when adequately interpreted.

To this someone may reply that Stewart was concerned not only with the moral judgments of himself and his fellow Scots, but also with those of alien peoples such as the Inuit and the Polynesians, but that contemporary academic moral philosophers who appeal to moral intuitions are concerned only with the judgments affirmed by themselves and by those in moral agreement with them, and that surely such persons can at least be treated as authoritative about the meaning and use of their own utterances. But here we need to notice the sometimes notable difference between what people say to themselves that they believe about moral and other practical issues, when they are by themselves and engaged in reflection in an abstract and general way – the situation in which most academic philosophy is written – and what the very same people show that they believe, when engaged in a variety of standard forms of activity, which involve sometimes uttering and sometimes presupposing, but not making explicit, a variety of particular moral judgments. Individuals vary a very great deal in the degree to which what they take themselves to believe and affirm on the basis of their reflections in the first type of

---

1 *Philosophy of the Active and Moral Powers* vol. I (Edinburgh, 1855), pp. 235–48.

situation coincides with what they actually believe and affirm in the second type of situation. Self-knowledge in this as in other respects is not just given; it has to be achieved, sometimes with difficulty. And its achievement often and perhaps characteristically involves learning about ourselves from the observations of others.

Indeed when our self-knowledge is not derived from the observations of others, it is a consequence of one's having made oneself with part of oneself into an observer, who behaves towards the relevant aspects of oneself and of one's activities as would a skilled external observer. First-person knowledge of one's self is thus either derived from or modeled upon the observation of others. And what is there to be observed, whether by others or by that part of oneself which has become an observing other, is characteristically and generally not an individual self in isolation, but an individual involved in some specific and particularized network of social relationships, whose modes of participation in those relationships express her or his moral commitments. Hence it is from the observation of networks of social relationships, and not from the introspective self-scrutiny of individuals reflecting upon themselves, that knowledge of one's moral judgments, including those which, if one was the relevant type of moral philosopher, one would call a moral intuition, is to be acquired. It remains therefore a striking fact that moral philosophers who appeal to moral intuitions should show as little interest as their colleagues do in socially and practically embodied moral concepts, restricting themselves as obstinately as any to a study of moral and other practical concepts conceived of as a purely theoretical subject matter, divorced from the actualities of practice, even including, so I have suggested, their own practice.

This is all the more surprising when we consider that the history of moral philosophy during the last thirty years has had a double aspect. There has on the one hand been the work done which has issued in those standard theories of justice and rights, of virtues and of utility, theories which constitute the achievement – the very great achievement – of academic analytic moral philosophy and which make of its practitioners the latest heirs of a range of Enlightenment and postEnlightenment thinkers from Bentham, Hume, and Kant to Sidgwick. But there has also by contrast been a set of contributions from a heterogeneous collection of writers – writers often viewed as mavericks by the academic establishment – who view this Enlightenment inheritance with attitudes which range from suspicion to hostility. Disagreeing radically among themselves on many issues, some of them have nevertheless sometimes agreed on the direction and focus of some of their criticisms of the type of moral philosophy now academically dominant, at least in the United States. Those critical agreements go beyond an accusation that contemporary academic analytic moral philosophy takes no account of the difference between moral and practical concepts, when abstracted from practice for the purpose of theoretical study in ways that may well disguise their character, when and as socially and practically embodied, and such concepts as actually embodied in social contexts. Their shared further claim is one for the primacy of practice. That is, they assert that a study of moral concepts detached from the political and social contexts in which they are put to work not only may, but does in fact inevitably distort our understanding of those concepts. It is not of course that there are not specific tasks for genuinely theoretical enquiry. But what theoretical enquiry needs to examine is precisely how moral and other practical concepts function, in directing and responding to activity in different types of social context, so that what theory abstracts from practice is not distorted by inattention to relevant key features of practice. About what those key features are such critics in large part disagree, but they have formulated a number of rival hypotheses, the truth of any one of which would put the enterprise of the dominant trend in contemporary academic moral philosophy in serious question.

Two very different and mutually antagonistic critical standpoints provide examples of such hypotheses. One is defined by the kind of use to which Nietzsche has been put by Foucault, Deleuze, and others, the other by the type of appeal to Aristotle and Aquinas made by some – as George Weigel has called us – NeoneoThomists, including myself. The genealogical hypotheses of the postNietzscheans are contributions to a narrative which not only claims to exhibit the utterance in practical contexts of standard, conventional moral judgments as characteristically reactive, giving corrupting expression to, while also disguising, the will to power, but also purports to show that the moral philosophy which underpins those judgments and takes them at their face value – in Nietzsche's own writings the key examples are drawn from the moral philosophy of German Kantians and postKantians and of English utilitarians, in those of Foucault from some of their later heirs – is the academic expression of those same reactive forces, in which the will to truth is yet another disguised transformation of the will to power. Let me translate these postNietzschean theses into another idiom.

What is being claimed is that there is a systematic discrepancy between on the one hand the meaning and the ostensible corresponding use of

moral concepts and judgments and on the other hand their actual use in
contexts of social practice. Meaning and ostensible use are such that the
use of moral concepts and judgments purports to involve an appeal to
some impersonal standard of right or good, neutral between the interests,
attitudes, preferences, and will of persons. Actual use is at the thereby
unrecognized service of highly specific interests, attitudes, preferences,
and will. This purported appeal to impersonality is made plausible by a
projection on to persons and situations of characteristics which they do
not in fact possess. To translate these postNietzschean claims into this
idiom is at once to recognize both the resemblances and the differences
between such claims and a type of theory in modern academic moral
philosophy advanced in different versions by C. L. Stevenson and by
Simon Blackburn.[2]

The resemblances reflect the agreement of both the postNietzschean
and the analytical emotivist or projectivist that morality as hitherto
understood is a psychological phenomenon whereby what are in fact
expressions of personal attitude and preference are presented in a very
different guise. The differences are in the conclusion drawn from this, for
the emotivist and the projectivist seem to believe that nothing in their
theories provides any good reason for abandoning the use of moral
concepts and judgments, as hitherto used, while the postNietzschean
affirms that anyone who has her or himself undergone the transformation
that will enable one to recognize how morality in fact functions will in
doing so have become unable to continue to use those concepts and
judgments. Underlying this difference is a more fundamental difference
about the social and psychological explanation of morality. Both Stevenson
and Blackburn, at least in their writings about morality, remain socially
and psychologically very much where Hume was. PostNietzscheans generally and Foucault more particularly by contrast not only understand the
genesis of morality in terms of a psychology and sociology of resentment,
frustration, and distortion, which puts in question unexamined Humean
assumptions, but also assert that the kind of moral philosophy which
leaves morality in place is a product of the same forces of resentment,
frustration, and distortion, able to uphold its intellectual positions only
because of a blindness to the dominant actual uses of moral concepts and
judgments in contexts of established social practice.

2 *Ethics and Language* (New Haven: Yale University Press, 1944); "Rule-Following and Moral
Realism" in *Wittgenstein: To Follow a Rule,* ed. S. H. Holtzman and C. M. Leich (London:
Routledge & Kegan Paul, 1981).

An external observer might therefore once again have expected that, challenged in this way on the nature and use of moral concepts in formally and informally institutionalized social practice, the practitioners of academic moral philosophy would have had to include the study of actual social practice in their deliberations. That external observer would once again have been disappointed. Why? Before I turn to sketch the outline of a possible answer to this question, it will be worthwhile to examine another case against recent academic moral philosophy, one framed from the very different standpoint of a Thomistic Aristotelianism.

Aristotle in the *Politics* and the *Nicomachean Ethics*, followed by Aquinas in his commentaries on these works, argued that it was only within a particular type of political and social order that rationally adequate practical and moral concepts could be socially embodied. This thesis was developed so that it had two aspects. Not only can and must we distinguish between social relationships which embody rationally adequate practical and moral concepts and those which embody only distorted and fragmented or otherwise counterfeit versions of those concepts, but it is also the case that only those who have been educated by and into the habits of character and mind integral to the former type of social relationships who are able adequately to recognize and to identify the difference between these two kinds of social relationship. Aristotle's own conjunction of empirical and normative theorizing, exemplified in his use of his collection of accounts of constitutions of *poleis* in the analyses of the *Politics* and the *Nicomachean Ethics*, provides a paradigm for any kind of study which aspires to present Aristotle's thesis in contemporary terms. But such a study will only succeed if it pays close attention to Aquinas's development of Aristotle's thesis, where the contrast has become one between types of social relationship which can be found in many different social orders, rather than one between the Greek *polis* and all other social orders.

Central to this Thomistic thesis about socially embodied moral concepts there is therefore a distinction between types of social milieu in which the conceptual organization of practical life can afford material for adequate and undistorted theoretical reflection and such contrasting types of milieu as those in which the fragmentation of any adequate conception and practice of virtues, rules, and of the achievement of goods has been such that they can provide material only for onesided and inadequate theoretical construction. And on a Thomistic view contemporary conventional academic moral philosophy is dominated by just such constructions.

I am not at this point arguing in favor of or against either the postNietzschean or the Thomistic type of hypothesis. I outline them only to take notice of the fact that they present recent academic analytic moral philosophy with a serious challenge. For if it is the claim of the proponents of such moral philosophy that the concepts which are elaborated within their theories, such concepts as those of rights and justice, of virtues and of utility, are one and the same set of concepts embodied in contemporary social reality, then they are committed thereby to a denial of all hypotheses of either a postNietzschean or a Thomistic kind. And we need to be provided with grounds for that denial. While if instead they assert that the concepts central to their theorizing can be fully understood quite independently of any relationship to such realities, they owe us and indeed themselves an account of why this is so, and of how it is that they have discovered a realm thus characterizable independently of reference to actual social practice. It is of course open to adherents of the contemporary academic analytic standpoint to adopt neither of these alternatives, but instead perhaps to reply that what they are engaged in delineating and analyzing is a set of normative idealizations. But, if this is the reply, we still need a specification of the relationship of those conceptual idealizations to embodied social realties. Are we being offered a blueprint for practice, designed to be translated more or less immediately into practice, perhaps by those engaged in so-called applied ethics? Or is what is being constructed an abstraction from practice, designed as much by its differences as its resemblances to instruct us about practice? Or is it instead that what such philosophy describes is a free-floating conceptual Utopia, innocent of any but the most idle aspiration to connect it with the real world?

These are once again generally unasked questions, so provoking the further question as to why they are thus systematically unasked. It was not so with Bentham and Hume, with Reid and Stewart, or with Mill and Sidgwick. Why is it now the case? What I am going to suggest is that the answer is not to be found by considering the present condition of academic moral philosophy as an isolated phenomenon, but rather as one aspect of the condition of the contemporary political, social, and cultural order. What distinguishes that order from its predecessors is both the extent and the character of the split between on the one hand those areas of social life, most signally, but not only those of the moral philosopher, in which an abstract and theoretical study of moral concepts is carried on, and those other much more extensive areas in which moral concepts and judgments enter into and inform the practical procedures and decision making of those institutionalized practices within which moral concepts take on socially embodied form. Where in the eighteenth and nineteenth centuries there was dialogue and interaction, sometimes more of it, sometimes less, between moral philosophers and the social order, and a closely related dialogue between moral philosophers who were defenders of some particular social and political order and those who were its antagonists, there are now barriers and obstacles. Unpractical philosophical theorizing confronts atheoretical social practice.

It is perhaps only by first understanding certain key features of that practice that we can best understand what has happened to academic moral philosophy. For it turns out to be the case that, were academic moral philosophers to attempt to find application for the central concepts which they have elaborated and defended at the level of theory in the realm of practice, they would encounter a kind of difficulty which arises not from the nature of contemporary moral philosophy, but from that of contemporary social practice. It is not, or at least not only, that moral philosophers restrict themselves to a theoretical enclave, but that contemporary social realities themselves offer obstacles to the project of embodying in practice the concepts central to contemporary academic moral philosophy. They do not to a significant degree provide the kind of matter which could become informed by those concepts. They are such that everyday plain persons could not in centrally important ways become responsive to the concepts and precepts of academic moral philosophy and remake and redirect their actions in accordance with them. The types of activity in which such everyday plain persons are inextricably involved nowadays have characteristics which preclude this possibility. And they preclude it because and insofar as they are types of individual activity and modes of institutionalized social practice which are already informed by distorted and distorting parodies of the concepts of modern moral philosophy. These socially embodied conceptual parodies effectively intervene between the theorizing of the moral philosopher on the one hand and on the other the responses of those plain persons whose lives would have to be informed by the concepts elaborated by and from that theorizing, if such theory were ever to be translated into practice.

What then are the features of distinctively contemporary social practice which thus intervene, transforming theoretical conceptions, either originally at home in moral philosophy or at least closely akin to those of the moral philosopher, into socially embodied counterparts which substitute themselves for genuine practical applications of the concepts articulated within philosophical theory? I shall here be concerned with three examples of such practice, but there are several others. The first is what I shall call *the professionalization of procedures* and I shall try to describe how this produces a socially effective distorting parody of what some moral philosophers have presented as a rationally justifiable conception of the person as autonomous and rightsbearing. The second is what I shall call *the compartmentalization of role-structured activity* and here I will suggest that in a parallel way what some other moral philosophers have presented as a rationally justifiable conception of the virtues is similarly distorted with similar results. I choose these first two examples from contrasting and often opposed types of contemporary academic moral philosophy, in order to emphasize that it is the condition of moral philosophy as such with which I am primarily concerned here and not any particular partisan standpoint within it. My third example likewise belongs to a type of moral philosophy very different in standpoint and methods from either of the first two. It concerns the evaluation of the consequences of actions or policies in terms of costs and benefits. The feature of social practice which intervenes so as to prevent on many occasions at least the application of certain key theoretical considerations I shall call *the negotiated aggregation of costs and benefits.*

I begin then with *the professionalization of procedures* and the effect of certain contexts of activity thereby professionalized upon the application of the concept of a right and of some closely related concepts. Let us begin with a type of situation often found in older forms of ordinary everyday social life in which rights were – as they sometimes still are – integral to relationships governed by customary institutionalized norms, relation-ships informed by mutual trust, a breach of which invited reproach by the characteristic utterance: "You had no right to do that." Sometimes – although only sometimes – appeals to put right what had been done wrong will have been made in the past not only to the perpetrator, but to some trusted authority, within the family or the local community, whose function it was both to pass judgment on the merits of the particular case, and also to do so in a way designed, if possible, to restore the relationship to its previous condition, so that the persons involved once again trusted each other. It has happened increasingly however that such authority is no longer available or is no longer trusted, so that there is no more or less assured remedy for wrongs. A wronged individual therefore will now generally be responsive to suggestions that she or he should refuse to respect or to trust in the particularities of local custom and should appeal instead to standards according to which certain rights belong to her or him qua human individual and not qua occupier of a particular role or possessor of a particular status. This appeal away from the local and particular to the universal requires just that kind of conception of the universal which it has been the aim of Enlightenment and postEnlightenment moral philosophers to supply. And we may plausibly suppose that such a philosopher, whether engaged in Kantian discovery or in Rawlsian construction, would recognize in the person responsive to this kind of appeal his or her own intended audience. But in what, if any, contemporary socially embodied form, we have to ask, does anything like a genuine version of the philosopher's discovery or construction actually become available to this kind of wronged plain person? Not, so it turns out, in any form which the relevant type of moral philosopher should be prepared to acknowledge.

What in fact becomes available is characteristically made so only through the bureaucratized procedures of some agency, court, or tribunal, appeal to which involves putting oneself into the hands of hitherto unknown others, so that one may be assigned the appropriate status. Documents of an unfamiliar kind will be made out, words will be put into one's mouth which are not one's own, the use of idioms which one has never before employed will be required of one and that these are one's own words and idioms will then be formally, and in an important way untruthfully, certified. The nature and gravity of the wrong complained of will be fixed, not by the preexisting, everyday shared understandings internal to those relationships whose norms were violated, but by the appropriate technical legal definitions. The plain person in search of a remedy is thereby to a significant degree alienated from the words and actions which are thus legally and bureaucratically imputed to her or him, and is able in any case to speak and act in this guise only as the more or less instructed and obedient client of someone whose professional expertise has officially licensed her or him to behave as required. So paradoxically what comes as close as social reality allows to the social recognition of a person as having the status of an autonomous rightsbearing individual is all too often inseparable from a new kind of alienated dependence, often enough a very expensive kind of dependence.

Moreover, suppose that this particular individual is in the end successful in obtaining whatever remedy for wrong is available from this particular agency, court, or tribunal. What she or he will then discover is that through the process of obtaining this remedy – and through the process whereby many others similarly situated have attempted to obtain and sometimes obtained such remedies – the original relationship has been transformed into something quite other than it at first was, so that the outcome of the complaint and its bureaucratic sequels cannot be the once hoped for restoration of the original relationship of trust, but must be instead a relationship informed by rules mandating an enforceable respect, rules always and only to be correctly grasped through dependent reliance upon someone else's professional expertise. Since these rules prescribe compensatory and punitive remedies, but are not in any way restorative, their prescriptions lead those taught to rely upon them to anticipate, so far as they can, future breakdowns of trust, and by acting in such anticipation to alter the character of the commitments with which as individuals they initially enter into relationships. So the relationship of wife and husband may become informed from the outset by not always recognized expectations of divorce and the relationship of patient to physician by anxieties which express an anticipation of malpractice, expectations and anticipations inevitably damaging to those relationships. A trust that was not always justified is replaced by a suspicion that too often has just the effects that seem to provide it with justification.

What matters for my present argument is however not at all whether these developments are welcome or unwelcome. What matters is that so much of the only social space available for any philosophical conception of the person as autonomous and rightsbearing to present itself in practical form is already occupied by this masquerading counterpart, a counterpart whose contingent and accidental negative features – accidental, that is, in relation to the moral philosopher's articulation of that conception in Kantian or in Rawlsian terms, not in relation to the determining forces of modern social life – distinguish it sharply from what the philosopher intended. So it is not just that a gap between the philosopher's conception and the actualities of social life remains, but that the counterpart to the philosopher's conception frustrates any possibility of the recognition of that conception as a genuine guide to practical activity and so effectively prevents the philosopher's conception from leaving a realm of theory now divorced from practice, a realm in which the academic division of labor had already made the moral philosopher all too comfortably at home.

The moral philosopher's conception of a right, should anyone attempt to introduce it into the practices of contemporary everyday social life and there find systematic application for it, would thus encounter a disfigured *Doppelgänger* barring its way. But is this true only of conceptions of rights elaborated in the course of postKantian or Rawlsian theoretical enterprises? I want to argue that this is something afflicting contemporary academic moral philosophy in general, rather than moral philosophy advanced from any one particular standpoint. Consider therefore another very different example, that of the concepts of the virtue theorist, whether avowedly Aristotelian, Humean, or whatever. The feature of contemporary social life which transforms notions of the virtues into something quite other than and alien to the virtue theorist's antecedent philosophical conceptions of them is a certain type of *compartmentalization of roles.*

By compartmentalization I mean that division of contemporary social life into distinct spheres, each with its own highly specific standards of success and failure, each presenting to those initiated into its particular activities its own highly specific normative expectations, each requiring the inculcation of habits designed to make one effective in satisfying those particular expectations and conforming to those particular standards. What is accounted effectiveness in the roles of the home is not at all the same as what is so accounted in the roles of the workplace. What is accounted effectiveness in the role of a consumer is not so accounted in the role of a citizen. The detailed specificity in the multiplicity of roles is matched by a lack of anything remotely like adequate prescriptions for the self which is required to inhabit each of these roles in turn, but which is itself to be fully identified with none of them. Yet it is this now attenuated core self, which when the compartmentalization of the distinctively modern self is carried to extremes, approaches the condition of a ghost, to which presumably the utterances of virtue theorists now have to be addressed. What happens when those utterances are heard by a multiplicity of selves, each inhabiting some particular role, rather than by the unified self envisaged by the virtue theorist?

What happens too often is that the precepts of the virtues come to be understood as prescriptions for habit-formation in the interests of achieving effectiveness in this or that particular role. And in so being heard and understood the crucial distinction between a virtue and a skill is obscured, if not obliterated. For within each role ends have been set to which the formation of habits are means. The virtues, as understood in the past, enabled us to identify the ends towards which good individuals are to direct themselves, and virtues, unlike skills, direct us only to good ends. But in social structures informed by role compartmentalization the ends of each role have already been to a remarkable degree socially and institutionally predetermined, so that virtues come to be understood only as more or less effective means to the achievement of those predetermined ends, that is, as socially relevant and effective skills. So the protagonists of virtue ethics, just like the rights theorists, find their conceptions in anything like their theoretical integrity to some large degree excluded from the realm of social actuality by those counterpart parodies which are at once barriers to the admission of theory into the realm of practice and substitutes for what the moral philosopher aspired to provide.

Consider now the confirmation that these theses receive from the predominant features of what is generally called "applied ethics." It is of course the official profession of the vast majority of the practitioners of the enterprises thus named that what they are doing just is applying the theory of the dominant standpoints of contemporary academic moral philosophy to the issues and problems arising in the practices of contemporary social life. And thus the very existence on so large and well-financed a scale of the enterprises of applied ethics may seem of itself to cast serious doubt upon the claims that I am making. For one thing it is from within those very spheres of activity which, so I have been suggesting, exclude genuine moral theory that the invitations to the practitioners of applied ethics have been most warmly extended. It has been from major figures in those private and public corporations within which, on the view that I have been taking, the phenomena of the professionalization of procedures and of the compartmentalization of rolestructured activity are most notably exemplified, that lavish endowment for applied ethics has flowed. Nonetheless the history of applied ethics, as it has developed through the last decades, strongly confirms my central thesis.

Begin by noticing two central aspects of its projects. First they are perhaps not exclusively, but almost so, focused upon the dilemmas or other predicaments confronting individuals within institutionalized and professionalized situations, rather than on the structures which determine the character of those situations. The questions consequently posed are: how is the individual within this type of situation or that to reason and what is such an individual to do? Neither the fundamental transformation of the dominant modes of social life nor the possibility of inventing modes of action outside them are generally taken seriously as options, and very understandably of course given the history of failed attempts to implement such radical solutions. But as a result it is only within the limitations and under the constraints imposed by *the professionalization of procedures* and *the compartmentalization of role-structured activity* that situations are described and alternative solutions propounded. The task of the applied ethicist thus becomes one of ameliorating particular types of problem situation, while leaving in place the underlying causes. In so doing applied ethicists come to be shaped by those same causes, so that we can observe an assimilation of the role of the applied ethicist to that of other managerial consultants and the growing professionalization of the activity of offering what purport to be solutions to the moral problems of business, the professions, and government. The moralist becomes one more technical expert, to be consulted by managers for a fee, just like other experts.

Secondly applied ethics has itself been transformed into one more set of specialized activities, bringing what those expert in it have to say to bear upon the particularized problems of a range of specialized contexts. So one type of expert deals with medical ethics, another with business ethics, a third with the ethics of government, and so on. Debates about the relevant credentials necessary for the recognition of expertise within each particular delimited area take place within that area. And once again it is in terms of constraints imposed by compartmentalization that applied ethics is structured. Two different questions have to be raised about the moral effects of such compartmentalization. A first concerns the nature of rules and how we are to identify the difference between a compartmentalized situation in which the application of a rule or set of rules has been such that the concrete particularities of the situation have been subjected to judgment in the light of the universality of the rule or rules and a compartmentalized situation in which the application of a rule has been such that the rule has been instead adapted to requirements imposed by the particularities of that situation, so that the rule provides not an independent standard of judgment, but an apologia for currently established forms of activity. How are we to discriminate between these when, for example, the rules about truth-telling and responsibility for disclosure are variously interpreted and rewritten in one way for physicians, in another for lawyers, in a third for salespersons or accountants?

The problem is not just that we can find grounds for alternative and incompatible answers to this question. It is that we have available to us no shared, public, incontestable standard for so discriminating. The difficulties thus posed are intensified when we consider a second effect of compartmentalization upon applied ethics, one that I have already noticed in a more general way in discussing how the compartmentalization of roles replaces the concept of a virtue by that of a socially effective character trait. What applied ethics by virtue of its specializations reinforces is a socially embodied conception of character as a locally effective set of traits, in which acceptability in a variety of particular professional contexts has replaced the moral philosopher's conception of character and of the virtues as belonging to the self as such, rather than to its compartmentalized roles, and as concerned with the relationship between the individual's good and the common good of the whole rather than with goods pursued in different and often largely independent spheres.

So-called "applied ethics" then is to some large degree not at all an application to actual social practice of the theories of academic moral philosophy, but is instead itself a substitute for those theories, providing ideological disguises for some of the limitations of the social settings in which moral discourse is deployed. And it is not only the rights theorist and the virtue theorist who can as a result no longer be heard in the realms of distinctively contemporary social practice; the very same inaudibility may on occasion afflict the utility theorist. What on such occasions has intervened between the utility theorist and the genuine application of her or his theories have been the effects of social practice structured *by the negotiated aggregation of costs and benefits* upon the application of theoretical conceptions of the evaluation of consequences of actions and policies by moral philosophers. What has generally informed such theorizing was an ideal inherited from classical utilitarianism, that of elaborating genuinely impersonal and therefore interest-neutral instruments for social measurement and evaluation, so that everybody should count for one and nobody for more than one. The achievement of this ideal in particular cases requires rationally justifiable and impersonal answers to such questions as: first, what factors in this particular case are to be included as relevant in assessing costs and benefits? What is it that is to be weighed and measured? Secondly what weight is to be assigned to different types of factor in assessing either costs or benefits, particularly when there are available radically different ways of commensurating them, none of them incontestable? That is, how do you weigh a thousand full-time jobs in an area already suffering from unemployment against three deaths from air pollution? Or forty thousand such jobs against the extinction of one species of owl? And thirdly over what time scale are consequences to be measured in this particular case, since the balance of costs over benefits or vice versa is often not the same over thirty years as over ten?

When such questions are posed nowadays, not in moral philosophy seminars but in the arenas where policy is made within corporations, private or public agencies, or government, it is crucial that answers are constructed through a process of negotiation, access to which and leverage within which depends upon the power and influence exerted by a variety of more or less organized interests. So out of the alternative and rival answers to these questions on particular issues a consensus will generally be reached, one for which a set of justificatory reasons can certainly be offered, just as another such set – with as much and as little rational justification – could have been offered for one or more rival conclusions, had the negotiations issued in a different outcome. The negotiated outcome is thus to a significant degree not at all an impersonal measurement of costs and benefits, but an index of the access to relative power within the negotiating processes of different groups. What is more, because cost-benefit analyses characteristically and generally concern only the effects of actions or policies within one particular delimited area of social life, actions or policies justified by appeal to them are rarely, if ever, evaluated in terms of the costs and benefits to the entire social and political community. Yet evaluation in such terms was what classical utilitarianism and its legitimate heirs have always required. So once again it is not the moral philosopher's theoretical concepts which have found application in the realm of practice, but instead a substitute counterpart informing a mode of practice which assists in preventing the intrusion of those theoretical concepts.

What this catalogue of examples – and there are of course others – suggests is that we inhabit an established social and cultural order which is in its central aspects resistant to, which has rendered itself largely immune to, critique from the standpoint of moral philosophy. Universities and colleges function in a twofold way in sustaining this order. They are on the one hand, through disciplines such as those of the applied natural sciences and economics, producers of techniques which can be put to the service of whatever ends are being pursued privately, corporately or governmentally. On the other hand the disciplines of the humanities and of the humaner of the social sciences provide reservations to which theoretical pursuits, such as those of the moral philosopher, can be relegated and within which any critical power that those disciplines might develop can be confined, so that whatever force moral philosophy might have had as criticism is neutralized by its status as professionalized theory, as belonging to a realm in which the victories and defeats of theorists have become irrelevant to the victories and defeats of everyday social life.

The moral concepts of contemporary professionalized theory are thus very different from those which inform practice. These latter are, as we have seen, able to function as well as they do in controlling moral expression within practical life, just because their parodying and distorting functions preserve them from representation in anything that would be recognized by the philosophical theorist as coherent theoretical form. And when someone does seriously attempt to embody the coherence of theory in her or his social relationships, then generally and characteristically her or his actions and their consequences will be so effectively shaped and strait-jacketed by the professionalization of procedures, by the compartmentalization of role structures, and by the negotiated aggregation of costs and benefits that even if that person should become aware of the discrepancies between their political profession or their standpoint in moral philosophy on the one hand and what actually happens in contemporary social practice on the other, that awareness will of itself have at most negligible power to alter matters.

I claim that this is what happens generally and characteristically, but not of course universally or inevitably. Under what conditions *can* this type of social deformation be avoided or escaped? Under what conditions is it escaped? Both Nietzsche and his genealogical heirs and modern Thomistic Aristotelians have provided answers to these questions. But they have done so in very different ways. Nietzsche had to resign his chair at Basel and Foucault lived for some of his intellectual life as a nomad on the margins of academia, striving even while at the Collège de France to ensure that "Nietzschean professor" was not an oxymoron. So from Nietzsche's beginnings until now the genealogical project has been to outwit and thereby to subvert the institutionalization of the gap between theory and practice, and the corresponding deformations of both, by a kind of intellectual and social guerrilla warfare.

Thomists by contrast have often enough created – and not only in the lives of seminaries or in those of religious orders, but sometimes also in secular communities – alternative institutions, to some degree insulated from the contemporary social order in an attempt to integrate intellectual, moral, and social formation in a way that would escape the deformations of their age. Today we are all too apt to stress the inadequacies of their projects, rather than the genuine insights that were at work in them. Nonetheless the inadequacies were real and damaging. But the moral is not to abandon the insights, but instead to reembark more forcefully on the task of creating alternative institutions, in which Aristotelian and Thomistic concepts are embodied in institutionalized forms of practical reasoning aimed at the achievement of a multiplicity of goods – those of the productive lives of the farmer and of the construction worker and of the philosopher both in their distinct enterprises and as together engaged in a single, common, complex task – all ordered to the achievement of the good.

The practical subversions of the genealogist and the practical constructions of the Thomist moral philosopher are of course themselves mutually antagonistic enterprises, even although each can learn much from the other. What they have in common is that any hope of success in them comes only from those of us not only content but anxious to be excluded from and marginalized by the dominant trends of our social life, so that they can escape the deformations which inform both it and academic moral philosophy. The aim of this essay has been to explain why.

# PART II

# The ends of philosophical enquiry

# CHAPTER 7

# The ends of life, the ends of philosophical writing

I

We are sitting with friends at a diner or standing in line to buy tickets for a movie, chatting idly, when suddenly one of us, unable to contain himself in the face of our trivialities, bursts out with some existential question which we might later on paraphrase in polite terms as "What is it to live a human life well or badly?" or one which we might paraphrase as "What law, if any, has authority over us?" or one which we might paraphrase as "What is the significance of death in our lives?" The questions that actually burst out on such occasions will be expressed in cruder and rawer terms, as much a scream as an utterance, whose obscenities can be heard as expressions of anger and pain. And the response by those who hear both the questions and the emotions expressed through them is likely to be deep embarrassment, a strong wish to change the subject, a will to behave as if the questions had not been asked. We think: what can have got into him to talk like *that*? Is he perhaps having a break-down?

Yet provide these very same questions with a different context, that, say, of a graduate seminar in philosophy, utter them in a quiet academic tone of voice and in a suitably purged vocabulary, and they no longer sound naive, they no longer evoke embarrassment. Discussing Aristotle's *Politics* Book I, where Aristotle contrasts the end of a political community with that of a village or a group of villages (1252b 27–30), Aristotle says that the end of a political community is not merely to live, to survive, but to live well. "What does Aristotle mean?" someone asks and someone else responds "So what is it to live a human life well or badly?" Aristotle's text has provided us with a pretext for asking a question that we might otherwise stammer nervously in uttering.

Or we are perhaps in a seminar on the philosophy of law, discussing skeptical arguments about the authority of law and how far they undermine

Aquinas's theses about that authority in qqu. 90–108 of the Ia-IIae of the *Summa Theologiae*, and someone asks "So what law, if any, has authority over us?" Or again we are reading in class sections 46 to 53 of Heidegger's *Sein und Zeit* and someone, while advancing an objection to Heidegger, asks "So what *is* the significance of death in our lives?" In each case the texts provide the questions with context and pretext. And without texts many of us would find it difficult, even impossible, to utter, let alone address them. But what of the writers of those texts? They after all present themselves to us as well able to ask and answer such questions in writing without anxiety or embarrassment. And what of those early thinkers who provided Aristotle and Aquinas and Heidegger with grist for their academic mills by posing these questions in talk long before there were any relevant texts? How did they succeed in first opening up this kind of question, questions that we may call questions about the ends of life?

The earliest answers to these questions were of course what we now call religious. They found expression in myth and ritual and most strikingly in words heard by humans as spoken by gods or by God. And religions have continued to provide one kind of context within which questions about life and death, hope and despair, and the ultimate nature of things have continued to receive answers. About such religious contexts, of supreme importance though they are, I will not speak further in this essay, except to note two things. First, in secularized societies, such as those of modern Europe, where the religious context has been largely removed, it is unsurprising that the asking of questions about the ends of life should have become so often something of an embarrassment, something even sometimes taken as a sign of psychiatric disorder. And, secondly, it was of course religious answers to such questions that were put in question by the earliest prephilosophical and philosophical theories. We all of us, both in the long histories of our cultures and in our own short histories as individuals, start out with some more or less well articulated set of beliefs and judgments, often, although not always, religious in form, and only later on recognize that we need to put some of those beliefs and judgments in question. What elicits this disturbance of our initial settled habits of belief is the impact of something that manifestly does not square with those beliefs. Only then are we apt to recognize that those beliefs are answers to questions, questions to which there are alternative and rival answers. But at this point a number of things may – or may not – happen.

We may make explicit those questions to which we had all along been giving answers without realizing it. And in considering different and rival answers, we may respond to each by asking "Is it true?" and "Do we have sufficiently good reasons for holding that it is true?" and "What would we mean by it, if we took it to be the answer to our question?" Someone may then take matters one stage further by asking "What do you mean by 'true'?" and "What are sufficiently good reasons for so judging?" and "How are we to understand the meaning of the various expressions that we use?" With this last set of questions philosophy has come on the scene.

Philosophy, that is to say, is generated only at this very late stage, after we have succeeded in standing back from those first-order life and death questions that give it much of its point and purpose. By standing back we distance ourselves both from those questions and from those who ask them, so generating the difference between the anguished and embarrassing utterances of those inescapably and painfully in the grip of those questions and the socially and academically acceptable utterances of those engaged in the professionalized and specialized enquiries of the philosophy seminar. What we often fail to acknowledge is that in doing so we are also distancing ourselves from ourselves. Philosophy inescapably involves some measure of self-alienation. And this remains true even of the kind of philosophy which makes this contrast between the existential anguish of the first-order questioner and the condition of those who stand back and think about these things in a distanced and impersonal way subject matter for their own philosophical enquiries, as Kierkegaard did in reflecting on Hegel, and as I am doing now.

So what then of philosophical writing? I suggested earlier that texts may provide us with pretexts for opening up questions about the ends of life. But this can happen in either of two very different ways. A text or set of texts may on the one hand engage those who read and discuss it, so that they become inhabitants of its conceptual world and formulate their questions only in its terms, so that, as it were, their world becomes text and their enquiries are no longer about the ends of life, even when these are the subject matter of the texts in question, but only about the-ends-of-life-as-conceived-within-this-particular-textual-universe.

Yet this way of putting matters is not quite right. It is rare for philosophical texts to have readers who are instructed only by texts. Characteristically it is through the interventions of teachers and interpreters that we come to understand texts, so that it is not that the world becomes text, but that the world becomes text-as-interpreted-by-so-and-so. And what comes between the reader and the questions that the author addressed is then not only the text, but the text read through layers of interpretation.

On the other hand there are philosophical texts and interpreters of such texts that, sometimes after some delay, send us from the text back into encounter with the world about which the text speaks. These are texts whose authors and interpreters succeed in distancing us their readers from the text and its interpretations, and by so doing return us to questions about the ends of life that we had earlier been unable or unwilling to confront, perhaps because they were too painful to ask, so enabling us to make these questions our own, and to pose them patiently and rationally. How do such texts achieve this? How do they, their authors and their interpreters differ from those who make of their readers inhabitants imprisoned within a textual world? These are questions that I address in this essay.

Someone may respond: these are the wrong questions. What you should be looking for is not differences between kinds of texts and kinds of author or interpreter, but rather differences between kinds of reader. It is readers who by their different ways of responding to texts produce such very different outcomes of philosophical reading. To this I reply that it is true that the collaboration between author and reader that takes place in the reading of a philosophical text is important. Nonetheless it is on the author's and perhaps the interpreter's contributions to this collaboration that I want to focus attention.

II

Consider first two philosophers of the kind who by their writing send us beyond philosophy into immediate encounter with the ends of life. I deliberately choose philosophers of different standpoints from different times and places: J. S. Mill and Thomas Aquinas. I begin with Mill. We cannot understand Mill's texts without also reading works by other authors, most importantly by Bentham and by Coleridge. Mill's own views emerged from and are fully intelligible only by reference to his dialogue with these and others, a dialogue whose starting-point was his nervous breakdown in 1826 when he was twenty years old. His early education had notoriously provided him with answers rather than questions. And he discovered the questions as his own only when his life's ends had become problematic. "Suppose," he asked himself, "that all your objects in life were realized, that all the changes in institutions and opinions which you are looking forward to, could be completely effected at this very instant: would this be a great joy and happiness to you?" And he tells us how "an irrepressible self-consciousness distinctly answered

'No!' At this my heart sank within me: the whole foundation on which my life was constructed fell down" (*Autobiography*, chapter 5).

The details of Mill's recovery need not concern us. But the controversies between Benthamites and Coleridgeans in which he first participated as a member of a debating society during this period were transformed into an internalized dialogue which became explicit in his essays on Bentham and Coleridge, but which is a subtext in many of his writings. It is because of this that Mill's readers are themselves cast in the role of participants in dialogue with Mill. Mill urges the answers at which he has presently arrived upon them, but he does so in such a way as to engage them primarily with the questions, whatever they may come to think of his particular answers.

It is a commonplace that within Mill's thought there are fissures and fractures, often partly concealed in passages where the compression of Mill's writing leaves it to his readers to spell things out further. And critics of Mill have sometimes identified these as providing grounds for rejecting some of Mill's central theses. The so-called proof of the principle of utility in chapter 4 of *Utilitarianism* is a case in point. What Mill says in this passage is at once highly compressed and highly suggestive and, before we interpret Mill as having committed not just fallacies in this argument, but obvious and blatant fallacies, as many of his critics have done – Sidgwick and Moore set us a very bad example in this respect – we need to ask what alternative ways there are of reconstructing Mill's argument.[1] And by providing the best, that is, the most cogent reconstruction possible, before we start quarreling with it, we become collaborators with Mill.

It does not follow that we will end up agreeing with Mill's conclusions. But even in disagreement we will still be attempting to answer versions of just those questions that Mill himself was posing. By returning us to them Mill directs us beyond his text, so that we now have the task of providing, if we can, a better response than Mill's to those problems about the ends of life by which he had been confronted at the time of his nervous breakdown.

Or consider a very different philosopher, Aquinas. Aquinas's method is more explicitly one of dialogue than is Mill's. On any question he assembles as wide a range of compelling arguments as he can, both for and against some particular answer, drawn from as wide a diversity of standpoints as he is aware of, and draws his own conclusions only after

---

1 For an excellent example of such a reconstruction see Elijah Millgram, "Mill's Proof of the Principle of Utility," *Ethics* 5, 110, no. 2, January 2000.

and from his engagement with these arguments. Where for Mill the tension is between Bentham and Coleridge, for Aquinas it is most importantly between the Averroistic Aristotelians of the Arts faculty and the Augustinians of the faculty of Theology in the University of Paris. Some of his most important treatises present in written form what were originally oral disputations, disputations in which a thesis had been publicly defended against any objection that might be advanced against it from any point of view. But even in treatises that do not belong to this genre Aquinas's treatment of arguments is that of a mind formed in part by the practice of commentary on texts, but also by the practice of disputation.

It is crucial that, just as in a disputation there is always the possibility of something more to say, so Aquinas's discussions of particular problems always leave open the possibility of the discovery of one more argument, of some hitherto unexpected formulation of at least apparently cogent premises, which entail a conclusion at odds with the conclusion that had up to this point prevailed. Readers who recognize this possibility and who are forced to ask the questions "Are the arguments advanced so far sufficient?" and "What are we to say next?" thereby become participants in the debate, just as they might have been at a disputation. And so they make Aquinas's questions their own questions and attempt to give more adequate answers than his.

It does not follow, any more than it did with Mill, that the outcome will be agreement with Aquinas. But Aquinas, like Mill, directs us beyond his text to the questions themselves. And those who happen to be close readers of both Aquinas and Mill will find themselves committed to constructing a new form of dialogue between those two very different standpoints on issues such as the nature of happiness, that is, on issues concerning the ends of life.

I have cited Mill and Aquinas as exemplary practitioners of a particular kind of philosophy and their examples enable us to say a little more about the kind. Three characteristics of their philosophical writing are defining characteristics of that kind. First both were engaged by questions about the ends of life as questioning human beings and not just as philosophers. It is not that either of them found any good way of posing these questions that did not already involve taking up an attitude to the answers that earlier philosophers – and others – had given to those questions. But the same questions about the ends of life continued to confront them as human beings throughout their not always straightforward development.

Secondly, both Mill and Aquinas understood their speaking and writing as contributing to an ongoing philosophical conversation, a conversation that had had a long history before they became a part of it and that would continue after they had fallen silent. This self-understanding enabled them to treat their readers and hearers as likewise contributing to that same conversation. Thirdly, it matters that both the end of the conversation and the good of those who participate in it is truth and that the nature of truth, of good, of rational justification, and of meaning therefore have to be central topics of that conversation, as both Mill and Aquinas insisted. But the technical or semitechnical treatment of those issues has to be subordinated to the purposes of the conversation.

So what is the condition of philosophy when it lacks these characteristics? It is first of all philosophy conceived as primarily and sometimes exclusively the exercise of a set of analytic and argumentative skills. Subject matter becomes incidental and secondary. Entering into philosophy is a matter of training in the requisite skills and questions about the ends of life are taken to be of interest to philosophers just insofar as they provide subject matter for the exercise of those skills. Secondly, philosophy may thereby become a diversion from asking questions about the ends of life with any seriousness. I use the word "diversion" as Pascal used it. On Pascal's view we try to conceal from ourselves how desperate our human condition is and how urgently we need answers to our questions about the ends of life by engaging in a variety of types of activity well-designed to divert our attention: engaging in the rituals of court and politics, hunting, gaming, and the like.

Hume, a more Pascalian character than we often realize[2] tells us how, when forced by his philosophical enquiries into painful reflection on the ends of life – "Where am I or what? From what causes do I derive my existence and to what condition shall I return? Whose favour shall I court, and whose anger must I dread? What beings surround me? and on whom have I any influence, or have any influence on me?" – he would cure himself of "this philosophical melancholy or delirium" by resorting to diversions: "I dine, I play a game of backgammon, I converse, and I am merry with my friends," so that his speculations appear "cold, and strain'd, and ridiculous" (*Treatise* I, iv, 7).

Yet, while Hume turned away from philosophical questions about the ends of life to the diversions of dining and backgammon, there has developed since a kind of philosophy that sometimes functions for those

---

2 As I have argued in "Hume, Testimony to Miracles, The Order of Nature, and Jansenism" in *Faith, Skepticism and Personal Identity*, ed. J. J. MacIntosh and H. Meynell (Calgary: Calgary University Press, 1994).

who engage in it just as dining and backgammon did for Hume. It reduces all questions to technical or semitechnical questions and it has the effect of making the serious and systematic asking of questions about the ends of life, rather than the asking of second-order philosophical questions about those first-order questions, appear if not cold, at least strain'd and ridiculous.

Thirdly, just because this kind of philosophy distances and defends those individuals who practise it from personal engagement with questions about the ends of life, it does not follow that they do not in their lives even if not in their philosophy, presuppose answers to those questions, answers all the more influential for being taken for granted and remaining philosophically unexamined. In fact in the lives of the practitioners of this kind of philosophy we may well find two different kinds of concern with questions about the ends of life that engage them in quite different ways. Qua philosophers, they may embark on second- or third-order enquiries about those questions. Qua human beings, they may take for granted, under the influence of whatever cultural ethos they inhabit, some unexamined type of first-order answer. And the relationship between these two, being contingent, will vary with their cultural situation.

Enough has now been said to suggest a remark about that well-established genre, the biography of philosophers, and that yet to be established genre, the history of philosophers (as contrasted with the history of philosophy). It is that both authors and readers of such biographies and such yet to be written histories would do well to attend to the relationship in the life of each philosopher between her or his mode of philosophical speech and writing and her or his attitude towards questions about the ends of life. Being a great philosopher is not at all the same thing as leading an exemplary philosophical life, but perhaps the point of doing philosophy is to enable people to lead, so far as it is within their powers, philosophical lives. And of course how individual philosophers work out in the detail of their lives the relationship between the ends of their philosophical writing and the ends of their lives always depends on a myriad of contingencies, so that any life may open up hitherto unimagined possibilities. And in this respect for anyone things may go either well or badly.

III

How then may things go wrong in relating the ends of life to the ends of one's philosophical writing? I shall make a beginning to answering this question by considering two philosophers, contemporary with each other and with this in common: that each took himself to have been imprisoned within a particular philosophical scheme of thought, one which by its way of treating questions about the ends of life had frustrated him from arriving at a true answer to them. Each therefore had to break with the mode of philosophical writing characteristic of that scheme of thought and to find a new mode of writing informed by different ends, so that the ends of his writing might become, if not subordinated to, at least consonant with those ends which he took to be the ends of life.

The philosophical scheme into which both had been educated in the first decade of the twentieth century was German NeoKantianism which had long since declined into its scholastic phase, something that characteristically happens to any mode of academic philosophy that becomes so well established that to those under its influence rival voices become inaudible, or if heard, are misinterpreted. The result was a large inability to think outside the framework of NeoKantianism, combined however with a variety of projects for extending its hegemony, both within philosophy, so that it might provide an account of the historical and social sciences as well as of the natural sciences, and in other academic disciplines, such as theology and sociology. It was not that there was no awareness of philosophical alternatives to NeoKantianism. But even for those anxious to break with NeoKantianism, the question was in which direction to make their exit. And this was not only a philosophical question.

For NeoKantianism was the philosophical face of Imperial German *Kultur*. The Kant of the NeoKantians was not just the philosopher who had defined the scope and limits of philosophy, he was also the culture hero of the *Reich*. From Otto Liebmann, who had understood himself to be serving the same ideals both as a Kantian professor and as a Prussian soldier in 1870–71, through the debates of the 1880s and 1890s, in which the contention that Kant's conception of the moral law had provided the philosophical foundation of the *Rechtsstaat* figures prominently, to Thomas Mann who identified the German cause in the First World War with that of Kant, the notion that Kantian philosophy in its various NeoKantian versions was *the* distinctively German philosophy had wide cultural currency. So that philosophers who broke with it also rejected a certain notion of what it was to be a German.

The two philosophers in question are Franz Rosenzweig (1886–1929) and Georg Lukács (1885–1971). And I shall contrast them in the following way. Rosenzweig's quarrels with particular philosophical views turned into a quarrel with philosophy as such, at least with philosophy as a form of abstract theorizing, and he in company with Eugen Rosenstock devised a type of dialogue that was intended to replace general and abstract theorizing by an engagement with the particular and the concrete. Lukács's quarrels with particular philosophical views turned into a quarrel with the whole German philosophical tradition and his conversion to Marxism, so he believed, enabled him to understand why that philosophical tradition was unable to solve its own problems. But each in trying to write so as to serve what they now took to be the ends of life no longer wrote in a way that served the ends of philosophy, Rosenzweig because his ends were no longer philosophical, Lukács because his Marxism became a philosophical straitjacket. I begin with Rosenzweig.

Rosenzweig was later to write of his own relatively brief immersion in NeoKantianism that

It is so long since I had any cause to bother myself over the Kantians. Even when I was reading Kant myself . . . I did not find any reason to turn to them. I mean the present "schools" have simply the significance of being schools. One must have passed through one of them – it doesn't matter which (I did the Southwest German one) – but afterwards one needs only to bother himself further with the Master, "the good Master, long since dead."[3]

Rosenzweig had already extricated himself from German Idealism when, at Leipzig in 1913, he encountered Eugen Rosenstock. Together they developed a conception of thinking designed to replace older philosophical conceptions. Three contrasts characterized this new conception. The first is between what Rosenzweig and Rosenstock took to be the monological character of older conceptions and their own view of thought as dialogue, dialogue through which truth emerges in ways that cannot be predicted. A second contrast is that, on what they took to be the traditional view, thought is primary, language use secondary, whereas in their view thought *is* the deployment of language, the conversational language of everyday life. Later Rosenzweig was to express these contrasts by saying "In actual conversation, something happens. I do not know in advance what the other will say to me because I myself do not even know what I am going to say; perhaps not even whether I am going to say anything at all."[4]

---

3  Letter of October 1916, trans. Dorothy M. Emmet in *Judaism despite Christianity: The "Letters on Christianity and Judaism" between Eugen Rosenstock-Huessy and Franz Rosenzweig* (New York: Schocken Books, 1971), p. 116.
4  "The New Thinking," *Philosophical and Theological Writings*, tr. and ed. Paul W. Franks and Michael L. Morgan (Indianapolis: Hackett, 2000), p. 136.

A third contrast is this: in traditional philosophy for the most part the thought is one thing, the thinker quite another. What is asserted, argued for, concluded is what matters. Who asserted it, argued it, arrived at the conclusion may be of historical, but is not of philosophical interest. But Rosenzweig's reading of Kierkegaard and Nietzsche had introduced him to the notion of thinkers as the embodiment of their thought, so that to reflect on the thought is impossible unless one enters into conversation with and comes to terms with the thinker.

Rosenzweig sometimes thought of himself as having espoused one philosophical standpoint against others, but sometimes as an antiphilosopher. The unpublished book in which he developed his critique and rejection of philosophy is entitled in German *Das Büchlein vom gesunden und kranken Menschenverstand* (the English translation's title is a very loose rendering of the German: *Understanding the Sick and the Healthy*.[5] If the words *"und kranken"* had been omitted from the title, the natural way to translate it would be *The little book of common sense* and what Rosenzweig succeeds in conveying by adding those words is that what is contrary to common sense is a symptom of a kind of sickness.

The movement away from common sense that results in this sickness is taken by philosophers who abstract themselves from the flow of life and set themselves timeless problems with systematically misleading answers. The philosopher "has forcibly extracted thought's 'object' and 'subject' from the flow of life and he entrenches himself within them" (p. 40). To ask in abstraction what the essential nature of things is is to lose one's grasp of the singularity and particularity of things. About what is essential – "no one but a philosopher asks this question or gives this answer. In life the question is invalid; it is never asked" (pp. 41–42). And so the philosopher, "suspicious, retreats from the flow of reality into the protected circle of his wonder. Nothing can disturb him there. He is safe. Why should he concern himself with the crowd of nonessences?" (p. 42).

What the philosopher protects himself from is encounter with the singular and particular. And one consequence is that he assimilates through his abstract use of terms and modes of argument what is in fact distinct and different. So he fails to recognize differences between three realities that we encounter, those of the world, of human beings, and of God. Some philosophers have reduced humanity to nothing more than an aspect of the natural world, while others have identified God with nature

---

5 Tr. Nahum Glatzer (Cambridge, Mass.: Harvard University Press, 1999).

or with *Geist*. The culmination of philosophy's misconceptions is Vaihinger's *Philosophie des Als-Ob*, written in 1876–78, although published only in 1911, described by Rosenzweig as "a synthesis of simplified Kant and stultified Nietzsche" (p. 44). "The last link in the chain has been snipped into its proper place. God, world, you yourself, all that is are woven into one great 'as if'" (p. 45).

The way to cure this sickness is not through rethinking the issues that the philosopher has raised. "Our enemy is not idealism as such; anti-idealism, irrationalism, realism, materialism, naturalism, and what not, are equally harmful" (p. 57). What has to happen is for the philosophically sick human being to learn to see things as they are. And this may be accomplished by a sudden shock, as when "in August 1914 the word 'fatherland' and all the theories of 'essence'" – that is, of the essential nature of the state – "dissolved into nothing" (p. 56). But it also may require more extended antiphilosophical therapy.

The transformation of Rosenzweig that has received and deserves the most attention is not of course his rejection of philosophy, but his conversion to Judaism that led to the writing of that extraordinary book *The Star of Redemption* (trans. W.W.W. Hallo, Notre Dame University: University of Notre Dame Press, 1985). Yet Rosenzweig himself saw a close connection between his rejection of philosophy and his openness to the truth that "There is in addition to the world and himself, He who turns His face towards both", the God of Judaism, the God of whom Rosenzweig said in *The Star of Redemption* that "Of God we know nothing. But this ignorance is ignorance of God" (pp. 93 and 23).

Rosenzweig's claim is then to pursue the ends of life in a way that is open to the truth about those ends by requiring us to step outside philosophy into a dialogue concerning the particular and the concrete. Philosophy cannot itself be or become dialogical. It is a frustrating alternative to such dialogue. What should we make of this claim? Before we examine it, it will be worth considering the very different path taken by Georg Lukács. Their starting-points were not dissimilar. Like Rosenzweig, Lukács had to overcome the prevailing NeoKantian ethics. Yet Lukács's intellectual development was very different from Rosenzweig's. I shall attend to only two aspects of that development, his encounter with Emil Lask's paradoxical conception of the philosophical theorist and the effect upon him of his reading of Kierkegaard and Dostoievski.

Lask, the last great thinker from the NeoKantian tradition, whom Lukács encountered when he went to Heidelberg in 1912, contrasted the realities of nature as we encounter them in lived experience and what we make of those realities, when we render them amenable to scientific investigation and technical control by conceptualizing and categorizing them. Nature as understood by the theorist is an artifact, an abstract conceptualized substitute for nature as it is. Philosophers too are theorists, whose peculiar task it is to understand the relationship between their own theorizing on the one hand and their lived experience on the other. I call Lask's view paradoxical because it presents philosophers as theorists whose theory discloses the inadequacy of theory, discloses, that is, the inadequacy of representing realities in abstract conceptualized terms, but does so by making use of just those abstract conceptualizations whose inadequacy it simultaneously discloses.

It would have been natural for any student of Lask to aspire to find some manner of theorizing that would enable him to move beyond this conception of theory. And something very like this became Lukács's ambition. But the sphere in which he hoped to satisfy this ambition was not that of the investigation of nature, but that of the moral, construed broadly so that it includes both the religious and the political. The theorists whose thought he wished to transcend were Kierkegaard and Dostoievski. For at this stage Lukács inhabited a moral universe that was in all essentials but one a Christian universe. What differentiated it from any Christian universe was the absence of God, His absence, that is, not His non-existence. To say that God is absent is to say that we live in a fallen world in which no possibility of divine redemption presents itself.

The burden of responding to evil is therefore borne by individual human beings. And Lukács took the present age, the period of history which he inhabited, to be what Fichte had characterized as "an age of absolute sinfulness," a thesis confirmed for Lukács by the outbreak of war in 1914. How might one then act with moral decisiveness against the powers that had brought about and continued the evils of the mass slaughter of the First World War? To confront evil one is required to be morally good. But the forces of evil are such that in order to overcome them one may have to perform actions that are morally prohibited. Kierkegaard had written that obedience to and faith in God required of Abraham "a teleological suspension of the absolute." What, Lukács asked, was required of him and his contemporaries by way of obedience to and faith in good? Was a teleological suspension of absolute moral prohibitions required?

Lukács had initially rejected the Bolshevism of the Hungarian communists. Their belief that good would issue from their acts of violence and terror had seemed to him no more than an unreasoned faith in a metaphysical assumption. But later with retrospective vision he took himself in so judging to have been imprisoned within modes of thought and action characteristic of bourgeois culture and bourgeois philosophy. He had been preoccupied with his own conscientious scruples rather than with the future of humankind. So in an existential moment late in 1918 he joined the infant Hungarian Communist Party, very much to the surprise of its members. By a teleological suspension of the absolute Lukács had succeeded in moving to a standpoint from which he could now, so he believed, see things as they are. For to see things as they are is on his new view to see them from the standpoint of the revolutionary proletarian, as that standpoint is articulated in the theorizing and the activity of the Leninist Party. And having changed his conception of the ends of life, Lukács now engaged in philosophical writing with different ends in view, writing the essays that became *History and Class-Consciousness*, essays that enabled him to give an account to himself of his own self-transformation as well as of the transformation of philosophy.

Yet once again his conceptions of the ends of life and of the ends of philosophical writing turned out to be incompatible. His commitment to the version of Marxism that he had elaborated required of him obedience to the decrees of the Communist Party's leadership. And that leadership decreed that the version of Marxism that he had elaborated was incompatible with the Marxism of the party. Lukács therefore had to make a choice, and what he chose was the party's understanding of philosophy. From within the party he at first argued in favor of his own positions. But in time his choice became – could not avoid becoming, so long as Lukács remained within the party – a choice of Stalinism. It is important that Lukács's Stalinism – like that of many others – was self-willed, not something imposed upon him.

Rosenzweig and Lukács thus exit from NeoKantianism in very different directions. Both turned their backs on philosophy as it had been hitherto understood. But, while Rosenzweig tried to open up a kind of dialogue, participation in which precludes the holding of large and general philosophical doctrines, Lukács exchanged one large and general doctrine for another. And the Marxism to which he had committed himself turned out to have no place for dialogue. (We should note that the younger Lukács had developed through dialogue both with his contemporaries and with the authors of the texts about which he wrote.) This is why Lukács's Stalinist writing – most notably *Die Zerstörung der Vernunft* – became the construction of a syllabus of errors from a point of view which could not itself be put in question. The Lukács of this period provides an extreme and tragic example of what happens to philosophy when it is no longer developed through dialogue with opposing points of view. And Lukács's life in this period exemplifies the situation of those for whom there are no longer questions about the ends of life, but only unquestioned and unquestioning answers.

Rosenzweig's case was of course very different. But he too, at least in the line of thought that moved through and beyond the *Büchlein*, pursued a philosophical phantom. Where Lukács in his Stalinist decline gave us theorizing without dialogue, Rosenzweig gave us dialogue without theorizing, a dialogue designed to enable us to encounter the concrete and the particular, while freeing us from the universal and the general. But neither in life nor in enquiry is it possible to encounter the concrete and particular except as instances of the universal and general. As we should have learnt from Aristotle, every "this" that we encounter is a "this-such." False abstractions are indeed one source of both philosophical and practical error. But abstraction and generalization are conditions of all and any understanding. When particulars present themselves to us as intelligible, they do so only insofar as they have characteristics that enable us to ask and answer just those kinds of questions that direct us towards large and general theories.

What Rosenzweig and Lukács share then is failure in relating their questions about the ends of life to the ends of their philosophical writing. Rosenzweig ostensibly, although not consistently, discarded philosophical theorizing in order to be free to ask and answer questions about the ends of life, while Lukács defined the ends of his philosophical writing in terms of an already given answer to every question about the ends of life. What neither understood is twofold: that beliefs about the ends of life are always inadequate and misleading, if they are detached from the questions to which they are the answer, and that, in order for us to continue to view them as answers to questions, we have to continue asking and reasking those questions in a dialogue that keeps those questions open. To pose and answer philosophical questions about the ends of life in detachment from such dialogue is to become a prisoner of the answers that one has already given, while to make the ends of one's philosophical writing something separate and distinct from the project of asking and answering questions about the ends of life is to turn philosophy into a diversion.

Why is this so? It is because beliefs and judgments about the ends of life can be of two very different kinds. I may hold a set of beliefs about the ends of life and be disposed to make judgments expressive of these beliefs just because I have somehow or other acquired them and I now take them for granted. I do not recognize them as answers to questions, let alone as answers to questions that have rival and alternative answers. I treat them as exempt from questioning. Or I may by contrast hold a set of beliefs about the ends of life and be disposed to make the corresponding judgments only because and insofar as those beliefs and judgments give the best answer that I am able to provide to some question or questions to which I badly need to find an answer. Where beliefs of the first kind are concerned, not only do I generally find no reason to put them in question, but issues of their truth or falsity characteristically do not arise for me. Where beliefs of the second kind are concerned, I cannot but be to some significant degree aware that those beliefs provide answers to questions to which there are significant alternative and rival answers and, even when the grounds that I have for such beliefs are, on the best judgment that I can make, sufficient, those grounds always invite my further scrutiny.

This actual or potential self-questioning becomes an inescapable feature of our reflective lives when we commit ourselves to philosophical dialogue with others, others who agree and others who disagree about some set of beliefs and the grounds for holding them. So dialogue rescues us both from inadequate scrutiny of the grounds for our beliefs and from insufficient awareness of the fact that our answers to questions are contested by others. By so doing dialogue returns us to our condition as reflective questioning and self-questioning animals, rather than as those helplessly in the grip of their own particular beliefs. Philosophical dialogue is a remedy for that loss of questioning and self-questioning which characterizes so much of belief in secularized societies, whether it is the unreflective and complacent unbelief of those who are tacitly and complacently dismissive of religious belief or the unreflective and complacent loud-mouthed belief of fundamentalists of every faith.

Yet to argue as I have done at once provokes a sharp question. For I have implied that, in order to continue asking questions about the ends of life, one has to think as a philosopher does by engaging in philosophical dialogue. But, if this is so, it may seem to follow that plain persons, just because they are not philosophers, are precluded from asking questions about the ends of life in a worthwhile way. Is this in fact a consequence of my conclusions? The answer is 'No' and this because the contrast between plain persons and philosophers is itself rooted in confusion. I have argued elsewhere[6] that plain persons – and we all start out as plain persons – who

6 "Plain Persons and Moral Philosophy: Roles, Virtues and Goods," *American Catholic Philosophical Quarterly*, 66, winter 1992, reprinted in *The MacIntyre Reader*, ed. Kelvin Knight (Cambridge: Polity Press, 1998).

pursue their own answers to the question "What is our good?" in their everyday lives to any significant extent inescapably become involved in reflective practices and, in reflecting on what their or rather our lives have been so far, they and we raise questions about those lives that are already philosophical questions. Plain persons are all of them potential and many of them actual philosophers, although not in the mode of professional philosophers, and every philosopher, whether professional or not, begins as a plain person. But this is matter for another discussion.

What needs to be remarked here is that we can perhaps now understand why any seriously intended utterance in a secularized culture of questions about the ends of life outside any context of ongoing philosophical dialogue and apart from any reading of philosophical texts, not only sounds like, but sometimes *is* a cry of pain, a symptom of some inner disturbance. For outside philosophical dialogue and the reading of texts these have become as a result of secularization questions addressed to a void, questions whose urgency brings with it no expectations of an answer. Psychiatric textbooks sometimes list among the symptoms of incipient psychiatric disorder the asking of metaphysical questions. It has been an incidental purpose of this essay to suggest why on occasion this might be an insight embedded in a confusion, rather than simply a confusion.

IV

Finally, something more can now be said about the tasks of the writer either of philosophical biography or of the history of philosophers. It matters first of all to ask about philosophers whether they, in giving answers to questions about the ends of life, either in their philosophical writing or in their lives, do or do not effectively forget the questions, so that the possibility of reopening them is no longer kept in sight. For those who forget the questions the answers, especially the "right" answers, that is, their own answers, become everything, the questions nothing, and so they never return to them as questions that might have been given radically different answers.

It matters secondly with whom philosophers are in dialogue and whether those with whom they are in dialogue are only the like-minded, or whether they also include those who see the world from different and incompatible standpoints. Are they, if they are our contemporaries, able to learn from both Davidson and Deleuze, from Confucian moral theorists as well as from Thomists, utilitarians, and Marxists? Those who are one-sided and refuse openness to the other, or who insist on imposing their own standards of intelligibility by reinterpreting the other, so that the other becomes Just Like Us – think of all those analytic domestications of so-called continental philosophy – lead interestingly one-sided philosophical lives. I have been careful not to say that those who thus insulate themselves against reopening large questions or considering alternative angles of philosophical vision are thereby precluded from notable achievement in philosophy. There are certainly examples that show otherwise. And to escape from such imprisonment by one-sidedness may only lead to philosophical sterility, as the examples of Rosenzweig and Lukács show.

A third dimension of philosophical biography concerns the relationship that philosophers have to the more extended philosophical conversations to which they are contributing. Of what history of philosophical dialogue, if any, do they take themselves to be a part? Whose projects are they carrying further? Why do they begin where they do and what is presupposed by beginning *there*? Whence did their standards of philosophical achievement originate and what light, if any, does knowledge of their origin throw on their authority?

It is by characterizing these dimensions that we are able to map the relationship between the ends that philosophers pursue qua human beings and the ends that determine the manner and the content of their philosophical writing. If we fail to enquire about these dimensions or if our enquiry is barren, then we will be forced to treat philosophers' lives as one sort of thing and their writings as something quite other. We will be forced to write the history of philosophy, including the history of our contemporaries, just as Russell wrote it, that is, with chunks of nonphilosophical biography followed by chunks of nonbiographical philosophy. There are of course, as I already noticed, philosophers for whom this treatment is apt, philosophers who by choice or otherwise have successfully fenced off their philosophical activity from the rest of their lives. But even they did not have to be like this and to understand why in particular cases this schism between the ends of life and the ends of philosophical writing may have occurred is itself one more task for the philosophical biographer.

I am indebted for criticism of what I said about Lukács in an earlier version of this essay to Stanley Mitchell, although he must not be held responsible for what I say now.

# CHAPTER 8

# First principles, final ends, and contemporary philosophical issues

I

Nothing is more generally unacceptable in recent philosophy than any conception of a first principle. Standpoints mutually at odds with each other in so many other ways, of analytic or continental or pragmatic provenance, agree in this rejection. And yet the concept of a first principle seems to have been for Aquinas, just as it had been for Aristotle, and before him for Plato, in itself unproblematic. For both Aquinas and Aristotle, of course, difficult questions do arise about such issues as the relationship of subordinate principles to first principles, the nature of our knowledge of first principles and the differences between the first principles of the different sciences. But in their writings debate even about such complex issues seems always to presuppose as not to be put in question, as never yet having been seriously put in question, the very idea of a first principle.

It is then unsurprisingly in the context of philosophical preoccupations and through the medium of philosophical idioms quite alien to those of either Aristotle or Aquinas that the very idea of a first principle has now been radically put in question, preoccupations which it is, therefore, difficult to address directly from a Thomistic standpoint with only the resources afforded by Aquinas and his predecessors. Hence it seems that, if this central Aristotelian and Thomistic concept is to be effectively defended, in key part it will have to be by drawing upon philosophical resources which are themselves – at least at first sight – as alien to, or almost as alien to, Thomism as are the theses and arguments which have been deployed against it. We inhabit a time in the history of philosophy in which Thomism can only develop adequate responses to the rejections of its central positions in what must seem initially at least to be unThomistic ways.

To acknowledge this is not to suggest that Aquinas's central positions ought to be substantially reworked or revised in some accommodation to the standpoints of those rejections. It is rather that, in order to restate and to defend those positions in something like their original integrity, it is necessary in our time to approach them indirectly through an internal critique of those theses and arguments which have displaced them, a critique dictated by Thomistic ends, but to be carried through in part at least by somewhat unThomistic means.

Yet if such a critique is genuinely to be directed by Thomistic ends it is worth reminding ourselves at the outset just how foreign to contemporary modes and fashions of thought the Aristotelian and Thomistic concept of a first principle is in at least two ways, one concerned with the firstness of first principles, the other with the difference between standard modern uses of the word "principle" in English – and its cognates in other contemporary languages – and the meaning given to "*principium*" by Aquinas and to "*archē*" by Aristotle. Let me begin with the latter.

"*Principium*" as a translation of "*archē*" preserves what from a contemporary English-speaking point of view seems like a double meaning. For us a principle is something expressed in language, something which in the form of either a statement or an injunction can function as a premise in arguments. And so it is sometimes for Aquinas who uses "*principium*" of an axiom furnishing a syllogism with a premise (*Commentary on the Posterior Analytics* I, 5) and speaks of a principle as composed of subject and predicate (*Summa Theologiae* I, 17, 3). But Aquinas also uses "*principium*" in speaking of that to which such principles refer, referring to the elements into which composite bodies can be resolved and by reference to which they can be explained as the "principium," of those bodies (*Exposition of Boethius De Trinitate* V, 4). In fact, "*principium*", as used by Aquinas, names simultaneously the principle (in our sense) and that of which the principle speaks, but not in a way that gives to "principium" two distinct and discrete meanings, although it can be used with either or both of two distinct references. For when we do indeed have a *principium*, we have to comprehend the principle and that of which it speaks in a single act of comprehension; we can only comprehend the principle as it refers us to that of which it speaks and we can only comprehend that of which it speaks as articulated and formulated in the principle.

The habits of speech required of us to say this go against the contemporary linguistic grain. And certainly sometimes it does no harm to speak of "principium" as though our contemporary conception of principle were all that is involved, yet we always have to remember that "principium," like "archē," is a concept which unites what contemporary idiom divides.

A concept with a similar structure is that of *aitia* or *causa*. We in the idioms of our contemporary speech distinguish sharply causes from explanations, but *causa* is always explanation-affording and *aitia* qua explanation is always cause-specifying. In both cases, that of *aitia/causa* and that of *archē/principium* the modern question: "Are you speaking of what is or of the mind's apprehension through language of what is?" misses and obscures the conceptual point, which is that the application of this type of concept, when sufficiently justified, gives expression to a coincidence of the mind with what is, to a certain kind of achievement in the mind's movement towards its goal. So it is that *causa* and *principium* are to be adequately elucidated only within a scheme of thought in which the mind moves towards its own proper end, its *telos*, an achieved state in which it is informed by an understanding of its own progress towards that end, an understanding completed by an apprehension of first principles. The meaning of these expressions is not independent of the context of theory within which they are employed.

In recognizing this we encounter a familiar truth about radical philosophical disagreements. Theory and idiom are to some significant degree inseparable. Insofar as I try to deny your theory, but continue to use your idiom, it may be that I shall be trapped into presupposing just what I aspire to deny. And correspondingly the more radical the disagreement over theory, the larger the possibility that each party will find itself misrepresented in the idioms of its rivals, idioms which exclude rather than merely lack the conceptual resources necessary for the statement of its position. So it has been to some significant degree with Thomism in its encounter with post-Cartesian philosophies.

This linguistic difficulty is reinforced by the barrier posed by the conviction which I noticed at the outset, one shared both by different, often mutually antagonistic schools of contemporary philosophy and by the culture of modernity at large, that no principle is or can be first as such. To treat a principle as a first principle is always, on this view, to choose to do so for some particular purpose within some particular context. So we in one type of formal system may wish to treat as a derived theorem what in another is treated as an axiom. Justificatory chains of reasoning generally terminate with what members of some particular social group are willing, for the moment at least, to take for granted; this type of agreement is all that is necessary to serve our contemporary justificatory purposes. But it is not just that the firstness of first principles has been relativized to social contexts and individual purposes. It is also that the range of such purposes is taken to be indefinitely various. And what the purposes of each of us are to be is taken to be a matter of our individual temperaments, interests, desires, and decisions.

This contemporary universe of discourse thus has no place within it for any conception of fixed ends, of ends to be discovered rather than decided upon or invented, and that is to say that it has no place for the type of *telos* or *finis* which provides the activity of a particular kind of being with a goal to which it must order its purposes or fail to achieve its own specific perfection in its activity. And this exclusion of the concept of *telos/finis*, I shall want to suggest, is closely related to the exclusion of the concept of *archē/principium*. Genuinely first principles, so I shall argue, can have a place only within a universe characterized in terms of certain determinate, fixed and unalterable ends, ends which provide a standard by reference to which our individual purposes, desires, interests and decisions can be evaluated as well or badly directed. For in practical life it is the *telos* which provides the *archē*, the first principle of practical reasoning: "Deductive arguments concerning what is to be done have an *archē*. Since such and such is the *telos* and the best . . ." (*Nicomachean Ethics* VI 1144a3235), says Aristotle; and Aquinas comments that this reference to the end in the first principle of practical syllogisms has a parallel in the way in which the first principle of theoretical syllogisms is formulated (*Commentary on the Ethics* VI, lect. 10, 17). And it could scarcely be otherwise since the *archai/principia* of theory furnish the theoretical intellect with its specific *telos/finis*. *Archē/principium* and *telos/finis*, so it must seem, stand or fall together.

II

Within distinctively modern schemes of thought they are, of course, taken to have fallen quite some time ago. And when Thomists, therefore, find their central theses concerning *archē/principium* and *telos/finis* rejected within contemporary culture at large as well as within philosophy, it may be tempting to proceed by way of an immediate rejection of the rejection, but this temptation must be resisted. For it will turn out that the considerations which in the context of contemporary discourse are taken either to support or to presuppose denials of the possibility of there being either first principles or final ends are in fact theses which for the most part a Thomist should have no interest in denying. What he or she must have the strongest interest in denying are the implications which are commonly nowadays supposed to follow from these.

The first of such theses denies that there are or can be what I shall call epistemological first principles, the type of first principle of which the

Cartesian cogito, as usually understood, provides a paradigmatic instance. Such a first principle was required to fulfill two functions. On the one hand, it gave expression to an immediate justified certitude on the part of any rational person who uttered it in the appropriate way, perhaps in the appropriate circumstances. It belongs, that is, to the same class of statements as "I am in pain," "This is red here now," and "I am now thinking." But, on the other hand, it had, either by itself or as a member of a set of such statements, to provide an ultimate warrant for all our claims to knowledge. Only in virtue of their derivation from it could other statements meet the challenge: How do you know *that*? And the importance of being able to answer this question is not just to rebut those who express skepticism. For since on this view knowledge involves justified certainty and justified certainty requires that, if I genuinely know, I also know that I know, then as a rational person I must be able to answer the question "How do I know?" in respect of each knowledge claim that I make.

Yet, as by now has often enough been pointed out, no statement or set of statements is capable of fulfilling both these functions. The kind of substantive content required for statements which could function as the initial premises in a deductive justification of the sciences, theoretical or practical, precludes the kind of justified immediate certitude required for this kind of epistemological startingpoint, and vice versa. Epistemological first principles, thus conceived, are mythological beasts.

Two kinds of reflection may be provoked in a Thomist by these by now commonplace antifoundational arguments. A first concerns the way in which they leave the Aristotelian or Thomistic conception of *archē/principium* unscathed. For where the protagonists of this type of foundationalist epistemological first principle, which is now for the most part, even if not universally rejected, characterized those principles so that they had to meet two sets of requirements, each of which could in fact only be met by some principle which failed in respect to the other, Aquinas, as a result of having reflected upon both Aristotle and Boethius, distinguished two different types of evidentness belonging to two different kinds of principle (see, for example, *Summa Theologiae* Ia–IIae 94, 2).

There are, on the one hand, those evident principles, the meaning of whose terms is immediately to be comprehended by every competent language-user, such as "Every whole is greater than its part," principles which are, therefore, undeniable by any such language-user. There are, on the other hand, principles which are to be understood as evident only in the context of the conceptual framework of some more or less large-scale theory, principles expressed in judgments known as evident only to those with an intellectual grasp of the theoretical framework in which they are embedded, that is, as Aquinas puts it, to the wise. It is such judgments which are used to state first principles with substantive content, and their function and the requirements which they have to meet are very different from those of the former type of principle. We should, of course, note that even the former type of principle can, in the light of its applications, be understood in greater depth by those who are theoretically sophisticated than it is by the merely competent language-user. But with the distinction between what is immediately apprehended, but not substantive in content, and what is substantive in content, but known as evident only through theoretical achievement, the Thomist distinguishes what the protagonist of epistemological first principles misleadingly assimilates and so remains untouched by this thrust at least of contemporary antifoundationalism.

Yet there is an even more fundamental way in which contemporary hostility to epistemological foundationalism misses the point so far as Thomistic first principles are concerned. For if the Thomist is faithful to the intentions of Aristotle and Aquinas, he or she will not be engaged, except perhaps incidentally, in an epistemological enterprise. The refutation of skepticism will appear to him or her as misguided an enterprise as it does to the Wittgensteinian. Generations of NeoThomists from Kleutgen onwards have, of course, taught us to think otherwise, and textbooks on epistemology have been notable among the standard impedimenta of NeoThomism. What in part misled their writers was the obvious fact that Aquinas, like Aristotle, furnishes an account of knowledge. What they failed to discern adequately was the difference between the Aristotelian or Thomistic enterprise and the epistemological enterprise.[1]

The epistemological enterprise is by its nature a first-person project. How can I, so the epistemologist enquires, be assured that my beliefs, my perceptions, my judgments connect with reality external to them, so that I can have justified certitude regarding their truth and error? A radical skeptic is an epistemologist with entirely negative findings. He or she, like other epistemologists, takes him or herself to speak from within his or her mind of its relationship to what is external to it and perhaps alien to it. But the Thomist, if he or she follows Aristotle and Aquinas, constructs an account both of approaches to and of the achievement of knowledge from

---

1 See Mark Jordan, *Ordering Wisdom* (Notre Dame: University of Notre Dame Press, 1986), pp. 118–19. I am deeply indebted to Mark Jordan and Ralph McInerny for their assistance at various points.

a third-person point of view. My mind or rather my soul is only one among many and its own knowledge of my self qua soul has to be integrated into a general account of souls and their teleology. Insofar as a given soul moves successfully towards its successive intellectual goals in a teleologically ordered way, it moves towards completing itself by becoming formally identical with the objects of its knowledge, so that it is adequate to those objects, objects that are then no longer external to it, but rather complete it. So the mind in finding application for its concepts refers them beyond itself and themselves to what they conceptualize. Hence the double reference of concepts which we already noticed in the cases of *archē/principium* and *aitia/causa*. The mind, actualized in knowledge, responds to the object as the object is and as it would be, independently of the mind's knowledge of it. The mind knows itself only in the second-order knowledge of its own operations and is known also by others in those operations. But even such knowledge when achieved need not entail certitude of a Cartesian sort.

"It is difficult to discern whether one knows or not," said Aristotle (*Posterior Analytics* I, 9, 76a26). And Aquinas glosses this by saying that "It is difficult to discern whether we know from appropriate principles, which alone is genuinely scientific knowing, or do not know from appropriate principles" (*Commentary on the Posterior Analytics*, lib. 1, lect. 18). The contrast with Cartesianism could not be sharper. If, on the view of Aristotle and Aquinas, one genuinely knows at all, then one knows as one would know if one knew in the light of the relevant set of first principles, but one may, nonetheless, genuinely know, without as yet possessing the kind of further knowledge of first principles and of their relationship to this particular piece of knowledge which would finally vindicate one's claim. All knowledge even in the initial stages of enquiry is a partial achievement and completion of the mind, but it nonetheless points beyond itself to a more final achievement in ways that we may not as yet have grasped. Hence, we can know without as yet knowing that we know, while for the Cartesian, as I remarked earlier, if we know, we must know that we know, since for the Cartesian it is always reference backwards to our starting-point that guarantees our knowledge and, hence, it is only through knowing that we know that we know. By contrast, for the Thomist our present knowledge involves reference forward to that knowledge of the *archē/principium* which will, if we achieve it, give us subsequent knowledge of the knowledge that we now have.

In this relationship of what we now know to what we do not as yet know, a relationship in which what we only as yet know potentially is presupposed by what we already know actually, there is to be observed a certain kind of circularity. This is not, of course, the type of circularity the presence of which vitiates a demonstrative argument. It is the circularity of which Aquinas speaks in endorsing Aristotle's view "that before an induction or syllogism is formed to beget knowledge of a conclusion, that conclusion is somehow known and somehow not known" (*Commentary on the Posterior Analytics*, lib. 1, lect. 3). The conclusion which is to be the end of our deductively or inductively (Aristotelian *epagōgē*, not Humean induction) reasoned enquiry is somehow already assumed in our starting-point. Were it not so, that particular type of starting-point would not be pointing us towards this particular type of conclusion (*Quaestiones Disputatae De Veritate* 11, 1).

Consider an example from the life of practice. Aquinas follows Aristotle in holding that one reason why the young are incapable of adequate reflective moral theorizing is that they have not as yet that experience of actions which would enable them to frame adequate moral and political arguments (*Nicomachean Ethics* I, 3, 1095a2–3, *Commentary on the Ethics*, lect. 3). But not any experience of human actions will provide adequate premises for sound practical reasoning. Only a life whose actions have been directed by and whose passions have been disciplined and transformed by the practice of the moral and intellectual virtues and the social relationships involved in and defined by such practice will provide the kind of experience from which and about which reliable practical inferences and sound theoretical arguments about practice can be derived. But from the outset the practice of those virtues in an adequately and increasingly determinate way already presupposes just those truths about the good and the best for human beings, about the *telos* for human beings, which it is the object of moral and political enquiry to discover. So the only type of moral and political enquiry through which and in which success can be achieved is one in which the end is to some significant degree presupposed in the beginning, in which initial actualities presuppose and give evidence of potentiality for future development.

This ineliminable circularity is not a sign of some flaw in Aristotelian or Thomistic conceptions of enquiry. It is, I suspect, a feature of any large-scale philosophical system which embodies a conception of enquiry, albeit an often unacknowledged feature. And it could only be thought a flaw from a standpoint still haunted by a desire to find some point of origin for enquiry which is entirely innocent of that which can only emerge later from that enquiry. It is this desire – for an origin which is not an origin – which plainly haunts much of the work of Jacques

Derrida[2] and which thus informs, even if somewhat paradoxically, the second major contemporary philosophical rejection of any substantive conception of first principles, one very different from its analytic antifoundationalist counterpart.

The most obvious difference is, of course, that, whereas the analytic rejection focuses upon epistemological considerations, the deconstructionist rejection formulated by Derrida focuses upon questions of meaning. What set the stage for Derrida's critique of what he took to be a metaphysical and, therefore, obfuscating understanding of meaning was the structuralist thesis, developed out of a particular way of interpreting Saussure, that in the structures of linguistic systems it is relationships of a certain kind which determine the identity and meaning of terms and not vice versa. It is in and through binary relationships of opposition and difference that such identity and meaning are constituted.

The stability of meaning is thus taken to depend upon the character of the oppositions and differences between terms. And a key part of Derrida's deconstructive work was to show that the oppositions between pairs of terms crucial to metaphysics, such counterpart pairs as form/matter, sensible/intelligible, and passive/active, seem to collapse into each other insofar as the meaning and application of each term already presupposes the meaning and applicability of its counterpart, and hence no term provides an independent, stable, unchanging point of definition for its counterpart. Insofar as this is so, any stable meaning is dependent upon something not yet said, and since these metaphysical oppositions are in relevant respects no different from the binary oppositions which on this type of poststructuralist view constitute language-in-use in general, it is a general truth that the meaning of what is uttered is always in a similar way dependent on some further not yet provided ground for meaning. There is however no such ground waiting to be attained, so that stable meaning is never achieved. So a deconstructive denial of first principles emerges from an analysis of meaning, as part of the denial of the possibility of metaphysical grounding for *anything*. But why does Derrida believe that there can be no such ground?

It is here that Derrida is open to more than one reading. For sometimes it seems that it is from the way in which the terms of his metaphysical pairs each presuppose the other, so that neither member of such pairs can

---

2 See, e.g., *Of Grammatology*, translated by G. C. Spivak (Baltimore: The John Hopkins University Press, 1976), p. 65 and the discussion by Peter Dews in chapter 1 of *Logics of Disintegration* (London: Verso, 1987).

provide an independent grounding for the meaning, identity, and applicability of the other, that Derrida is arguing to the conclusion that there can be no grounding for metaphysical thought and theory of the kind which he takes it to require. But at other times he seems to move from the denial of the possibility of such a grounding, on occasion referring us to Heidegger and to Nietzsche, towards conclusions about the consequent instability of meaning exemplified in such terms.

Yet in either case what Derrida presents us with is a strange mirror-image inversion of Thomism. For the Thomist has no problem either with the notion that, where such pairs as form and matter or potentiality and act are concerned, each term is and must be partially definable by reference to the other, or with the view that when such terms are applied at some early or intermediate stage in an enquiry the full meaning of what has been said is yet to emerge and will only emerge when the relevant set of first principles is as fully specified as that particular enquiry requires. Terms are applied analogically, in respect both of meaning and of use, and the grounding of meaning and use through analogy is by reference to some ultimate *archē/principium*. So that stability of meaning, on a Thomist view, is tied to a metaphysically conceived ground, just as Derrida asserts, and the denial of that ground, it follows equally for the Thomist and the deconstructionist, could not but issue in systematic instability of meaning. Yet, if the entailments are the same, the direction of the arguments which they inform is, of course, different. So why move in the deconstructive rather than in the Thomistic direction?

To state Derrida's answer to this justly and adequately would require me to go further into the detail of his position than is possible on this occasion. What is possible is to sketch one central relevant deconstructive thesis which may illuminate what is at stake in the disagreement. For Derrida as for deconstructive thought generally, any metaphysically conceived ground, such as an *archē/principium* would supply, would have to function in two incompatible ways. It would have to exist outside of and independently of discourse, since upon it discourse is to be grounded, and it would have to be present in discourse, since it is only as linguistically conceived and presented that it could be referred to. But these are plainly incompatible requirements, the first of which in any case violates Derrida's dictum that there is nothing outside text. (Notice the instructive resemblances between Derrida's denials and Hilary Putnam's attacks on what he calls external or metaphysical realism.[3]). So the binary oppositions

---

3 See, e.g., chapter 3 of *Reason, Truth and History* (Cambridge: Cambridge University Press, 1981).

of meaning cannot be referred beyond themselves to some first principle and meaning must be unstable.

This deconstructive rejection of first principles raises some of the same questions which arise from the analytic antifoundationalist's rejection. To what kind of reasoning is each appealing in justifying and commending their rejection? Is it a kind of reasoning which is itself consistent with those rejections? Or do those rejections themselves destroy any basis for the reasoning which led to them? Consider the impasse into which thought is led by the difficulties involved in two rival types of answers to those questions. On the one hand, it is easy to construe both the analytic antifoundationalist and the deconstructive critic as offering what are taken to be compelling arguments as to the impossibility of grounding either justificatory argument or discourse itself by means of appeal to some set of first principles. But if these arguments have succeeded in respect of cogency, it can surely be only in virtue of their deriving their conclusions from premises which are in some way or other undeniable. Yet the impossibility of such undeniable premises seems to follow from the conclusions of these same arguments. So can those arguments be construed in a way which will avoid self-deconstruction? This is a more than rhetorical question.

On the other hand, if we begin by taking seriously the thought that there are no in principle undeniable premises – whatever the type of principle – for substantive arguments, then the undeniability claimed must be of some other kind. But the most plausible attempts hitherto to elucidate the notion of an undeniability for the premises of deconstructive and antifoundationalist argument, which is not an undeniability in principle, have resulted in some conception of an undeniability rooted in some particular kind of social agreement. Characterizations of the nature of the social agreement involved have differed widely: more than one of the rival views contending in this area appeals to Wittgenstein, others to Kuhn, others again to Foucault.

Disagreement on these issues by a multiplicity of contending parties, grounded in their shared rejection of metaphysical first principles, indeed of first principles as such, is pervasive in its effects and manifestations both within academic philosophy and outside it, both in the literary and social scientific disciplines and in the rhetorical modes of the culture at large. In the latter it appears in the now, it seems, perpetually renewed debates over continually reformulated end-of-ideology theses; the end of ideology is in politics what the refutation of metaphysics is in philosophy. Within academia it appears in the unsettled and, as I shall claim, unsettlable debates which are now carried on between historicists and antihistoricists, realists and antirealists, pragmaticists and antipragmaticists.

It is at this point that the Thomist has to resist the temptation of premature self-congratulation. For, if it is indeed the case, as I have suggested, that the Aristotelian and Thomistic conception of *archē/principium* survives unscathed both the analytic antifoundationalist and the deconstructive critique of first principles, it would be all too easy to announce victory. Yet this would be a serious mistake. For it is not so much that Thomism has emerged unscathed from two serious philosophical encounters as that no serious philosophical encounter has as yet taken place. The Thomistic conception of a first principle is untouched by contemporary radical critiques in key part because the cultural, linguistic, and philosophical distance between it and them is now so great, that they are no longer able seriously to envisage the possibility of such a conception. If then serious encounter is to occur, and the Thomistic understanding of the tasks of natural human reason functioning philosophically makes such encounter mandatory, it can only occur insofar as Thomism can speak relevantly of and to those critiques and the debates which arise out of them. The question which I am posing then is that of what light the Aristotelian and Thomistic conception of *archē/principium* can throw on such critiques and debates. But a necessary preliminary to that question is a more adequate statement of what that conception is and involves.

III

Aquinas introduced his commentary on the *Posterior Analytics* by distinguishing the task of analyzing judgments within a science, with a view to explaining their warrant and the kind of certitude to which we are entitled by that warrant, from the task of giving an account of investigation. In so distinguishing he pointed towards the resolution of a problem about what Aristotle was trying to achieve in the *Posterior Analytics* which has engaged the attention of some modern commentators.

This problem arises from an evident contrast between the account of the structure of scientific understanding and of how it is achieved which is provided in the *Posterior Analytics* and the way in which Aristotle carries out his own scientific enquiries in the *Physics* and in the biological treatises. If, as has often enough been assumed by modern commentators, the *Posterior Analytics* is Aristotle's theory of scientific method, while the *Physics* and the biological treatises are applications of Aristotle's scientific method, then the discrepancy between the former and the latter is obvious and striking. What the first expounds is just not what the second practices. There have indeed been scholars who have, nonetheless, attempted to deny that there is any problem here. But their arguments have not withstood the test of debate, and it would now be generally agreed that, whatever the methods of enquiry put to work in the *Physics* and the biological treatises, they are not the methods described in the *Posterior Analytics*. How then is the discrepancy to be explained?

Is it perhaps that Aristotle changed his mind some time after writing the *Posterior Analytics*? Is it, as some scholars have maintained, that the *Posterior Analytics* is an account only of the mathematical sciences? Or is it, as Jonathan Barnes has argued,[4] after decisively refuting this latter suggestion, that the *Posterior Analytics* is not designed to teach us how to acquire knowledge, but rather how to present knowledge already achieved, that is, that the *Posterior Analytics* is a manual for teachers? There is no problem in agreeing with much of what Barnes says in favor of this view, provided that we do not take the criteria of sound scientific demonstration to be upheld primarily or only because of their pedagogical effectiveness. It is rather that we can learn from the *Posterior Analytics* how to present achieved knowledge and understanding to others only because of what that text primarily is: an account of what achieved and perfected knowledge is.

Why do I say this? Not only because everything in the text is consistent with this view, but also because Aristotle's system of thought requires just such an account and it is nowhere else supplied. The *Physics* and the biological treatises report scientific enquiries which are still in progress, moving towards, but not yet having reached the *telos* appropriate to, and providing implicit or explicit guidance for, those specific types of activity. Clearly there must, on an Aristotelian view, be such a *telos*. And we need to know what it is, something only to be found, if anywhere, in the *Posterior Analytics*. So my claim is that the *Posterior Analytics* is an account of what it is or would be to possess, to have already achieved, a perfected science, a perfected type of understanding, in which every movement of a mind within the structures of that type of understanding gives expression to the adequacy of that mind to its objects.

Of course, in furnishing an account of what perfected and achieved understanding and knowledge are, Aristotle could not avoid the task of specifying, in part at least, the relationship between prior states of imperfect

---

4 See "Aristotle's Theory of Demonstration" in *Articles on Aristotle*, edited by J. Barnes, M. Schofield, and R. Sorabji, vol. I (London: Duckworth, 1975).

and partial understanding and that final state. And it was perhaps by attending too exclusively to what he tells us about this relationship and these prior states that earlier commentators were led to misconstrue Aristotle's intentions. But what matters about his discussions of understanding still in the process of formation, still in progress, in the *Posterior Analytics* is the light cast thereby on the way in which the *telos* of perfected understanding is already presupposed in partial understanding, and this is a concern very different from that of the *Physics* or of the biological treatises. So that when Aquinas in the introduction to his commentary distinguished the subject matter of the *Posterior Analytics* from any concern with the nature of investigation, he correctly directed our attention to the place of the *Posterior Analytics* within Aristotle's works.

The *telos/finis* of any type of systematic activity is, on an Aristotelian and Thomistic view, that end internal to activity of that specific kind, for the sake of which and in the direction of which activity of that kind is carried forward. Many types of activity, of course, are intelligible as human activities only because and insofar as they are embedded in some other type of activity, and some types of such activity may be embedded in any one of a number of other types of intelligible activity. So it is, for example, with tree-felling, which may as an activity be part of and embedded in an architectural project of building a house or a manufacturing project of making fine papers or an ecological project of strengthening a forest as a habitat for certain species. It is these more inclusive and relatively self-sufficient forms of systematic activity which serve distinctive human goods, so that the *telos/finis* of each is to be characterized in terms of some such good. So the *Posterior Analytics* in its account of scientific demonstrative explanations as the *telos/finis* of enquiry furnishes us with an account of what it is to understand, that is, of the distinctive human good to be achieved by enquiry as a distinctive type of activity.

Achieved understanding is the *theoretical* goal of the *practical* activity of enquiry. Neither Aristotle nor Aquinas themselves discuss the theory of the practical activity of theoretically aimed enquiry in a systematic way, although some of Aristotle's discussions in the *Topics* are highly relevant and Aquinas rightly understood the *Topics* as a partial guide to such activity. Moreover, elsewhere in both Aristotle and Aquinas incidental remarks and discussions abound (see especially *Exposition of Boethius De Trinitate* VI, 1). But to make use of those remarks and discussion we must first say what, on the view taken by Aristotle and Aquinas, achieved understanding is. In so doing we shall find both that Aquinas, while generally endorsing Aristotle, goes beyond Aristotle's theses, and that later discussions of enquiry by nonAristotelian and nonThomistic writers can be put to good use in extending the Aristotelian account still further. So that although I shall be going over largely familiar and even over familiar ground, it will not always be in an entirely familiar way.

A perfected science is one which enables us to understand the phenomena of which it treats as necessarily being what they are, will be, and have been, because of the variety of agencies which have brought it about that form of specific kinds has informed the relevant matter in such a way as to achieve some specific end state. All understanding is thus in terms of the essential properties of specific kinds. What those kinds are, how they are to be characterized, what the end state is to which those individuals which exemplify them move or are moved, those are matters about which – it seems plain from Aristotle's own scientific treatises as well as from modern scientific enquiry – there may well have been changes of view and even radical changes of view in the course of enquiry. The final definition of these matters in a perfected science will generally be the outcome of a number of reformulations and reclassifications which have come about in the course of enquiry.

The mind which has achieved this perfected understanding in some particular area represents what it understands – the form of understanding and the form of what is understood necessarily coincide in perfected understanding; that is what it is to understand – by a deductive scheme in whose hierarchical structure the different levels of causal explanation are embodied. To give an explanation is to provide a demonstrative argument which captures part of this structure. What causal explanation enables us to distinguish is genuine causality from mere coincidence. The regularities of coincidence are striking features of the universe which we inhabit, but they are not part of the subject matter of science, for there is no necessity in their being as they are. It follows from this account that in each distinctive form of achieved understanding, in each science, there is a set of first principles, *archai/principia*, which provide premises for demonstrative arguments and which specify the ultimate causal agencies, material, formal, efficient, and final for that science. It follows also that, insofar as the perfected sciences are themselves hierarchically organized, the most fundamental of sciences will specify that in terms of which everything that can be understood is to be understood. And this, as Aquinas remarks in a number of places, we call God.

There is then an ineliminable theological dimension – theological, that is, in the sense that makes Aristotle's metaphysics a theology – to enquiry conceived in an Aristotelian mode. For enquiry aspires to and is intelligible only in terms of its aspiration to finality, comprehensiveness, and unity of explanation and understanding, not only in respect of the distinctive subject matters of the separate subordinate sciences, but also in respect of those more pervasive and general features of contingent reality, which inform those wholes of which the subject matter of the subordinate sciences supply the constituent parts – nature and human history. And, as the most radical philosophers of postEnlightenment modernity from Nietzsche to Richard Rorty have recurrently insisted, in the course of polemics against their less thorough-going colleagues, the very idea of a unified, even if complex, ultimate and final true account of the order of things in nature and human history has hidden – and perhaps not so hidden – within it some view of the relationship of contingent beings to some ground beyond contingent being.

What the substantive first principles which provide the initial premises of any perfected science achieve then is a statement of those necessary truths which furnish the relevant set of demonstrative arguments with their first premises, but also exhibit how if something is of a certain kind, it essentially and necessarily has certain properties. The *de re* necessity of essential property possession is represented in and through the analytic form of the judgments which give expression to such principles.[5] It is their analyticity which makes it the case that such principles are evident *per se*, but their evidentness is intelligible only in the context of the relevant body of perfected theory within which they function as first principles, and only an understanding of that body of theory will enable someone to grasp their analytic structure.

That first principles expressed as judgments are analytic does not, of course, entail that they are or could be known to be true a priori. Their analyticity, the way in which subject-expressions include within their meaning predicates ascribing essential properties to the subject and certain predicates have a meaning such that they necessarily can only belong to that particular type of subject, is characteristically discovered as the outcome of some prolonged process of empirical enquiry. That type of enquiry is one in which, according to Aristotle, there is a transition from attempted specifications of essences by means of prescientific definitions, specifications which require acquaintance with particular instances of the relevant kind (*Posterior Analytics* II, 8, 93a21–9), even although a definition

---

5 For an overview of disputed questions on this topic and a view at some points different from mine, see chapter 12 of R. Sorabji, *Necessity, Cause and Blame* (London: Duckworth, 1980).

by itself will not entail the occurrence of such instances, to the achieve-ment of genuinely scientific definitions in and through which essences are to be comprehended. To arrive at the relevant differentiating causes which are specific to certain types of phenomena thus to be explained, empirical questions have to be asked and answered (*Posterior Analytics* I, 31 and 34, II, 19). But what results from such questioning is not a set of merely *de facto* empirical generalizations, but, insofar as a science is perfected, the specification through analytic definitions of a classificatory scheme in terms of which causes are assigned, causes which explain, in some way that subsequent enquiry cannot improve upon, the ordering of the relevant set of phenomena. So the analyticity of the first principles is not Kantian analyticity, let alone positivist analyticity. The first principles of a particular science are warranted as such if and only if, when conjoined with whatever judgments as to what exists may be required for that particular science, they can provide premises for a theory which tran-scends in explanatory and understanding-affording power any rival theory which might be advanced as an account of the same subject matter. And insofar as the judgments which give expression either to the first principles or to the subordinate statements deriving from them, which together constitute such a theory, conform to how the essential features of things are, they are called true. About truth itself Aristotle said very little, but Aquinas has a more extended account.

Truth is a complex property. "A natural thing, therefore, being consti-tuted between two intellects, is called true with respect to its adequacy to both; with respect to its adequacy to the divine intellect it is called true insofar as it fulfills that to which it was ordered by the divine intellect," and Aquinas cites Anselm and Augustine and quotes Isaac Israeli and ·Avicenna. "But a thing is called true in respect of its adequacy to the human intellect insofar as concerning it a true estimate is generated . . .," and here Aquinas quotes Aristotle (*Quaestiones Disputatae De Veritate* 1, 2). The complexity of Aquinas's view is a consequence of his having integrated into a single account theses both from Aristotle and Islamic and Jewish commentary upon Aristotle and from Augustine and Anselm. But the integration is what is most important. Different kinds of predica-tion of truth each received their due within a genuinely unified theory of truth, in which the analogical relationship of different kinds of predication becomes clear.

What emerges then from the discussion of the rational justification of particular judgments within a perfected science by Aristotle in the *Poster-ior Analytics*, followed closely by Aquinas in his *Commentary*, and from the discussion of truth by Aquinas, in which Aristotelian theses are synthesized with Augustinian, is that both truth and rational justification have their place within a single scheme of perfected understanding and that the relationship between them depends upon their respective places within this scheme. But, as I emphasized earlier, what this conception of a perfected science supplies is a characterization of the *telos/finis* internal to and directive of activities of enquiry. What then is the nature of progress in enquiry towards this type of *telos/finis* and how are truth and rational justification to be understood from the standpoint of those still at early or intermediate stages in such a progress?

IV

In the progress towards a perfected science first principles play two distinct parts. Those which are evident to all rational persons do indeed provide standards and direction from the outset, but only when and as conjoined with initial sketches of those first conceptions and principles towards an ultimately adequate formulation of which enquiry is directed. Examples of the former type of first principle, evident to us as to all rational persons, are, of course, the principle of noncontradiction and the first principle of practical rationality, that good is to be pursued and evil avoided, and these are relatively unproblematic. But how are we even to sketch in outline at the outset an adequately directive account of a first principle or set of first principles, about which not only are we as yet in ignorance, but the future discovery of which is the as yet still far from achieved aim of our enquiry?

It is clear that, if we are able to do so, this will be the kind of case noticed earlier in which we shall be somehow or other already relying upon what we are not as yet fully justified in asserting, in order to reach the point at which we are fully justified in asserting it. But how then are we to begin? We can begin, just as Aristotle did, only with a type of dialectical argument in which we set out for criticism, and then criticize in turn, each of the established and best reputed beliefs held amongst us as to the fundamental nature of whatever it is about which we are enquiring: for example, as to the nature of motion in physics, or as to the human good in politics and ethics. As rival views are one by one discarded, leaving as their legacy to enquiry either something in them which withstood criticism or that which turned out to be inescapably presupposed by such criticism, so an initial tolerably coherent and direction-affording conception of the relevant first principle or principles may be constructed.

The criticism of rival opinions about the human good in a way which leads on to an account of *eudaimonia* as that good in Book I of the *Nicomachean Ethics* is a paradigmatic case.

Yet, as enquiry progresses, even in these initial stages we are compelled to recognize a gap between the strongest conclusions which such types of dialectical argument can provide and the type of judgment which can give expression to a first principle. Argument to first principles cannot be demonstrative, for demonstration is *from* first principles. But it also cannot be a matter of dialectic and nothing more, since the strongest conclusions of dialectic remain a matter only of belief, not of knowledge. What more is involved? The answer is an act of the understanding which begins from but goes beyond what dialectic and induction provide, in formulating a judgment as to what is necessarily the case in respect of whatever is informed by some essence, but does so under the constraints imposed by such dialectical and inductive conclusions. Insight, not inference, is involved here, but insight which can then be further vindicated if and insofar as this type of judgment provides just the premises required for causal explanation of the known empirical facts which are the subject matter of that particular science.

Moreover, the relationship between the different sciences and their hierarchical ordering becomes important at this point. Initially the shared beliefs which provide premises for dialectical arguments cannot but be beliefs prior to any particular science; such are the beliefs criticized and corrected in Book I of the *Nicomachean Ethics*. But once we have a set of ongoing established sciences, the shared set of beliefs to which appeal can be made include in addition the beliefs presupposed in common by the findings and methods of those sciences.[6] And what those sciences presuppose are those judgments and elements of judgments understanding of which provides the key to Aristotle's metaphysical enterprise, by directing his and our attention beyond the kinds of being treated by the subordinate sciences to being qua being.

Aristotle has sometimes been thought to have undergone a radical change of mind between the earlier *Posterior Analytics* and the later *Metaphysics*, not least because in the first he denies that there can be a supreme science, while in the latter he not only affirms there can be, but provides it. Yet this discrepancy is less striking than at first seems to be the

---

6 The book which states the central issues most fully is T. H. Irwin, *Aristotle's First Principles* (Oxford: Clarendon Press, 1988); I suspect that, if my account were less compressed, it would be more obviously at variance with Irwin's.

case. For what Aristotle means by what he calls "the demonstrative sciences" in the *Posterior Analytics* (e.g., I, 10, 76a37, 76b11–12) are such that none of *them* could be a supreme science: each is concerned with a distinct genus and each is demonstrative and any supreme science would have to be neither. So what Aristotle denied in the *Posterior Analytics* is not what he affirmed in the *Metaphysics*, and Aquinas, who construed the relevant passages of the *Posterior Analytics* not as a denial of the possibility of a supreme science, but as a specification of its character, had understood this very well (*Commentary on the Posterior Analytics*, lib. 1, lect. 17).

More than this, we can in this light understand more adequately how dialectic even within the developing subordinate sciences can, by drawing upon those same presuppositions informing all scientific activity, bring us to the point at which the transition can be made from merely dialectical to apodictic and necessary theses. For the goal of such uses of dialectic thus reinforced is not to establish that there are essences – that is presupposed, not proved, by dialectic and its further investigation is a matter for metaphysics – but to direct our attention to how the relevant classifications presupposing essences are to be constructed, by providing grounds for deciding between the claims of rival alternative formulations of apodictic and necessary theses. Such theses cannot, as we have already noticed, follow from any dialectical conclusion any more than any law in the natural sciences can follow from the interpretation of any experimental result (and interpreted experimental and observational results often have in modern natural science the status assigned by Aristotle to dialectical conclusions), but they can be vindicated against their immediate rivals by such conclusions, just as formulations of natural scientific laws can be vindicated against rival formulations by experiment or observation.

We have then within any mode of ongoing enquiry a series of stages in the progress towards the *telos* of a perfected science. There will be dialectical conclusions both initially in the first characterizations of the *archē/principium* of that particular science, which provide the earliest formulations of the *telos/finis* of its enquiries, and later on in the arguments which relate empirical phenomena to apodictic theses. There will be provisional formulations of such theses, which in the light of further evidence and argument, are displaced by more adequate formulations. And, as enquiry progresses, the conception of the *telos* of that particular mode of enquiry, of the type of perfected science which it is its peculiar aim to achieve, will itself be revised and enriched.

Such a mode of enquiry will have two features which coexist in a certain tension. On the one hand, progress will often be tortuous, uneven, move enquiry in more than one direction, and result in periods of regress and frustration. The outcome may even be large-scale defeat for some whole mode of enquiry. These are the aspects of enquiry not always recognized in adequate measure by either Aristotle or Aquinas and, consequently, their crucial importance to enquiry also needs a kind of recognition by modern Thomists which cannot be derived from our classical texts. Only types of enquiry, we have had to learn from C. S. Peirce and Karl Popper, which are organized so that they can be defeated by falsification of their key theses, can warrant judgments to which truth can be ascribed. The ways in which such falsification can occur and such defeat become manifest are very various. But in some way or other falsification and defeat must remain possibilities for any mode of enquiry and it is essential to any theory that claims truth, and to the enquiry to which it contributes, that they should be vulnerable in this regard.

Hence, it was in one way a victory and not a defeat for the Aristotelian conception of enquiry when Aristotelian physics proved vulnerable to Galileo's dialectical arguments against it. And it is a mark of all established genuinely Aristotelian modes of enquiry that they too are open to defeat; that is, what had been taken to be adequate formulations of a set of necessary, apodictic judgments, functioning as first principles, may always turn out to be false, in the light afforded by the failure by its own Aristotelian standards of what had been hitherto taken to be a warranted body of theory. Lesser partial failures of this kind are landmarks in the history of every science.

It is in this context that we can provide an account of how epistemological crises can be generated and how they can be resolved, including that particular epistemological crisis which the sixteenth century heirs of Aristotelian physics, the impetus theorists – among them the young Galileo – encountered and its resolution by Galileo's creative rejection of Aristotelian physics and cosmology. For one achievement characteristic of the scientific movement from less to more adequate ways of understanding is the ability to explain in the light of our present theorizing just what was inadequate in our past theorizing. Galileo not only provided a better explanation of natural phenomena than did the impetus theorists, but he was also able to explain precisely why, given that nature is as it is, impetus theory could not but fail – by its own standards – at just the points at which it did fail. The continuity of the history of physics and astronomy from impetus theory through and beyond Galileo's work is the continuity of a movement towards a perfected scientific understanding, towards the *telos/finis* of physics. And so it is with progress in each of the sciences.

To understand this conception of scientific progress better we need to remind ourselves that, on an Aristotelian and Thomistic view, enterprises which issue in theoretical achievement are practical enterprises, partially embedded in and having many of the central characteristics of other practical enterprises. Or, to put the same point in another way, the *Nicomachean Ethics* and the *Politics* – and correspondingly Aquinas's commentaries upon and uses of those works – provide a context in terms of which the activities which resulted in the various types of science described in the *Posterior Analytics,* the *Physics,* and the biological treatises – and indeed in the *Metaphysics* and the *Summa Theologiae* – have to be understood.

So when Aristotle distinguishes genuine enquiry, *philosophia,* from dialectic and sophistic (*Metaphysics* 1004b17–26), he does so by contrasting the *power* of philosophy with that of dialectic, but by contrasting philosophy with sophistic as the project (*prohairesis*) of a different life, that is, by a moral contrast. And Aquinas comments that the philosopher orders both life and actions otherwise than does the practitioner of sophistic (*Commentary on the Metaphysics,* lib. 4, lect. 4). So the life of enquiry has to be structured through virtues, both moral and intellectual, as well as through skills. It is more than the exercise of a *technē* or a set of *technai.* But in spelling out how this is so, we have to go beyond what we are explicitly told by either Aristotle or Aquinas.

The central virtue of the active life is the virtue which Aristotle names "*phronēsis*" and Aquinas "*prudentia.*" Three characteristics of that virtue are important for the present discussion. First, it enables its possessor to bring sets of particulars under universal concepts in such a way as to characterize those particulars in relevant relationship to the good at which the agent is aiming. So it is a virtue of right characterization as well as of right action. Secondly, such characterization, like right action, is not achieved by mere rule-following. The application of rules may indeed be and perhaps always is involved in right characterization as in right action, but knowing which rule to apply in which situation and being able to apply that rule relevantly are not themselves rule-governed abilities. Knowing how, when, where, and in what way to apply rules is one central aspect of *phronēsis/prudentia.* These two characteristics of this virtue are sufficient to show its epistemological importance for enquiry; the lack of this virtue in those who pursue, and who teach others to pursue, enquiry always is in danger of depriving enquiry of the possibility of moving towards its *telos/finis.*

So enquiry involves not only a teleological ordering of the activities of enquiry, but also a teleological ordering of those who engage in it and direct it, at least characteristically and for the most part. And it is here that a third characteristic of *phronēsis/prudentia* as an epistemological virtue becomes important. Both Aristotle and Aquinas stress the way in which and the degree to which the possession of that virtue requires the possession of the other moral virtues in some systematic way. In doing so they anticipate something of what was to be said about the moral and social dimensions of the natural sciences in one way by C. S. Peirce and in another by Michael Polanyi.

It is then within a social, moral, and intellectual context ordered teleologically towards the end of a perfected science, in which a finally adequate comprehension of first principles has been achieved, that the Aristotelian and Thomistic conceptions of truth and rational justification find their place, and it is in terms of such an ordering that the relationships between them have to be specified. Consider now how they stand to each other, if we draw upon Aquinas's extended account.

The intellect, as we have already noticed, on this account completes and perfects itself in achieving finality of understanding. Truth is the relationship of the intellect to an object or objects thus known, and in predicating truth of that relationship we presuppose an analogy to the relationship of such objects as they are to that which they would be if they perfectly exemplified their kind. Rational justification is of two kinds. Within the demonstrations of a perfected science, afforded by finally adequate formulations of first principles, justification proceeds by way of showing of any judgment either that it itself states such a first principle or that it is deducible from such a first principle, often enough from such a first principle conjoined with other premises. For such perfected demonstrations express in the form of a scheme of logically related judgments the thoughts of an intellect adequate to its objects. But when we are engaged in an enquiry which has not yet achieved this perfected end state, that is, in the activities of almost every, perhaps of every science with which we are in fact acquainted, rational justification is of another kind. For in such justification what we are arguing to is a conclusion that such and such a judgment does in fact have a place in what will be the final deductive structure. We are engaged in the dialectical construction of such a structure, and our arguments will be of a variety of kinds designed first to identify the conditions which a judgment which will in fact find a place in the final structure must satisfy, and then to decide whether or not this particular judgment does indeed satisfy those conditions.

That truth which is the adequacy of the intellect to its objects thus provides the *telos/finis* of the activities involved in this second type of rational justification. And the deductively ordered judgments which provide the first type of justification with its subject matter are called true in virtue of their affording expression to the truth of the intellect in relation to its objects, since insofar as they afford such expression they present to us how things are and cannot but be. Each type of predication of truth and each type of activity of rational justification stand in a relationship to others specifiable only in terms of their place within the overall teleological ordering of the intellect's activities of enquiry.

Those activities, it should be noted, involve a variety of types of intentionality. And were we to attempt to specify those intentionalities adequately, we should have to learn not only from what Aquinas says about intentionality, but from Brentano, Husserl, and Edith Stein. But it is important to recognize that a Thomistic account of types of intentionality, while it will be as much at variance with those who wish to eliminate intentionality from its central place in the philosophy of mind as are the phenomenologists, will be an integral part of, and defensible only in terms of, a larger Thomistic account of the mind's activities, relating types of intentionality to types of ascription of truth and of rational justification, in an overall scheme of teleological ordering. And any rational justification of the place assigned to *archai/principia* in that perfected understanding which provides the activities of the mind with its *telos/finis* is likewise inseparable from the rational justification of that scheme of teleological ordering as a whole.

There are, however, two objections which may be advanced against understanding enquiry in this Aristotelian and Thomistic mode. First, it may be said that on the account which I have given no one could ever finally know whether the *telos/finis* of some particular natural science had been achieved or not. For it might seem that all the conditions for the achievement of a finally perfected science concerning some particular subject matter had indeed been satisfied, and yet the fact that further investigation may always lead to the revision or rejection of what had previously been taken to be adequate formulations of first principles suggests that we could never be entitled to make this assertion.

My response to this objection is not to deny its central claim, but rather to agree with it and to deny that it is an objection. The history of science shows both in the case of geometry, which was widely supposed to be a perfected science until the eighteenth century, and in that of physics, supposed to be approaching that state by Lord Kelvin and others in the late nineteenth century, that this is an area in which error is never to be ruled out. And it is important that any philosophical account of enquiry should be confirmed rather than disconfirmed by the relevant episodes in the history of science.

We ought, however, at this point to note one remarkable feature of Aquinas's account of enquiry, one which differentiates it from Aristotle's. Aquinas, like Aristotle, asserted that enquiry moves towards a knowledge of essences, but unlike Aristotle he denies that we ever know essences except through their effects. The proper object of human knowledge is not the essence itself, but the *quidditas* of the existent particular through which we come to understand, so far as we can, the essence of whatever it is (*De Spiritualibus Creaturis* II, ad 3 and ad 7). So our knowledge is of what is, as informed by essence, but this knowledge is what it is only because of the nature of the causal relationship of the existent particular and its quiddity to the intellect.[7] Aquinas's affirmation of realism derives from this type of causal account. And such realism is quite compatible with a variety of misconstruals in their causal inferences by enquirers.

A second objection may appear to have been strengthened by my answer to the first. For I there appealed to the verdict of the history of science, and yet the history of science makes it plain, as do the histories of philosophy, theology, and the liberal arts, that the actual course of enquiry in a variety of times and places has proceeded in a variety of heterogeneous ways, many of them not conforming to, and some radically at odds with this particular philosophical account of enquiry. What point can there be, it may be asked, to a philosophical account of enquiry so much at variance with so much of what actually occurs?

The answer is that it is in key part by its power or its lack of power to explain a wide range of different types of episode in the history of science, the history of philosophy and elsewhere, including episodes which are from an Aristotelian and Thomistic standpoint deviant, that the Aristotelian and Thomistic account is to be tested. For, if the Aristotelian view, as extended and amended by Aquinas, is correct, then specific types of departure from enquiry so conceived and specific types of denial of its central theses can be expected to have certain equally specific types of consequence. Intellectual failures, resourcelessnesses, and incoherences of various kinds will become intelligible, as well as successes. A particular way of writing the history of science, the history of philosophy and intellectual history in general will be the counterpart of a Thomistic conception of rational enquiry, and insofar as that history makes the

7 See chapter 8 of E. Gilson, *Thomist Realism and the Critique of Knowledge,* translated by M. A. Wauck (San Francisco: Ignative Press, 1986), especially pp. 202–04.

course of actual enquiry more intelligible than do rival conceptions, the Thomistic conception will have been further vindicated.

The *locus classicus* for a statement of how that history is to be written is the first and second chapters of Book A of the *Metaphysics*, supplemented by Aquinas's commentary. What Aristotle provides is not a narrative, but a scheme for the writing of narratives of that movement which begins from experience and moves through the practices of the arts and sciences to that understanding of *archai* which provides the mind with its terminus. And in succeeding chapters Aristotle writes a series of narratives, some very brief, some more extended, of those among his predecessors who failed or were only in the most limited way successful in their search for *archai*. At the same time Aristotle is providing indirectly a narrative of his own movement through the positions of his predecessors to his achievement of the positions taken in the *Metaphysics*. In so doing he reveals something crucial both about particular enquiries and about philosophical accounts of enquiry.

Of every particular enquiry there is a narrative to be written, and being able to understand that enquiry is inseparable from being able to identify and follow that narrative. Correspondingly every philosophical account of enquiry presupposes some account of how the narratives of particular enquiries should be written. And indeed every narrative of some particular enquiry, insofar as it makes the progress of that enquiry intelligible, by exhibiting the course of its victories and its defeats, its frustrations and endurances, its changes of strategy and tactics, presupposes some ordering of causes of the kind that is only provided by an adequate philosophical account of enquiry.

Aquinas in his commentary endorses and amplifies Aristotle. Indeed, where Aristotle had said, referring to the early myths as precursors of science, that the lover of stories is in some way a philosopher, Aquinas says that the philosopher is in some way a lover of stories. And at the very least, if what I have suggested is correct, a philosopher will, in virtue of his or her particular account of enquiry, always be committed to telling the story of enquiry in one way rather than another, providing by the form of narrative which he or she endorses a standard for those narratives in and through which those engaged in particular sciences cannot but try to make intelligible both to themselves and to others what they are doing, in what direction they are moving, how far they have already moved and so on. Thomism, then, like all other specific philosophical accounts of enquiry, has implicit within it its own conception of how narratives of enquiry are to be constructed. Yet to introduce the Thomistic conception of enquiry into contemporary debates about how intellectual history is to be written would, of course, be to put in question some of the underlying assumptions of those debates. For it has generally been taken for granted that those who are committed to understanding scientific and other enquiry in terms of truth-seeking, of modes of rational justification and of a realistic understanding of scientific theorizing must deny that enquiry is constituted as a moral and social project, while those who insist upon the latter view of enquiry have tended to regard realistic and rationalist accounts of science as ideological illusions. But from an Aristotelian standpoint it is only in the context of a particular socially organized and morally informed way of conducting enquiry that the central concepts crucial to a view of enquiry as truth-seeking, engaged in rational justification, and realistic in its selfunderstanding, can intelligibly be put to work.

To have understood this, and why Thomists are committed to this way of understanding enquiry, is to have reached the point at which Thomism becomes able to enter certain contemporary philosophical debates by explaining, in a way that the protagonists of opposing standpoints within those debates are themselves unable to, how and why the problems posed within those debates are systematically insoluble and the rival positions advanced within them untenable. I do not, of course, mean that those protagonists would be willing or able to accept a Thomistic diagnosis of their predicament. Indeed, given the fundamental assumptions which have conjointly produced their predicament, it is safe to predict that to the vast majority of such protagonists it will seem preferable to remain in almost any predicament rather than to accept a Thomistic diagnosis. Nonetheless it is only by its ability to offer just such a diagnosis, and one, as I have suggested, that will involve a prescription for writing intellectual history, that Thomism can reveal its ability to participate in contemporary philosophical conversation. What then is it that Thomism has to say on these matters?

v

Consider in a more general way than previously the unresolved disagreements and unsettled conflicts which characterize those contemporary philosophical theses, arguments, and attitudes from which issue both the analytic and the deconstructive rejection of first principles. Those disagreements and conflicts are, I want to suggest, symptoms of a set of underlying dilemmas concerning concepts whose status has now been put in question in new and more radical ways.

So, for example, truth has been presented by some as no more than an idealization of warranted assertibility and by others as an entirely dispensable concept. Standards of warrant and justification have, as I noticed earlier, been relativized to social contexts, but the philosophers who have so relativized them have themselves been at odds with each other in multifarious ways. The intentionality of the mind's relationship to its objects, whether as understood by Thomists or otherwise, has been dismissed by some as a misleading fiction, while others have treated it as a pragmatically useful concept, but no more.

Debate over these and kindred issues has proceeded on two levels and on both it has been systematically inconclusive, perhaps in spite of, but perhaps because of the shared background beliefs of the protagonists of rival standpoints. At a first level, where debate has been directly about truth, rationality, and intentionality, the difficulties advanced against earlier metaphysical conceptions – conceptions dominant from the seventeenth to the nineteenth centuries – have appeared sufficient to render such conceptions suspect and questionable for many different reasons, yet insufficient to render them manifestly untenable, an insufficiency evident in the need to return again and again and again to the task of disposing of them. And so, at a second level, debate has opened up among those committed to rejecting or displacing or replacing such conceptions as to why what they have had to say has proved less conclusive in the arenas of philosophical debate than their protagonists had expected.

At this level too disagreements are unresolved and rival views remain in contention. It has been argued, for example, that the antimetaphysical case has seemed less cogent than it is, because its protagonists have been insufficiently ruthless in purging their own positions of metaphysical residues. And it has been further asserted that, so long as the polemic against metaphysical conceptions of truth, rationality, and intentionality is carried on in a conventional philosophical manner, it is bound to be thus burdened with what it ostensibly rejects, since the modes of conventional philosophy are inextricably tied to such conceptions. So the modes of conventional philosophical discourse must be abandoned. This is why Richard Rorty has tried to find a way of going beyond Davidson and Sellars.[8] This is why Derrida has had to go beyond Nietzsche and Heidegger.

---

8 See R. Rorty, *Contingency, Irony and Solidarity* (Cambridge: Cambridge University Press, 1989), pp. 8–9.

Yet to follow Rorty and Derrida into new kinds of writing would be to abandon the debate from which the abandonment of debate would derive its point. So there is a constant return to the debate by those who still aspire to discover an idiom, at once apt for negative philosophical ōpurposes in refuting metaphysical opponents, but itself finally disentangled from all and any metaphysical implications. As yet they have failed.

This is a philosophical scene, then, of unsolved problems and unresolved disagreements, perhaps because these particular problems are insoluble and these particular disagreements unresolvable. Why might this be so? It may be because within contemporary philosophy the concepts which generate these divisions occupy an anomalous position. They are radically discrepant with the modes of thought characteristic of modernity both within philosophy and outside it, so that it is not surprising that relative to those modes of thought they appear functionless or misleading or both. Yet they keep reappearing and resuming their older functions, most notably perhaps in those narratives of objective achievement in enquiry, by recounting which philosophers make what they take to be the progress of their enquiries, and the activities of debate which are so central to that progress, intelligible to themselves and to others.

Within such narratives, narratives of a type which, so I suggested earlier, are ineliminable constituents of philosophical, as of other enquiry, but which nowadays are characteristically deleted and even denied when the outcomes of enquiry are presented in the genre of the conference paper or the journal article, there occurs a return of the philosophically repressed, which reinstates for a moment at least ways of understanding truth, rationality, and intentionality which it was a principal aim of the philosophical activities recounted in the narrative to eliminate. We may note in passing that it is perhaps only in terms of their relationship to such narratives – narratives which still embody, even if in very different forms the narrative scheme of Book A of the *Metaphysics* – that most contemporary philosophers are liable to lapse into something like a teleological understanding of their own activities, even if only for short times and on relatively infrequent occasions.

What I have asserted then is that there is a tension between that in contemporary philosophy which renders substantive, metaphysical, or quasimetaphysical conceptions of truth, rationality, and intentionality not merely questionable, but such as to require total elimination, and that in contemporary philosophy which, even when it is only at the margins of philosophical activity and in largely unacknowledged ways, prevents such total elimination. This thesis is capable of being sustained only insofar as it can be developed as a thesis about contemporary philosophy, elaborated from some standpoint external to the standpoints which dominate and define contemporary philosophy, for only thus can it be itself exempt from the condition which it describes. But from what point of view then can such a thesis be advanced? And, if it is from a point of view genuinely external to that of the kinds of philosophy which it purports to describe, how, if at all, can it be advanced as part of a conversation with the practitioners of those kinds of philosophy?

*Ex hypothesi* anyone who advances such a thesis must, it would seem, share too little in the way of agreed premises, beliefs about what is problematic and what is unproblematic, and indeed philosophical idiom with those about whose philosophical stances he or she is speaking. The depth of disagreement between the two parties will be such that they will be unable to agree in characterizing what it is about which they disagree. We are debarred, that is to say, from following Aristotle and Aquinas in employing any of those dialectical strategies which rely upon some appeal to what all the contending parties in a dispute have not yet put in question. How then are we to proceed? It is at this point that we have to resort to unThomistic means, or at least to what have hitherto been unThomistic means, in order to achieve Thomistic ends. What means are these?

Although I have identified the thesis which I have propounded about the nature of distinctively contemporary philosophy as one that can only be asserted from some vantage point external to that philosophy, I have up to this point left it, as it were, hanging in the air. I now hope to give it status and substance by suggesting – and in this essay I shall be able to do no more than suggest – how, by being elaborated from and integrated into an Aristotelian and Thomistic point of view, it might become part of a theory about the predicaments of contemporary philosophy, providing an account of how those predicaments were generated and under what conditions, if any, they can be avoided or left behind.

The provision of such a theory requires the construction of something akin to what Nietzsche called a genealogy. The genealogical narrative has the function not of arguing with, but of disclosing something about the beliefs, presuppositions and activities of some class of persons. Characteristically it explains how they have come to be in some *impasse* and why they cannot recognize or diagnose adequately out of their own conceptual and argumentative resources the nature of their predicament. It provides a subversive history. Nietzsche, of course, used genealogy in an assault upon theological beliefs which Thomists share with other Christians and upon philosophical positions which Aristotelians share with other philosophers, so that to adopt the methods of genealogical narrative is certainly to adopt what have hitherto been unThomistic means. How then may these be put to the service of Thomistic ends?

What I am going to suggest is that the predicaments of contemporary philosophy, whether analytic or deconstructive, are best understood as arising as a long-term consequence of the rejection of Aristotelian and Thomistic teleology at the threshold of the modern world. I noticed earlier that a teleological understanding of enquiry in the mode of Aristotle and Aquinas has as its counterpart a certain type of narrative, one through the construction of which individuals are able to recount to themselves and to others either how they have achieved perfected understanding, or how they have progressed towards such an understanding which they have not yet achieved. But when teleology was rejected, and Aristotelian conceptions of first principles along with it, human beings engaged in enquiry did not stop telling stories of this kind. They could no longer understand their own activities in Aristotelian terms at the level of theory, but for a very long time they proved unable, for whatever reason, to discard that form of narrative which is the counterpart to the theory which they had discarded. It is only within the last hundred years that it has been recognized by those who have finally attempted to purge themselves completely of the last survivals of an Aristotelian conception of enquiry and of its goals that, in order to achieve this, narratives which purport to supply accounts of the movement of some mind or minds towards the achievement of perfected understanding must be treated as acts of retrospective falsification. But even those, such as Sartre, who have embraced this conclusion have themselves been apt to yield to the temptation to construct just such narratives, a sign of the extraordinary difficulties involved in repudiating this type of narrative understanding of the activities of enquiry.

It is not, of course, that such narratives themselves find an explicit place for distinctively Aristotelian, let alone Thomistic conceptions of truth, rationality, and intentionality. It is rather that they presuppose standards of truth and rationality independent of the enquirer, founded on something other than social agreement, but rather imposing requirements upon what it is rational to agree to, and directing the enquirer towards the achievement of a good in the light of which the enquirer's progress is to be judged. These presuppositions can be elucidated in a number of different and competing ways, but it is difficult and perhaps impossible to do so without returning to just that type of framework for narrative provided in the early chapters of *Metaphysics* A. It is thus unsurprising that, so long as this type of narrative survives in a culture, so long also Aristotelian and Thomistic conceptions are apt to recur even among those who believe themselves long since liberated from them.

One strand in the history of what followed upon the rejection of Aristotelian and Thomistic teleology would therefore be an account of how, under the cover afforded by a certain kind of narrative, some Aristotelian and Thomistic conceptions survived with a kind of underground cultural life. Another and more obvious strand in that same history concerns the way in which in the history of philosophy and the history of science those conceptions were first displaced and marginalized, undergoing radical transformations as a result of this displacement and marginalization, and then even in their new guises were finally rejected. What were the stages in that history?

In the account that I gave of the Aristotelian and Thomistic account of enquiry, framed in terms of first principles, I emphasized the way in which a variety of types of predication of truth and a variety of modes of rational justification find their place within a single, if complex, teleological framework designed to elucidate the movement of the mind towards its *telos/finis* in perfected understanding, a movement that thereby presupposes a certain kind of intentionality. It is within that framework and in terms of it that not only are the functions of each kind of ascription of truth and each mode of rational justification elucidated, but also the relations between them specified, so that what is primary is distinguished from what is secondary or tertiary and the analogical relationships between these made clear. Abstract these conceptions of truth and reality from that teleological framework, and you will thereby deprive them of the only context by reference to which they can be made fully intelligible and rationally defensible.

Yet the widespread rejection of Aristotelian teleology and of a whole family of cognate notions in the sixteenth and seventeenth centuries resulted in just such a deprivation. In consequence conceptions of truth and rationality became, as it were, free floating. Complex conceptions separated out into their elements. New philosophical and scientific frameworks were introduced into which the older conceptions could be fitted only when appropriately and often radically amended and modified. And naturally enough conceptions which had been at home in Aristotelian and Thomistic teleological contexts in relatively unproblematic ways were now apt to become problematic and questionable.

Truth as a result became in time genuinely predicable only of statements; "true" predicated of things came to seem a mere idiom of no philosophical interest. New theories of truth had, therefore, to be invented, and they inescapably fell into two classes: *either* statements were true in virtue of correspondence between either them or the sentences which expressed them, on the one hand, and facts – "fact" in this sense is a seventeenth-century linguistic innovation – on the other, *or* statements were true in virtue of their coherence with other statements. The protagonists of a multiplicity of rival versions of correspondence and coherence theories succeeded in advancing genuinely damaging critiques of their rivals' theories and so prepared the way for a further stage, one in which truth is treated either as a largely redundant notion or as an idealization of warranted assertibility.

In a parallel way conceptions of rational justification also underwent a series of transformations. With the rejection of a teleological understanding of enquiry, deductive arguments no longer had a place defined by their function, either in demonstrative explanations or in the dialectical constructions of such explanations. Instead they first found a place within a variety of epistemological enterprises, either Cartesian or empiricist, which relied upon a purported identification of just the type of epistemological first principle which I described earlier. When such enterprises foundered, a variety of different and mutually incompatible conceptions of rational justification were elaborated to supply what this kind of foundationalism had failed to provide. The outcome was a de facto acknowledgment of the existence of a variety of rival and contending conceptions of rationality, each unable to defeat its rivals, if only because the basic disagreement between the contending parties concerned which standards it is by appeal to which defeat and victory can be justly claimed. In these contests characteristically and generally no reasons can be given for allegiance to any one standpoint rather than to its rivals which does not already presuppose that standpoint. Hence it has often been concluded that it is the socially established agreement of some particular group to act in accordance with the standards of some one particular contending conception of rational justification which underlies all such appeals to standards, and that such agreement cannot itself be further justified. Where rationalists and empiricists appealed to epistemological first principles, their contemporary heirs identify socially established forms of life or paradigms or epistemes. What began as a rejection of the Aristotelian teleological framework for enquiry has, in the case of conceptions of truth, progressed through epistemology to eliminative semantics and, in the case of conceptions of rational justification, through epistemology to the sociology of knowledge.

What I am suggesting then is this: that certain strands in the history of subsequent philosophy are best to be understood as consequences of the rejection of any Aristotelian and Thomistic conception of enquiry. To construct the genealogy of contemporary philosophy – or at least of a good deal of contemporary philosophy – in this way would disclose three aspects of such philosophy which are otherwise concealed from view. First, such a genealogical account would enable us to understand how the distinctive problematic of contemporary philosophy was constituted and what its relationship is to the problematics of earlier stages in the history of modern philosophy. The history of philosophy is still too often written as if it were exclusively a matter of theses and arguments. But we ought by now to have learned from R. G. Collingwood that we do not know how to state, let alone to evaluate such theses and arguments, until we know what questions they were designed to answer.

Secondly, once we understand how the questions and issues of contemporary philosophy were generated, we shall also be able to recognize that what are presented from within contemporary philosophy as theses and arguments about truth as such and rationality as such are in fact theses and arguments about what from an Aristotelian and Thomistic standpoint are degenerated versions of those concepts, open to and rightly subject to the radical critiques which have emerged from debates about them, only because they were first abstracted from the only type of context within which they are either fully intelligible or adequately defensible. Hence, in important respects Thomists need have no problem with much of the contemporary critiques; if indeed truth and rationality were what they have for a long time now been commonly taken to be, those critiques would be well-directed. And in understanding this the Thomist has resources for understanding contemporary philosophy which the dominant standpoints within contemporary philosophy cannot themselves provide.

To this, however, it may well be retorted that the protagonists of those standpoints have no good reason to concede that the history of modern philosophy should be construed as I have attempted to construe it, even if they were to grant for argument's sake that the very bare outline sketch which I have provided could in fact be filled in with the appropriate details. Nothing in their own beliefs, it may be said, nothing in the culture which they inhabit gives them the slightest reason to entertain any conception of enquiry as teleologically ordered towards an adequate understanding of an explanation in terms of *archai/principia*. They therefore cannot but understand the sixteenth- and seventeenth-century rejections of Aristotelianism, whether Thomistic or otherwise, as part of a progress towards greater enlightenment. And in this perspective the accounts which they have given of truth, rationality, and intentionality are to be understood as culminating achievements in a history of such progress. Where the Thomist sees stages in a movement away from adequate conceptions of truth and rationality, stages in a decline, the protagonists of the dominant standpoints in contemporary philosophy, so it will be said, will see stages in an ascent, a movement towards – but the problem is: towards what?

The defender of contemporary philosophy is at this point in something of a dilemma. For if he or she can supply an answer to this last question – and it is not too difficult to think of a number of answers – what he or she will have provided will have been something much too like the kind of narrative account of objective achievement in enquiry whose structure presupposes just that type of teleological ordering of enquiry the rejection of which is central to the whole modern philosophical enterprise. But if he or she cannot supply an answer to this question, then philosophy can no longer be understood to have an intelligible history of achievement, except in respect of the working out of the details of different points of view. It will have become what David Lewis has said that it is: "Once the menu of well-worked out theories is before us, philosophy is a matter of opinion . . ."[9] Yet, the question arises once again about *this* conclusion: is it an achievement to have arrived at it or not? Is it superior in truth or rational warrant to other opinions? To answer either "Yes" or "No" to these questions revives the earlier difficulty.

It is no part of my contention that a protagonist of one of the dominant trends in contemporary philosophy will lack the resources to frame a response to this point, adequate in its own terms. It is my contention that such a protagonist will even so lack the resources to explain the peculiar predicaments of contemporary philosophy and to provide an intelligible account of how and why, given its starting-point and its direction of development, to be trapped within these predicaments was inescapable. Thomism enables us to write a type of history of modern and contemporary philosophy which such philosophy cannot provide for itself.

9 See *Philosophical Papers*, vol. I (Oxford: Oxford University Press, 1983), pp. x–xi.

In the course of writing this kind of genealogical history Thomism will be able to open up possibilities of philosophical conversation and debate even with standpoints with which it shares remarkably little by way of agreed premises or shared standards of rational justification. It will be able to do so insofar as it can show how an Aristotelian and Thomistic conception of enquiry, in terms of first principles and final ends, can provide us with an understanding and explanation of types of philosophy which themselves reject root and branch the possibility of providing a rational justification for any such conception. But that is, of course, work yet to be done.

# CHAPTER 9

# Philosophy recalled to its tasks: a Thomistic reading of Fides et Ratio

*Fides et Ratio* is both an encyclical about philosophy and an exercise in philosophy, a contribution to the very same debates about which it speaks. As an encyclical, it insists on the autonomy of philosophical enquiry: "philosophy must remain faithful to its own principles and methods. Otherwise there would be no guarantee that it would remain oriented to truth and that it was moving towards truth by way of a process governed by reason" (section 49 of the encyclical). And by so insisting it deliberately opens itself up to questioning. Certainly, like other encyclicals, it invites obedient assent from Catholic readers. But we would be disobedient to its distinctive message, if we did not subject it to philosophical questioning.

My own questioning is from the standpoint of a Thomist. And, since the highest praise in the encyclical is accorded to St. Thomas Aquinas, it might seem that for Thomists there should be little to question. But there is something philosophically problematic about this encyclical. For it proceeds boldly and instructively in the direction of some of the most deep-cutting and divisive issues within philosophy and then at certain points stops short, exhibiting on the one hand an evident reluctance "to demand adherence to particular theses" within philosophy (38) and a corresponding emphasis on the legitimacy from a Catholic standpoint of a range of diverse and mutually inconsistent philosophical positions of which Thomism is only one, but also voicing unqualified approval for Thomistic realism (44). How are these two attitudes related? The encyclical presents us with a question, and although it does not provide us with an answer, it points us towards an answer.

A second area in which we are also left with questions concerns the relationship between on the one hand the enquiries of those of us who are philosophers by vocation and profession and on the other the search for meaning and understanding that informs the lives of plain persons. Here again the encyclical stops short. It characterizes that relationship in illuminating, but general terms, and leaves it to us to ask how that relationship is to be understood by us here now in the particular and specific context of our own present social and cultural situation. I shall claim that, in order to understand that situation more adequately, it is indeed to Thomistic realism that we have to look for resources, and perhaps one implication of this is that it may be more difficult to be a Catholic philosopher and not to be a Thomist than the encyclical suggests. But I shall not now pursue this thought. I begin instead by considering how philosophical enquiry is characterized in *Fides et Ratio.*

I

*Fides et Ratio* draws our attention to four characteristics of philosophical enquiry. First, its primary tasks are to articulate and to pursue answers to questions posed by human beings in general, and not only by professional philosophers. It is characteristic of human beings that, whatever our culture, we desire to know and to understand, that we cannot but set ourselves the achievement of truth as a goal. And among the truths to which we aspire truth about the human good is of peculiar importance. We move towards that truth by asking what, if anything, the meaning of our lives is, what place suffering has in our lives, and whether or not death is the terminus of those lives (25, 26). So all human beings "are in some sense philosophers and have their own philosophical conceptions with which they direct their lives" (30). Philosophy is a matter of concern for plain persons before it is a matter of concern for professional philosophers.

Those of us who are philosophers by profession, whose daily work is philosophy, are therefore carrying further a kind of questioning that is also of importance to those whose work is farming or fishing or making steel. We do so as ourselves plain persons and on behalf of other plain persons, contributing to the common good by our work, just as do farmers or fishermen or steel workers by theirs. But this is something that we professional philosophers often forget, perhaps because of a second characteristic of our activities that is emphasized by the encyclical. Philosophy, as I already noted, is defined as an autonomous form of practice with its own principles and methods, its own standards of success and failure, its own idioms and semitechnical vocabularies, its own specializations. And to become a professional philosopher in Europe or North America now requires a particular type of extended education and initiation into the specializations of the profession, one effect of which is that the professional philosopher often appears strange and unintelligible to the plain person, an irrelevant, oddly useless figure of obscure utterance.

Philosophers do in fact become irrelevant to others not only by making their utterances inaccessible, but also by losing sight of the often complex and indirect connections between their own specialized, detailed and piecemeal enquiries and those larger questions which give point and purpose to the philosophical enterprise, which rescue it from being no more than a set of intellectually engaging puzzles. Part of what is needed to remedy this is to call to mind a third salient characteristic of philosophy identified in the encyclical, its systematic character. Philosophy does not consist of a set of independent and heterogeneous enquiries into distinct and unconnected problems: the characterization of space and time, the nature of the human good, the relationship of perceived qualities to the causes of perception, how referring expressions function, what standards govern aesthetic judgment, the nature of causality, and so on. For the answers that we give to each of these questions impose constraints upon what answers we can defensibly give to some at least of the others. And when from collaborative work in a number of areas the logical, conceptual, empirical, and metaphysical relationships between each of these sets of answers begin to emerge, we commonly find that we have at least an outline of a system, a system that will inescapably have implications for how the philosophical questions posed by plain persons are to be answered. We will have reached a point at which we are able to recognize the need for a comprehensive vision of the human good and of the order of things (30, 46). System-building however can itself degenerate into a form of philosophical vice against which the encyclical warns us (4). Philosophers who are aware of the systematic character of their enterprise may always fall in love with their own system to such an extent that they gloss over what they ought to recognize as intractable difficulties or unanswerable questions. Love of that particular system displaces the love of truth. If the vice of reducing philosophy to a set of piecemeal, apparently unconnected set of enquiries is the characteristic analytical vice, this vice of system-lovers may perhaps be called the idealist vice.

Both vices have their representatives in present-day academic philosophy. Yet neither they nor the condition of academic philosophy more generally is sufficient to explain the radical marginalization of philosophical concerns in our culture. This marginalization has several aspects. In part it is a matter of the relegation of philosophy in the vast majority of colleges and universities to a subordinate position in the curriculum, an inessential elective for those who happen to like that sort of thing. But this itself is a symptom of a more general malaise. For to a remarkable extent the norms of our secularized culture not only exclude any serious and systematic questioning of oneself and others about the nature of the human good and the order of things, but they also exclude questioning those dominant cultural norms that make it so difficult to pose these philosophical questions outside academic contexts in any serious and systematic way. We have within our social order few, if any milieus within which reflective and critical enquiry concerning the central issues of human life can be sustained and the education to which we subject our young is not well-designed to develop the habits of thought necessary for such questioning. This tends to be a culture of answers, not of questions, and those answers, whether secular or religious, liberal or conservative, are generally delivered as though meant to put an end to questioning. So it is not just that the philosophy of the academic philosopher has been marginalized in the college curriculum. It is also and more importantly that, when plain persons do try to ask those questions about the human good and the nature of things in which the philosophical enterprise is rooted, the culture immediately invites them to think about something else and to forget those questions.

To this it may be retorted that the point of asking questions is to arrive at answers, that the teaching of the church is after all an authoritative source of answers. When those answers have been accepted, then presumably the time for philosophical questioning is over. Yet just this is trenchantly denied by the encyclical. Philosophical questioning, when it encounters the mystery of God's self-revelation, does not come to an end, but is entrusted with new and additional tasks, for which it is provided with new and enriched resources. So, on the encyclical's account, philosophy has a fourth important characteristic, its ability to learn from God's self-revelation still further questions to ask and new directions to take.

There are two conceptions of the relationship of faith to reason in general and to philosophy in particular which the encyclical rejects. One is that which affirms that the fact of revelation puts a decisive end to the rational enquiries of philosophy, by exposing the false claims made on behalf of reason by philosophy and by showing philosophy to be at best redundant and unnecessary. Faith, on this rejected view, displaces and replaces reason. The other rejected view is that which allows that reason does indeed have its due place and with it philosophy, but only as prologue. Philosophical enquiry can take us so far, but must stop short and become silent before the fact of revelation. Against both these views the encyclical directs our attention to "a genuinely novel consideration for philosophical learning" that has emerged from the two Vatican Councils.

It is that revelation "impels reason continually to extend the range of its knowledge" (14). From the New Testament, especially from St. Paul's letters, we learn that "revealed wisdom disrupts the cycle of our habitual patterns of thought, which are in no way able to express that wisdom in its fullness" (23). And that disruption makes it possible for philosophy to renew its enquiries, instructed by faith. I take it that the encyclical does not mean by this that the philosopher is now to argue from premises accepted only by faith. It is rather that philosophy confronts new possibilities and has the task of giving a rationally justifiable account of those new and hitherto unthinkable possibilities, one that never permits reason to take the place of faith, but that makes visible not just the agreement of faith and reason, but also the illumination of reason by faith. The encyclical commends Anselm as a model for Christian philosophers in this respect, but it is perhaps worth considering briefly another example, one not discussed in the encyclical.

Self-knowledge provides familiar matter for philosophical enquiry and the need to understand self-deception, if we are to understand self-knowledge, is generally recognized. St. Paul tells us however in his letter to the Ephesians (4: 17–24) that it is our sinful alienation from God and our consequent hardness of heart that darkens our understanding and makes us accomplices in our victimization by our own deceitful desires. And Aquinas, in his commentary on this passage, assembles from elsewhere in scripture an array of texts in which there is to be found this same diagnosis of self-knowledge as systematically corrupted by a will not to acknowledge that law of which God is the author and the self's dependence on that law. So philosophers whose faith enables them to learn from St. Paul will suspect insufficiently complex accounts of self-knowledge that do not allow for the possibility of the mind perversely and systematically defending itself against self-knowledge. They will ask how far and in what ways theories of the mind that do not allow for this possibility are not merely philosophical mistakes, but are themselves further defenses against the acknowledgment of this possibility. They will enquire how far and in what ways the mind's reflections upon itself are informed by willfulness.

In so doing they remain philosophers, that is, they are still subject to the requirement that they provide adequate rational justification for their conclusions without appeal to revealed truths and, that they formulate those conclusions, so that every objection to them may be given sufficient weight. But their thought has been given a direction that only revelation could have afforded. That revelation can inform philosophical enquiry in this way is not of course a new thought. But the encyclical gives it an added significance by its theological and scriptural emphasis on philosophical questioning as so central to human nature that, when that nature is through faith transformed by grace, it does not and should not cease to question. A life that is one of growth in holiness does not thereby cease to be a life of philosophical enquiry, something exemplified for us in our own time by Edith Stein, and most notably by St. Thomas Aquinas.

Of the four characteristics of philosophical enquiry thus considered in the encyclical, three have as much to do with philosophy's external relationships as with its own internal concerns. The assertion of the autonomy of philosophy and the recognition of its indispensability safeguard it from the imperialism of theology on the one hand and of the social sciences on the other. The recognition that the questions central to philosophy are questions asked by plain persons and that philosophers conduct their enquiries on behalf of other plain persons raises urgent questions about the place of philosophy within our overall culture and the harm done to that culture by the marginalization of philosophical questioning. And the insistence that the tasks of philosophers do not end with their encounter with revealed truth is a salutary reminder of philosophy's due place in the life of the church as well as in that of secular culture. Yet the encyclical is concerned with much more than philosophy's external relations. One of its central preoccupations is with the obstacles to understanding that arise from a range of currently influential philosophical standpoints and programs. What those standpoints and programs have in common is a failure to provide an adequate account of truth. They include relativism and historicism (87), both understood, it seems, as doctrines that err by contextualizing the application of truth predicates. And it is against them that the encyclical invokes and praises Aquinas's realism and its recognition of "the objectivity of truth" (44). So I turn to some of the philosophical issues that arise when questions concerning truth are posed.

II

Most discussions of truth in recent analytic philosophy turn out to be almost exclusively discussions of the predicates "is true" and "is false" when said of asserted sentences. And those discussions take the form that they do, because of a widely shared assumption that semantic questions can be and should be answered prior to and independently of metaphysical questions. So, on this view, we can enquire into the meaning and use of truth predicates without any prior consideration of the full range of uses and applicants of the notion of truth. It is simply taken for granted that the primary and sometimes, it appears, the only subjects of which truth is predicated are asserted sentences. It is unsurprising that those who begin from this assumption have sometimes concluded that the predicates "is true" and "is false" are redundant and could be eliminated from language without loss. For in asserting that it is true that such and such is the case, I seem to have asserted no more than that such and such is the case, and in asserting that it is false that such and such is the case, I seem to have asserted no more than that such and such is not the case. So "it is true that" and "it is false that" have seemed to add nothing to our assertions and so to be redundant expressions. Many of those who do not take this radical eliminativist view of truth predicates, who acknowledge that we do need such expressions as "That is true" in our language, have nonetheless agreed with the eliminativists in denying that "is true" is a genuine predicate whose meaning adds anything to the meaning of that of which it is predicated.

These are not the only minimalist theories of truth, but they will serve to highlight the contrast between any such minimalism and Aquinas's account. I take that account to involve three central contentions, set out in the opening articles of the first of the *Quaestiones Disputatae de Veritate*. First, Aquinas recognizes that "is true" and "truth" are used in a number of ways and that these are related analogically, but he takes the primary uses to be those in which truth is predicated of a relationship between the intellect and those realities which the intellect encounters and concerning which the intellect judges theoretically and practically. To those realities the intellect may be more or less adequate. It is adequate insofar as its conceptions and judgments of how things are identical with how things in fact are (I, 1; for the formula "Truth is the adequacy of thing and intellect" Aquinas refers us to the Jewish philosopher Isaac Israeli).

Secondly, Aquinas holds that to conceive and judge truly of how things are is to understand and understanding is the goal of the intellect, an end in itself, even if incidentally on occasion a means to further ends. Every rational animal by its nature desires to understand. The intellect therefore has to understand itself as goal-directed in its movement from inadequacy towards adequacy. And the measure of its achievement of or of its failure to achieve adequacy is external to it and independent of it, for those things which are the objects of its understanding and about which it judges are the measure of its adequacy in understanding and judgment. Truth is thus primarily a property of the intellect (I, 2), yet the things which provide the intellect with the measure of its adequacy may themselves also be said to be true or false.

Thirdly a thing is said to be true, insofar as it is adequate to some intellect. It is adequate to the divine intellect, insofar as it fulfills that to which the divine intellect orders it. And it is adequate to a human intellect insofar as it causes a true judgment of itself (I, 2). So the truth of some particular human individual's judgment is to be explained by a causal relationship that holds between the relevant subject matter and the judging mind. And the characterization of that subject matter for the purpose of such an explanation will refer us to properties of things which things possess as parts of the divine ordering of the universe. To conceive of things as they are we have to be able to discriminate those properties that they have by reason of their essential nature – those properties that define the part that they play in the order of things – from those that they possess only incidentally. It is then a presupposition both of our judgments of truth and falsity, rightly understood, and of activities aimed at achieving a perfected understanding of any subject-matter that there is such an order of things, existing independently of its apprehension by this or that particular mind. So, on Aquinas's account, we cannot characterize the semantic properties of truth-predicates adequately without having already made metaphysical commitments, commitments also presupposed by our explanations. For to explain some particular just is to identify its place in the order of things. Explanation and understanding, thus understood, are not interest-relative.

This understanding of understanding is exemplified in the mind's understanding of itself. The mind does not arrive at an understanding of itself by beginning from some act of introspection, from some inwardly directed self-scrutiny. It does so rather by considering how human beings are, as rational beings, goal-directed, so that they not only in general correct their judgments in the light of new evidence, but move towards arriving at a more and more adequate understanding of particular subject matters. To function well in this respect they need to exercise intellectual virtues as well as intellectual powers.

What distinguishes Aquinas's account of the progress of the speculative intellect from modern accounts of scientific progress is that, while for the latter scientific progress consists exclusively in the development of more and more adequate theories, through a process of rejection, revision, and conceptual invention, for the former it is a matter not only of thus perfecting our theories, our sciences, but also of the perfecting of the minds of the enquirers, of the theorists. For, until we have understood intellectual progress in this second way, we have not understood the place that enquiring minds have in the order of things. And here Aquinas marks another distinction not found in modern accounts of scientific progress, that between those intellectual virtues that enable their posses-sors to move towards and to achieve perfected understanding within particular sciences and the first and highest intellectual virtue, *sapientia*, wisdom, the virtue without which one cannot grasp those first principles that enable us to understand how the different sciences relate to each other and how each contributes to an integrated understanding of the natural universe and of the place of human beings within it (*Summa Theologiae* Ia-IIae 57, 2).

It is in recognizing this integrative understanding as the end to which by its nature the human intellect is directed that we return to a central thesis of *Fides et Ratio*. For the questions to which philosophers and scientists cannot expect to find an answer, unless they become wise, are in substance just those questions posed by plain persons about the universe that they inhabit and their own place within it. On a Thomistic view, as on the view taken by the encyclical, the questions proper to philosophers are reformulations of questions that are inescapable for plain persons, insofar as they are rational agents. And just as philosophers need both the intellectual virtues and those moral virtues without which the intellectual virtues cannot be exercised, so too do plain persons. The intellectual virtues are not virtues peculiar to intellectuals.

The wisdom achieved by plain persons is of course exhibited in a kind of grasp of the nature and meaning of things which differs importantly from that of philosophers and scientists. But the necessary qualities of character and mind are in substance the same. Consider one set of such qualities, those habits of mind that are expressed in an openness to difficulties in and objections to the theses and theories that one currently accepts. Aquinas, in his dialectical practice, shows himself well aware of how it is only through giving their due weight to all such difficulties and objections that intellectual progress is to be made. And the internal structure of each article of the *Summa* testifies to this. But it was left to recent nonThomistic philosophers, especially to C. S. Peirce and Karl Popper, to identify the crucial place that an emphasis on falsifiability has in scientific progress from less adequate to more adequate theories and to show that corrigibility and refutability are necessary properties of any theory for which truth can be claimed. There are here two distinct, even if closely related, theses which invite our assent, one concerning theories, the other concerning theorists.

For the latter, as I have already noticed, it is a matter of their willingness to confront in full measure difficulties and objections, so that they are not tempted to employ protective strategies to preserve their beliefs from correction or refutation. When such willingness is lacking, we obscure from ourselves an important property of our theories, a property that derives from the character of judgments and assertions. To assert is, as minimalists correctly point out, to assert as true. And of true assertions it is always true that, had things been in this or that respect otherwise than they are, those assertions would have been false. Even assertions about what is necessarily the case in respect of members of some species or genus – at least if they are understood as Aristotle and Aquinas understood them – may fail in respect of truth. For their truth depends on the contingent fact that this particular genus or species does have members. So the true is always to be understood as a counterpart to the false. And in consequence I understand what it is for some particular judgment to be true, only if I understand what would have to be the case for that particular judgment to be false, that is, if I understand what difference in things corresponds to the difference between the truth and the falsity of that judgment.

When my judgments are in fact false, it is because some factor has intervened which prevents the objects about which I am judging from impacting first on my senses and then on my mind in such a way that my thoughts about how things are become identical with how they are. If I am to revise or to reject those judgments, I will need to ensure that the objects about which I am judging do impact on me without such interference. And this may require active intervention, so that I make myself open to those experiences which may afford me a reason for revising or rejecting my present judgments. It is only because and insofar as my judgments are falsifiable, that they are capable of being true. And it is only because and insofar as I expose those judgments to the verdict of experiences that may show them to be false, that I can hope to move purposefully from falsity to truth, towards a relationship in which my mind is more adequate to its objects than it formerly was.

What reasons someone has, then, for revising or rejecting their judgments, whether theoretical or practical, depends upon what causal relationships she or he stands in to objects that are external to and independent of her or his senses or mind, objects whose properties have to be understood, if they are to be understood rightly, with reference to their place in the order of things. For those causal relationships determine the character of our reason-affording experiences and of the judgments that the mind makes on the basis of those experiences. And here we may pause to note that if we proceed further in elaborating this version of Aquinas's theory of truth we will at once become involved in at least three areas of contemporary philosophical controversy: the relationship between reasons and causes, the nature of experience, and the question of what it is for our judgments to agree with or be discrepant with their subject matter. It is a distinctive characteristic of Aquinas's account of truth that, unlike both its minimalist rivals and some other correspondence theories of truth, it cannot be developed and evaluated without entering into these areas of controversy. What conclusions we arrive at about truth depends in part on what conclusions we arrive at on these other questions and vice versa. So here is a program of systematic philosophical work to be done. What is at stake in its outcome?

The conception of a perfected understanding, of a mind whose relationship to the subject matter about which it thinks is one of adequacy, is the conception of a mind that has rendered some particular subject matter intelligible. And the attempt to arrive at a perfected understanding of the mind and of the nature of its directed movement from inadequacy to adequacy in its thinking is the conception of a mind that may succeed or fail in making itself intelligible to itself. To make something intelligible is to recognize it as a distinct object or set of objects and to identify its place in the order of things by understanding it in terms of the first principle or principles to which it must be referred, so distinguishing what it is necessarily and essentially from what it is only contingently. It is to identify those formal, final, material, and efficient causes which not only make it the kind of thing that it is, but also determine how perfectly or imperfectly and in what ways it exemplifies that kind. And someone may at this point remark that in so doing we are rendering the object about which we are judging intelligible by means of our categories and concepts, we are placing it within our conceptual scheme. This apparently harmless remark – how after all could the categories and concepts through which we understand not be ours? – has however become a premise for some recent antirealist arguments, arguments whose conclusions are antithetical to the Thomist position. If we understand objects only as categorized and conceptualized by us, then, so it has been claimed, we can have no knowledge of them, can indeed form no conception of them, apart from and independently of our categories and conceptual schemes. Anyone who asserts that there are realities that exist independently of and prior to any apprehension of them that we may have is, on this view, claiming to be able to conceive of things as they are apart from our conceiving of them. But this claim is, so it is claimed, absurd. How should we respond to this type of argument?

On Aquinas's view we are only able to conceive of and to categorize the objects of our understanding truly by reason of certain characteristics that those objects themselves possess, the characteristics in virtue of which they impact on us causally so that they become perceptible and intelligible by us. Objects that exist prior to and independently of our apprehension of them are potentially, even if not yet actually, objects of perception by us and of understanding by us, and they are already actually whatever they must be in order to be perceptible and intelligible. Were it not so, we would not, when we do encounter those objects, be able to perceive and understand them. Our potentialities as perceivers and thinkers match their potentialities as perceptible and intelligible. It is not just that, or primarily that, we make objects intelligible by categorizing them and conceptualizing them. It is rather that objects are intelligible per se and that we are able to categorize and conceptualize them truly because they have properties that make them apt for categorization and conceptualization in this way rather than that. We may of course and often enough do miscategorize or misconceive (for Aquinas's catalogue of different types of error, see *Summa Theologiae* Ia 85, 6), so that we have to revise our conceptual schemes and not merely our particular judgments. And we have already noticed the importance of such revision for the intellect's progress towards perfected understanding. But it is precisely in moving from less adequate to more adequate categorical and conceptual schemes and judgments that we recognize that the realities which we formerly categorized and conceptualized in one way, and now recategorize and reconceptualize in another are the same realities, and that they exist and have the characteristics that warrant or fail to warrant our categories and our conceptualizations independently of those categories and conceptualizations. We need therefore to be able and we do have the ability to identify and to reidentify objects independently of those categorizations and conceptualizations, whether mistaken or accurate. So Thomistic realism, if it can make good on these claims, unlike, say, the metaphysical realism once espoused and later repudiated by Hilary Putnam, has a compelling response to this kind of antirealism.

It is however a response that is at odds with some of the basic presuppositions of many contemporary academic philosophers. For the notion that, if we succeed in understanding our world and ourselves, we discover an intelligible order of things, whose ordering is independent of our desires, wills, choices, and projects, but by reference to which alone significance attaches to those desires, wills, and choices, entails a denial of theses central to contemporary pragmatism and contemporary nominalism.

A central thesis of contemporary pragmatism is that the categories, concepts, and classificatory schemes by reference to which our experience is ordered are to be justified by the uses to which they are put. All explanation is relative to our purposes and interests. A central thesis of contemporary nominalism is that there is no ordering of things independent of the human mind and of its conceptual conventions. There are no natural kinds. And these two theses complement each other, providing support for the view that intelligibility is a mental artifact, that to understand some phenomenon is no more than to assign a place to it within some scheme which we have constructed. We are able to make whatever it is intelligible only by imposing upon it our categories and classifications and our fundamental conceptual schemes can be afforded no justification by reference to anything external to themselves.

There are of course rival and alternative versions of both pragmatism and nominalism. Not all pragmatists adopt the positions of Richard Rorty, not all nominalists those of Gilles Deleuze. But even the adherents of a modified and qualified pragmatism and nominalism are committed to the rejection of anything like the interrelated Thomistic conceptions of truth, intelligibility, and a human-mind-independent order of things. And this rejection is reinforced by a further characteristic of the ordering of things, as understood by Aquinas, its teleological character. It is not just that generally and characteristically each individual belongs to a kind and has the essential properties of members of that kind, but that, at least so far as plants and animals, including rational animals, are concerned, individuals are by their natures each directed towards their specific end. Each has its own natural line of development, each is directed in accordance with that line towards its own specific mode of flourishing. And our understanding of that directedness remains incomplete until we recognize that it can be explained only by reference to God as first and final cause. It is sometimes said contemptuously by those who are deeply sceptical about the notions of natural kinds and of essential natures that the use of these notions presupposes the possibility of there being a God's eye view of things. And this throwaway remark is intended to counteract any temptation to find a use for these notions. But for a Thomist it embodies a deep insight concerning the nature of explanation and understanding.

What I have tried to do so far is to spell out some of the implications of the Thomistic realism affirmed in the encyclical and to take note of the commitments of that realism to a set of particular theses concerning truth, understanding, and explanation. But to have done this makes the question of the encyclical's attitude to Thomism inescapable. For to praise Thomistic realism is to commit oneself to the truth of a set of particular assertions and the soundness of a set of particular arguments. Yet the encyclical insists that its praise of Aquinas as an exemplar for all those concerned with the relations between faith and reason "has not been in order to take a position on properly philosophical questions nor to demand adherence to particular theses" (78), an insistence that is re-inforced by the praise accorded to such unThomistic or antiThomistic thinkers as Bonaventure, Pascal, Newman, Rosmini, Edith Stein, Soloviev, Florensky, Chaadaev, and Lossky. There thus seems, as I said at the outset, to be an unresolved ambiguity in the encyclical's attitude towards Thomism.

How might this ambiguity be resolved? We need at this point to return to the encyclical's account of human beings as beings one of whose essential characteristics is that they are moral and metaphysical question-ers and self-questioners, beings inescapably engaged in practical enquiry and often compelled into theoretical enquiry too. Were we incapable of arriving at intellectually satisfying answers to our questions, were we incapable of completing our enquiries, then the human condition would be one of predestined disappointment, of absurdity. But the necessary conditions for its not being absurd, the necessary conditions for the possibility of the completion of the human questioning enterprise, are just those specified by Thomistic realism in its account of what is required for perfected understanding and of what it is that makes such understand-ing possible. Thomistic realism is in this way a doctrine presupposed by the questioning of plain persons. And its vindication is a vindication of that questioning as well as of the enquiries of philosophers, Thomistic and nonThomistic alike, who extend further the questioning of plain persons. It follows that any type of philosophy that is to be able to function as philosophy must function, if it is to achieve its own ends, may be nonThomistic or even antiThomistic in many respects – as were the philosophies of Scotus and Pascal and Newman, as are the philosophies of the phenomenological and of the Eastern Orthodox traditions – but that they will have to find some place for those truths that were classically articulated as the doctrine of Thomistic realism.

III

The significance of Thomistic realism is not exhausted by its contribu-tions to metaphysical and semantic enquiry and debate. It also has implications for the interpretative perspective that we bring to our study of cultures, both of alien cultures and of our own. For it teaches us to understand all cultures as embodying complex attempts to apprehend and represent the order of things, to engage with things as they are rather than as they merely appear to be, attempts that have had varying degrees and kinds of success or failure. Cultures are on this view projects, projects whose strikingly different and often incompatible modes of activity and presentation – differences in rituals, stories, kinship structures, modes of production, and games that are also differences in concepts and in beliefs – may disguise from us the extent to which those who inhabit other and alien cultures share concerns with us, concerns that may properly be called philosophical and theological, and this even when they are the concerns of those for whom "philosophy" and "theology" are unknown names. For every culture is an attempt to make the natural and social world habitable by making it intelligible and in such attempts there is always an appeal, characteristically implicit and unspelled out, to standards of truth and goodness, to standards by which this set of beliefs is judged more adequate than that and this way of life better than that (28–33).

There are of course many disagreements between cultures, disagreements that sometimes extend to disagreement about how truth and goodness are to be understood. And the resolution of such disagreements is notoriously difficult. Here there is much philosophical work yet to be done. But we can never rule out the possibility that what we most need to learn, in order to advance further towards the true and the good, may have to be learned from the insights, arguments, and practices of some alien culture. Openness to the culturally embodied beliefs, insights, and arguments of other cultures is required for reasons analogous to those which make it important for us as truth-seekers to be open in general to difficulties in and objections to our own present beliefs. So the cultural pluralism of the encyclical is complementary to its philosophical concerns. In his 1993 encyclical, *Veritatis Splendor*, John Paul II had reminded us of "the moral sense present in peoples and . . . the great religious and sapiential traditions of East and West, from which the interior and mysterious workings of God's spirit are not absent" (94). Now in *Fides et Ratio* he refers us to a range of Asian religious and philosophical traditions as exemplifying our common quest for answers to fundamental questions (1). Indeed his most incisive critical and negative remarks are reserved for features of the Western cultures of advanced modernity. But here perhaps the encyclical does not go far enough. For it treats those features primarily as features of mistaken theories advanced by philosophers rather than as features of the culture itself, of attitudes that are exhibited in the actions and transactions of everyday life. What attitudes do I have in mind?

To understand human beings as having their place within an intelligible order of things is to understand them as possessing, like members of other species, a determinate and given nature. To what ends they are directed by that nature, to what norms they must conform if they are to achieve those ends, what relationships between them are required by those norms, and what their natural mode and direction of development is, so that they may pass from conception and birth through education to the achievement of their flourishing, are all aspects of that determinate and given nature. In different types of social order those aspects may appear in very different cultural guises. But the recognition of a common humanity enables us to recognize the expression in varying cultural forms of a single human nature.

To understand oneself as having such a determinate and shared nature and correspondingly a well-defined place in the order of things is, on a Thomistic view, to understand oneself as a part of more than one whole, constituted as what one is not only by the relation of oneself as individual human being to one's household and family, and to the good of that household and family, and of oneself *and* one's family to the local political community, and to the good of that community, and of oneself, one's family, *and* one's political community to the whole natural order and to the good to which nature is ordered. I am therefore in key part constituted as who I am, and what I am by the social roles to which I find myself assigned and by the relationships within which my life is embedded. During a lifetime, of course, individuals occupy different roles and over time both roles and relationships are to some degree transformed. What it is to be a parent now in North America is significantly different from what it was to be a parent five hundred years ago in Europe or a thousand years ago in China. But households and families as the milieus in terms of which individuals understand themselves and political communities as the milieus in terms of which individuals and families understand themselves have persisted through many types of change.

Nothing however prevents individuals from misunderstanding themselves and their relationships to family and to political community and such misunderstandings often find cultural and social expression in everyday practice. So individuals in some particular culture might over time learn to think of themselves as free to redefine and to remake their relationships to family and to political community and this to an indefinite extent. Those relationships would be, on this new view, whatever individuals might choose to make of them and any attempt to insist upon the givenness and determinateness of those relationships would appear as the provision of a metaphysical disguise for an imposition of arbitrary limitations upon their freedom of choice. And just this has of course happened in our own culture, so that what were once understood as unconditional relationships have increasingly assumed a conditional and temporary character. They have become roles and relationships that many individuals feel free to assume and discard at will. The consequences are unsurprising. Any determinate conception of the family has become contestable and commitment to the family has been increasingly undermined. "Politics" has become the name not of a dimension of the normal life of every member of a political society, but of an optional activity engaged in only by those who at this or that particular time choose to engage in it. And, when there is a conservative reaction to the consequent damage to family life or to a consequent lack of widespread participation in political activity, that reaction is itself characteristically expressed in exhortations to make a different and opposing set of choices, choices to espouse family values or to undertake political responsibilities. So conservative choices confront liberal choices in debate. But what such debate characteristically fails to put in question is the shared underlying conception of the nature of choice and its place in human life. Yet it is this shared contemporary conception of choice that has played a key part in displacing older understandings of the determinateness of the order of things and of the relationship of individuals, families, and political communities to that order.[1]

The narrative of the stages through which the concept of choice was transformed, so that it became available to play this central part in the culture of advanced modernity is a complex one. And it cannot be told here.[2] But its culmination is a culture among whose dominant images is that of the individual human being as one who defines her or himself through her or his acts of choice, choices which determine for her or him not only what use to make of this or that object and what attitude to take to this or that other human being, but also how to describe or to redescribe, to classify or to reclassify the objects and the uses, the other

---

1 I am much indebted in this part of the essay to an unpublished essay by Grace Goodell on "The Social Foundations of Realist Metaphysics."

2 For an account of one important stage in the history of that transformation see chapter 10 of *The Sources of Christian Ethics* by Servais Pinckaers, O.P. (Washington, D.C.: Catholic University of America Press, 1995).

human beings and the attitudes. So there is a pragmatism and a nominalism of everyday life as well as a pragmatism and a nominalism of
the philosophers. But, while the pragmatism and the nominalism of the
philosophers take the form of theories, the pragmatism and nominalism
of everyday life take the form of a socially powerful way of reimagining
the self.

Individuals who learn to reimagine themselves in this way, so that they
become what they imagine, are prevented thereby from understanding
themselves as having an ultimate end, a final good to which they are
directed by their essential nature. For their way of imagining themselves is
incompatible with there being a good towards which they might be
directed prior to and independently of their choices and incompatible
with their having an essential nature defined by that good as its end. But it
is not just that this way of imagining oneself is an obstacle to the
achievement of understanding. It may even inhibit the asking of those
questions and the systematic pursuit of answers to those questions that are
directed towards the achievement of understanding. For the very asking of
those questions presupposes a goal towards which the agent's life is
directed and a conception of that life as a quest for understanding of
oneself and one's place in the order of things. And this presupposition is
undermined whenever the influence of the pragmatist and nominalist
imagination is too powerful.

It is not of course that the habit of asking the perennial questions can
ever be extinguished. That habit is too deeply embedded in human
nature. But the attempt to answer these questions through enquiry is
much less likely to be sustained in a culture in which even the adoption of
a *Weltanschauung*, of any particular view of the nature of things, is itself
often presented as matter for individual choice, so that individuals go
shopping for an ethics or a metaphysics much as they go shopping for
other objects of consumer choice. To the extent that choice becomes
sovereign, philosophical enquiry in general will come to seem
eccentric and enquiry informed by the theses and arguments of
Thomistic realism almost unintelligible. To speak from the standpoint
of Thomistic realism in a way which recognizes the importance of
philosophical enquiry for the questions posed by plain persons is therefore
to put oneself at odds not only with a variety of rival philosophical
theories, but also with some of the most influential attitudes of contemporary Western culture. Here too there is work to be done.

# CHAPTER 10

# *Truth as a good: a reflection on* Fides et Ratio

In the encyclical *Fides et Ratio* John Paul II remarks that he will be "concentrating on the theme of truth itself" (6) and the argument of the encyclical returns recurrently to questions about truth and about the place of a concern for truth in human life. These questions presuppose that truth is a good and indeed *the* good of the human intellect. And it is with this presupposition that I shall be most concerned, noting that *Fides et Ratio* not only is an encyclical about philosophy, as was *Aeterni Patris*, but is also, as *Aeterni Patris* was not, itself a contribution to philosophy, inviting philosophical scrutiny of its arguments and assertions in a way that is rare, perhaps unique, among encyclicals. It does so just because the questions which are central to it are in part philosophical questions and the encyclical insists that in pursuing them "philosophy must remain faithful to its own principles and methods" (49). "A philosophy which did not proceed in the light of reason according to its own principles and methods would serve little purpose" (49).

So philosophy is to be accorded an inviolable autonomy within the sphere of its own enquiries. And the teaching church recognizes the possibility of alternative and rival philosophical approaches in the exercise of this autonomy (74). Yet at the same time the truths of faith presuppose the truth of some particular philosophical theses and the falsity of others. Relativism with regard to truth, for example, is condemned (82) and Aquinas's realistic account of truth is commended (44), and this in such a way that a tension may seem to emerge. What is this apparent tension? It is perhaps best initially identified by an unfriendly caricature of the encyclical's positions. As caricatured, the encyclical would be read as saying to philosophers: "You are free to pursue your enquiries about truth to whatever conclusions the arguments may lead and here now are the conclusions about truth to which your arguments are to lead." And thus read the encyclical might seem to be in grave danger of imposing on philosophy a set of constraints that would seriously violate its autonomy.

An incidental aim of this essay is to provide a reading of the encyclical that will show what is distorted and mistaken in this caricature and to do so by focusing on what is centrally important, its concern with the nature of truth and more particularly with truth as a good. So I begin by asking whether there is in fact a line of purely philosophical argument that would take us from the current preoccupations of philosophers with truth in the direction of the conclusions endorsed in the encyclical.

I

What should philosophers hope for from a theory of truth? What should it enable us to understand? There are three conditions that any adequate theory must satisfy. First, it should account for a range of different uses of "true" and "false" and of other related expressions, distinguishing primary uses from those that are secondary and derivative. Secondly, it needs to explain why we cannot but take truth to be a good, so that "false," whether predicated of a belief, a judgment, testimony, or a coin, or a friend, always has the gerundive force of "This is something to be rejected." And thirdly, among the uses of "true" and its cognates that require particular attention in respect of this gerundive force are such expressions as "the truth about such and such" or more simply "the truth."

Some analytical philosophers who have written about truth have ignored all three of these conditions, flouting the first by focusing exclusively on "true" and "false" as predicated of asserted sentences, and taking it for granted that these are the primary uses of "true" and "false." It is an undeniable commonplace that the utterance of the assertion "p is true" communicates no more information about the subject matter of which "p" speaks than does the utterance of the assertion "p" and from this some philosophers have concluded that "p is true" has no more assertive content than "p." Hence they have sometimes further concluded that "is true" is a redundant predicate, one that could be eliminated from our language without significant loss, one whose use is expressive only of an endorsement of "p." But it was very soon recognized that these latter contentions must be mistaken, if only because there are common uses of "is true" which are plainly not endorsements, as well as uses in which "is true" is plainly not redundant: types of example often cited are "If what he said is true, I should be surprised"; "For every asserted sentence, either it is true or it is false"; and "What John asserts is sometimes false."

Examples of this kind led the Pittsburgh philosophers, Grover, Camp, and Belknap to argue that such expressions as "It is true" and "That is true" function as prosentences, referring us to some antecedent asserted sentence, as when someone responds to someone else's assertion by saying "*That* is true."[1] As Grover, Camp, and Belknap spell out their theory, "is true" is not a redundant predicate – there are things that cannot be said without it – but it is nonetheless never a genuine predicate, functioning instead only as a fragment of some prosentence. It is evident that this prosentential theory of truth is able to give an account of examples that redundancy theories cannot explain. So is there then any good reason not to accept such a minimal theory of truth, a theory free from any metaphysical commitments?

One reason for rejecting it is that, like redundancy theories, the prosentential theory passes too easily over the possibility that "p is true" *is* a genuine assertion and indeed a significantly different assertion from "p." Consider, for example, the obvious differences between "The nightingale is singing" and "It is true that the nightingale is singing." It is true that whatever confirms or disconfirms the truth of the former confirms or disconfirms the truth of the latter. But it seems difficult to deny that they are sentences with different subject matters. One is about a bird, saying of it that it is singing, while the other is about an asserted sentence, saying of it that it is true. The former is true, if it is true, in virtue of some relationship that holds between the sentence "The nightingale is singing" and something else, but it says nothing about that relationship. The latter asserts that the relevant relationship between the sentence and whatever it is of which the sentence speaks holds. Whether and how this is philosophically important depends on the nature of such relationships and correspondence theories of truth are attempts to characterize the nature of this relationship.

Correspondence theorists, however, like redundancy theorists and like adherents of the prosentential theory, have all too often attended too exclusively to those uses of "true" and "false" in which they are predicated of asserted sentences. And the importance of what we have to learn from them has also been obscured by misunderstandings about the nature of the correspondence to which correspondence theorists are or ought to be committed, misunderstandings which have too often led to a lock, stock, and barrel rejection of *all* correspondence theories.

---

1 Dorothy L. Grover, Joseph L. Camp, Jr., and Noel D. Belknap, Jr., "A Prosentential Theory of Truth', *Philosophical Studies*, vol. 27, 1975.

For it has been erroneously supposed that what a true asserted sentence must correspond to, on a correspondence theory of truth, is some non-linguistic item whose components and structure match the components and structure of the sentence. But nonlinguistic realities just do not have the components and structure of sentences and the realities that have been alleged to have such components and structure, such as facts or states-of-affairs, are in fact disguised linguistic items, characterizable only by reference to the true asserted sentences which report them. The fact that John has red hair cannot be identified independently of and has no existence apart from the truth of the asserted sentence "John has red hair." So there is no fact independent of the sentence to which the sentence corresponds and from which it derives its truth. The expression "the fact that John has red hair" is a useful nominalization of the sentence "John has red hair," but it refers to nothing and characterizes nothing that is not already referred to and characterized in the sentence. Facts, it has been rightly said, are shadows cast by sentences.

What is important is that the discrediting of this conception of truth as correspondence-to-fact should not be allowed to discredit any conception of truth as correspondence. And a first step towards an adequate conception of truth as correspondence is to remind ourselves that it is not sentences as such that are truth-bearers, but asserted sentences, sentences used by a particular speaker to make a particular assertion on a particular occasion. And the relationships in which some particular asserted sentence may stand to the subject matter of which it speaks cannot be adequately characterized, if we do not also consider the relationships in which someone who sincerely asserts that sentence may stand to that subject matter. Consider an example.

Someone arrives at a judgment by exercising his powers of perceptual discrimination and recognition. Examining the blue jug he sees that it is broken. The belief at which he thus arrives, a belief which need not have been put into words, as to how things are agrees with, corresponds to (one of the primary meanings of "correspondence to," according to the *Oxford English Dictionary* is "agreement with") how things are. That is to say, the words that would have to be used to specify the content of his thought are the same words that would tell us how things are. How things are and how he takes them to be are identical. If he himself gives verbal expression to his belief by saying "The blue jug is broken," the uttered sentence both expresses his belief and says how things are.

Yet this identity of the content of a particular thought with how things in fact are does not make it any less the case that the mind that has this thought, indeed the thought itself, is one thing and the reality thought of quite another. A mind thinking about a jug is not a jug. And that this is so is crucial to a second aspect of true judgment. When we take our assertions to be true, when we take it that their content is identical with how things are, we also take it that this is *because* our thoughts in the assertive mode have been made what they are by that same reality about which we are thinking. We presuppose, that is, that some causal relationship holds between our mind and the realities external to it about which we judge and that our thoughts are in this particular case determined to be what they are by those realities being as they are.

About this of course we may always on occasion be mistaken. For it may be that our thoughts in the assertive mode agree with how things are only by accident, perhaps because reality just happens to coincide with the outcome of our wishful thinking or perhaps because from two premises, false but believed to be true, we have inferred to a true conclusion. But in judging on any particular occasion that such and such is true, we always presuppose that this is not one of these accidental cases. Speaking of someone else we may say "What he believes is true, but he believes it not because that is how things are, but only because of his wishful thinking." But we cannot say coherently of ourselves "What I believe is true, but I believe it not because that is how things are, but only because of my wishful thinking."

So we always understand someone's thoughts of how things are as determined in one of two ways, either by how things are or instead by something else, by some aspect of that mind's receptivity or activity that influences it, so that determination by how things are is to some significant degree excluded. In the former case the mind is receptive to external reality in such a way and to such a degree that its judgments, at least on this occasion and concerning this subject matter, are true and true because of this receptivity. In the latter case the mind may judge either truly or falsely, but, if truly, only by accident. And insofar as a mind judges truly only by accident, it exhibits the same lack of receptivity to things as they are as does a mind that judges falsely.

We have then identified so far two features of any adequate theory of truth: first, it needs to supply an account of the identity that obtains between the mind's thought of how things are and how those same things are and, secondly, it needs to characterize the kind of causal relationship that must hold between things and the mind's thought of them, when our beliefs and judgments are nonaccidentally true. To these two features of an adequate theory of truth a third must be added, concerning the relationship between belief and truth. To assert of any asserted sentence that it is false is to assert that it is not to be believed, that it is unworthy of judgmental assent. It is to appeal to a norm governing belief and judgment. So we need an account of why we cannot but treat false beliefs and false judgments as violations of a norm. What then is it that is bad about falsity?

A false asserted sentence misrepresents, fails to agree with how things are. An assertion may of course fail in respect of truth in more than one way. It may use a name or a singular referring expression, such as "unicorn" or "the king of the United States," which names or refers to nothing, it may ascribe a property to something that does not possess that property, or it may deny that some particular individual has a property which it does in fact have, it may deny that anything has some property which some individuals do in fact have, or it may involve even more complex types of misrepresentation. False asserted sentences are necessarily as various in type as true asserted sentences. But false assertions, when believed, interpose themselves between the individuals who assert them and the realities of which they speak. In so doing they are always apt to disable those individuals in their everyday activities as well as in their enquiries.

For the objects about which we speak, the objects concerning whose properties and relationships we make judgments, are the very same objects with which we also and antecedently enter into nonlinguistic relationships, with which we interact, which we identify and recognize, about which we make and sometimes correct mistakes. It is what we encounter as independent, causally effective realities in active and responsive experience that we also designate as independent realities in speech acts of reference and assertion. And just as the real is what impacts upon us independently of our willing, what is true of that reality is so independently of our thinking it to be so. "That which is such that something true about it is either true independently of the thought of any *definite* mind or minds or is at least true independently of what any person or any definite individual group of persons think about that truth, is real."[2]

So all our transactions, theoretical or practical, with independent realities are put at risk by false judgments, by our believing and thereby being disposed to act on the basis of false assertions. Therefore to say truly of p that "p is false" is to say something significantly different from saying

2 C. S. Peirce to Lady Welby, Ash Wednesday, 1909, in *Values in a Universe of Chance*, ed. P. P. Wiener (New York: Doubleday, 1958), p. 420.

truly that "It is not the case that p," even although to assert that "p is false" is to be committed also to asserting "It is not the case that p." For to assert that "p is false" is to ascribe to the assertion of p and to belief that p an injurious causal property, something that is not ascribed by asserting that "It is not the case that p." So long as I believe and judge that p, when p is in fact false, I debar myself from recognizing how things are.

Notice that in acts of assertion it is whole sentences that function to such good or bad effect. Names, referring expressions, and predicates so function only as parts of and in the context of sentences. And an adequate theory of, say, referring expressions would be a theory of how such expressions contribute to sentences which are capable of truth and falsity, when uttered as assertions. The importance of division and composition within an asserted sentence is this: that about any asserted sentence we may ask two distinct questions: "To the existence or nonexistence of what are those who assert it committed?" and "What properties or relations does it ascribe to that to whose existence or nonexistence those who assert it are committed?" For different parts of an asserted sentence contribute differently to the answers to these two questions. Whether an asserted sentence is true or false depends of course upon the answers to two further and corresponding questions: "Does what according to the asserted sentence exists exist?" and "Does it possess the properties or relations ascribed to it by the assertion of that sentence?" So it is individuals and their properties and relations, not facts or states of affairs, that make asserted sentences true or false. And false beliefs and judgments, as I have already suggested, are of peculiar importance in our lives. Human beings have a capacity for getting things wrong and for blundering in their dealings with their environment that makes them unique among animal species. And it is false belief and false judgment that most often involve us in this kind of failure. For this reason alone we could scarcely avoid treating truth as a good.

To say that truth is a good is not of course to define truth in terms of the utility of a belief to those who hold it. False beliefs are sometimes useful. Albert O. Hirschman has argued compellingly, for example, that because we underestimate our own creativity, "it is desirable that we underestimate to a roughly similar extent the difficulties of the tasks we face, so as to be tricked . . . into undertaking tasks that we can, but otherwise would not dare, tackle."[3] And this important contingent truth,

3 Albert O. Hirschman, *Development Projects Observed* (Washington, D.C.: The Brookings Institute, 1967), p. 13.

that false beliefs *are* sometimes useful, itself entails that the true is not to be equated with the useful.

Yet one can recognize this and still question whether or not truth is a good, as Stephen Stich has done.[4] Stich argues that, in valuing truth as we do, and indeed in evaluating beliefs in terms of their truth or falsity, we are presupposing one particular way of mapping words on to the world, one particular way of interpreting the sentences that we utter to each other, the presently established way. But there are, so Stich argues, an indefinitely large number of different and attractive ways in which such mapping and such interpretation could take place and, so Stich claims, it needs to be shown that we are better off with the modes of interpretation and belief that are bound up with our present evaluations in terms of truth and falsity than we would be with some of these alternatives.

To this there should be a twofold response. First, what Stich has offered us is no more than an outline proposal. When, and only when, he or others are able to propose some particular alternative mode of discourse, characterizing it in detail, and to show by some justifiable standard that it would be better for us to adopt this alternative mode, will we be in a position to evaluate this kind of proposal. But even then it is difficult to understand how we could avoid evaluating it except as "true" or "false," for either it will be true that the adoption of this alternative carries with it the advantages claimed for it or it will be false that it does so. And, if we adopt it only because and insofar as and for as long as we take it to be true, we will in fact not have abandoned either our present uses of "true" and "false" or our present conception of truth as a good.

Secondly, Stich himself presupposes a commitment to those present uses and that present conception. Both in his account of the constraints that would have to govern any acceptable way of mapping words on to the world and in his thesis about those actual and possible features of brain states, beliefs, and types of reference to which he appeals in constructing his argument, there is no way to understand his argument, unless we take him to be claiming that that account and those theses are true – as we presently understand "true" – and that we would do well to accept them, just because they are true. Stich, as a user of language rather than a theorist about language, seems to be as committed to the goodness of truth and the badness of falsity quite as seriously as the rest of us are.

4  *The Fragmentation of Reason* (Cambridge, Mass.: MIT Press, 1990).

The good of truth is however not merely a matter of the badness in general of falsity and falsehood. It also has to do more specifically with the contribution that true judgments make to enquiry and to understanding. The mind's characteristic activity is enquiry and at the core of any enquiry is the task of distinguishing between the true and the false in order to arrive at "the truth" about some particular subject matter. To have arrived at *the* truth about some subject matter is to have achieved understanding, the terminus of enquiry. And to have achieved understanding is of course more than to have achieved a set of true beliefs, a capacity to make true judgments. For all one's judgments on a particular subject can be true and yet one can still fail to understand. And the mere accumulation of further truths will not necessarily take one any further towards the goal of understanding. So what more is required? What differentiates those true beliefs and judgments that constitute understanding from those that do not?

The mind that understands is such that its thoughts not only of how things are, but also of why they are as they are, are identical with how they are *and* with why they are as they are. And that is to say once again that the words that would have to be used to specify the content of such thoughts are the very same words that would tell us how things are *and* why they are as they are. The distinction between how things are and why they are as they are is of course a rough and ready one. A mind that has formed an adequate conception of some particular object or set of objects will have already recognized that among their key properties are those which render them explicable and intelligible in this way rather than that. We do indeed encounter and describe objects that we do not as yet know how to explain. But to know that we cannot as yet explain some object is to know that we have not yet identified some of its key properties, that our description of it up to this point is inadequate, because it omits at least some of just those properties that would render this particular object or set of objects intelligible: perhaps that, although it is actually such and such, it is potentially so and so, or that this particular feature belongs to this kind of thing in virtue of its nature, while that other feature needs to be characterized as an effect of accidental causation.

That is to say, a mind whose thoughts are adequate to the subject matter about which it thinks not only makes and is disposed to make true judgments and only true judgments about that subject matter, but it judges truly in such a way as to present that subject matter as intelligible. And the mind, when adequate to some subject matter, finds that subject matter intelligible only insofar as that subject matter *is* intelligible, is, prior to its being understood by you or me, apt to be understood in virtue of those characteristics which give it its place in the order of things. For to explain some subject matter, to render it intelligible, just is to identify its place, function, and relationship within the overall order of things.

It is then a metaphysical presupposition of this view of truth that there is an order of things and that this order exists independently of the human mind, just as do the objects and sets of objects that find their place within it. And to make true judgments about the order of things is for the mind to be receptive to that order, so that its judgments about that order agree with how things are just because it is how things are in respect of that order that determines how the mind thinks about it and this not accidentally. But to have recognized this is also to have understood more adequately why truth is a good. For the goodness of truth is in key part a matter of the contribution that particular true judgments make to acts of understanding. For the mind to understand is for it to have achieved its principal good, to have arrived at "the truth" in some area. And it is from the relationship of particular truths to "the truth" that the goodness of particular truths is in part derived. In order therefore to characterize the gerundive force of "true" and "false" adequately we need a theory of truth that takes account both of the relationship between particular true judgments and that of which they speak and of the part that those same true judgments play both in the transactions of everyday life and in the enquiring life of the mind as it moves towards the achievement of its theoretical and practical goals, that is, as it becomes more rather than less adequate to the subject matters about which it enquires.

What enables us to connect these various aspects of truth, truth as judgment in agreement with how things are, the truth as the goal of enquiry, truth as a good that confers gerundive force on our judgments, is a conception of the mind as standing in more or less adequate relationships to those realities about which it judges. It is insofar as the mind's thoughts about how things are agree with how things are *because* these particular thoughts are determined by how these particular realities are – and the same holds of the mind's thoughts about *why* things are – that the mind may be said to be adequate to those realities.

The causal relationship is crucial for this account. Earlier I spoke of a judgment perhaps being true by accident. What would be an example of this? Consider someone in a windowless room, who receives no information about the state of the weather outside, but at frequent intervals utters judgments about the weather: "Now it's raining"; "Now there is fog"; "Now it is dry, but cloudy." Given the random relationship between this set of utterances and the current state of the weather, if those judgments are made over a long enough period of time some of them will correspond with how the weather is at the moment of utterance. They may certainly therefore be said to be true, but only accidentally, and in qualifying our predication of truth in this way, we treat this particular use of "true" as a peripheral extension of our central uses. For those central uses refer us to a relationship between the mind and that of which it speaks which in this type of case does not hold.

What is fundamental to our conception of truth then is the notion of a type of relationship that may hold or fail to hold between a mind and those subject matters about which it passes judgments. And it is characteristic of the mind that it is capable of discriminating and classifying and explaining, so that it becomes more and more adequate in respect of those subject matters about which it judges. So the mind achieves its goals not only by discarding false judgments and replacing them by true, but by doing so in such a way that it moves towards a final and completed grasp of the truth concerning the place of the objects about which it judges in the overall order of things.

To understand truth in this way removes any temptation to assimilate truth to rational justifiability, to warranted assertibility. Crispin Wright has provided the so far most ambitious and compelling account of truth in terms of justification by considering what it would be to equate truth with a property to which he has given the name "superassertibility."[5] "A statement is superassertible . . . if and only if it is, or can be, warranted and some warrant for it would survive arbitrarily close scrutiny of its pedigree and arbitrarily extensive increments to or other forms of improvement of our information."[6] And it is of course true of superassertibility thus defined that if p is true, then p is superassertible. But what this type of theory obscures is the difference between two distinct sets of questions to both of which we need answers. Questions about truth are as I have argued, questions about the relationship between minds and their judgments on the one hand and the subject-matters of those judgments on the other. And in answering questions about whether or not this relationship holds in particular cases there need be no mention of or allusion to superassertibility or indeed any other conception of warranted assertibility. The question of warrant or justification is quite other than the question of truth.

So, if someone asserts that p, I may ask "Is this indeed how things are?" – and this is a question about truth " or else I ask "What kind and degree of

5 *Realism, Meaning and Truth* (Oxford: Basil Blackwell, 1987), pp. 295–302.
6 *Truth and Objectivity* (Cambridge, Mass.: Harvard University Press, 1992), p. 48.

justification does this particular speaker have for making this judgment?" –
and this is a question about warranted assertibility. To equate truth with
superassertibility is thus to confuse the answers to two distinct questions.
But, if so, why does Wright think otherwise? It is perhaps because he shares
with proponents of minimalist theories of truth a belief that the standards
governing the assertion of the truth or falsity of some particular statement
must be no other than the standards that in fact govern whatever is taken to
be the justified assertion of that statement within some particular kind of
established discourse. So Wright declares that

> superassertibility is . . . an *internal* property of the statements of a discourse – a
> projection, merely, of the standards, whatever they are, which actually inform
> assertion within the discourse. It supplies no external norm – in a way that truth is
> classically supposed to do – against which the internal standards might *sub specie
> Dei* themselves be measured and might rate as adequate or inadequate. (p. 61)

What this remark brings out is the extent to which Wright is offering a
revision of what was traditionally meant by truth, an abandonment of an
older realistic view – and one held not only by theorists, but presupposed
in our long-standing practices of enquiry – and its replacement by a new,
fabricated notion. What might philosophically motivate such a revisionist
project? Perhaps that truth, as realistically conceived, does indeed involve
a notion of how things are "sub specie Dei," as Wright says, a conception
of an absolute standpoint that is not our standpoint. If so, then a rejection
of the possibility of such a standpoint would indeed require some radical
revision of our understanding of truth.

Conversely it is the possibility of such a standpoint that renders intelligible the notion of a directed movement of our enquiries towards an
ultimate end. For if we lacked any conception of such an absolute
standpoint, we might well conclude that there is no such thing as a final
terminus for enquiry concerning any particular subject matter. What
directs enquiry on this alternative view are whatever may happen to be
our explanatory interests and in taking this or that as the goal of enquiry
in some particular area we are only giving expression to our interests as
they happen to be now, but may not be in the future, interests that may
also differ from social group to social group. Hence there is no such thing
as "the truth" about any subject matter, but only different sets of truths
that are answers to different questions posed about that subject matter
by those with different explanatory interests. But this view of
explanation itself leaves certain matters unexplained. For we may
always ask about the subject matter of our enquiries what characteristics

it must have as the kind of subject matter it is, quite apart from our enquiries, if the answers to our questions are to be *true* answers. And we may ask about ourselves what characteristics *we* must have, apart from and antecedent to our enquiries, if our interests in enquiry are to be what they are. And in posing such questions about how things are and about how we are, prior to our enquiries, we already presuppose an order of things realistically conceived, an order of things which is itself the ultimate object of enquiry.

To apprehend the truth about some subject matter then is to judge truly what place the objects and properties and relations that constitute that subject matter have in the order of things. It is always a good to have true rather than false beliefs and to make true rather than false judgments; but it is the specific good of a mind to have just those true beliefs and to make just those true judgments that make that mind adequate to its objects by understanding their place in the order of things. And part of the progress of a mind towards its goal is a progress from less to more adequate theories of truth. About truth too we need the truth and why this should be so is a question on which too many theories of truth are silent. So in moving from less to more adequate theories of truth we are exemplifying just that historical progress which can be made intelligible only by taking "the truth" to be the *telos* towards which the mind moves. But whether the account that I have given so far is indeed such a progress is of course still an open question and not only because I may well have failed to identify mistakes in my arguments. At best I have provided no more than an outline sketch of how a set of arguments might run, rather than the arguments themselves. I have provided an agenda of work to be done rather than the work itself.

Yet such an outline sketch may have some value. For it may enable us to identify the difficulties that confront us, the obstacles that will have to be overcome, if we are to move argumentatively from a rejection of current minimalist theories of truth to something that is at least close to Aquinas's realistic view. For this is the direction in which the line of argument that I have sketched so inadequately has taken us, something that becomes evident, if we consider what Aquinas's view was.

II

Some relevant aspects of Aquinas's theory of truth are perhaps best addressed by bringing into relationship two of his central theses, theses that we have already found some reason to accept. (Note that I shall not here be concerned with what Aquinas says about the truth or falsity of practical judgments; and also that nothing in what I say turns on the differences between Aquinas's successive accounts of truth.[7] The first is that truth is the specific good of the human mind, something that Aquinas asserts in a number of contexts. So, for example, in cataloguing the intellectual virtues, he argues that only those qualities can be virtues that enable that of which they are the virtues to achieve its good. But the good of the mind is truth, and so habits that are not concerned with truth cannot be intellectual virtues (*Summa Theologiae* Ia-IIae 57, 2 ad 3). Earlier Aquinas had said that "Virtue designates a certain perfection of a power" (Ia-IIae 55, 1 resp.) and so we are to understand the mind as perfecting the development of its powers through the achievement of truth.

A second central thesis had initiated the discussions of the disputed questions on truth. It is Aquinas's endorsement of the definition of truth advanced by Isaac Israeli, "Truth is the conformity (*adaequatio*) of thing and intellect" (*De Veritate* 1, 1 resp.), a definition which Aquinas proceeds to interpret, so that it is mind which has to conform itself to how things are, if its judgments about things are to be true. Truth and falsity are properties of mind, of thoughts as to how things are. Yet it is not only beliefs and judgments that may be said to be true or false. Things too may be said to be true or false. How so?

The standard by which the truth or falsity of human beliefs and judgments is measured is provided by the things about which human beings form beliefs and make judgments. And Aquinas cites Aristotle (*Metaphysics* 1053a 33): "natural things from which our mind gets its scientific knowledge measure our mind" (1, 2, resp.). But he immediately adds: "Yet these things are measured by the divine mind" and a natural thing "is said to be true with respect to its conformity with the divine mind insofar as it fulfills the end to which it was ordered by the divine mind." So we judge truly only insofar as we judge how things truly are, discounting misleading appearances and distinguishing what something is by its nature from what it is only accidentally in its particular contingent circumstance. And we judge how things truly are when we think of them as they are thought of by God.

The mind, in order to arrive at a comprehension of how things are, begins from sense experience. But the judgments of sense are of

---

7 On this latter see Lawrence Dewan, "St. Thomas's Successive Definitions of the Nature of Truth" in *Sanctus Thomas de Aquino: Doctor Hodiernae Humanitatis*, ed. D. Ols (Vatican City: Libreria Editrice Vaticana, 1995).

themselves unreflective. The mind has to go beyond sense in discriminating those appearances which are a reliable guide to what is from those that are deceptive. And it is insofar as something is the cause of deceptive appearances that it is called false: "as something is called false gold, which has the external color of gold and other accidents of this kind, but which lacks the underlying nature of gold" (1, 10, resp.). In moving beyond sense-experience towards adequacy of judgment the theoretically enquiring mind moves towards its good. It achieves that good in arriving at a perfected understanding of what things are essentially, an understanding that exhibits particulars as exemplifying universal first principles.

There are then three obvious respects in which Aquinas's theory of truth closely resembles the account that emerged from the line of argument that I sketched earlier. First, there is the conception of truth as *adaequatio*, as consisting in the agreement of the mind's judgments as to how things are with how things are, an agreement which results from the mind being causally influenced by how things are. For because the mind "is receptive in regard to things it is, in a certain sense, moved by things and in consequence measured by them" (1, 2, resp.). Secondly, the mind in moving to achieve truth thus defined not only cannot but treat truth as a good, but has a conception of "the truth" to be achieved as its specific goal. And thirdly the mind cannot dispense with a conception of an absolute standpoint, a divine standpoint, that from which things would be viewed as they truly are. Aquinas's account, that is to say, realizes Crispin Wright's worst fears.

Some of Aquinas's philosophical preoccupations were of course very different from ours, although Anthony Kenny has usefully pointed out parallels between Aquinas's discussions of truth and recent debates, noting, for example, that the issues raised for Aquinas by the view that to be true just is to be are much the same as those raised for us by those redundancy theorists who have held that to say " 'Snow is white' is true" is to say no more than "Snow is white."[8] But, as Aquinas moves from his starting-point through the questions of the *De Veritate*, there is an important parallel between his investigation and that which I sketched earlier, as well as an equally important difference. The parallel is that both investigations not only arrive at an account of truth, but in so doing exemplify just the kind of account at which they arrive. For in each investigation there is a movement from a set of initial problems and

---

8 *Aquinas* (Oxford: Oxford University Press, 1980), p. 6.

difficulties, some of them arising from well-established theories of truth, through a set of increasingly adequate formulations, towards a final account the best test of whose truth is that it is able to withstand the strongest objections available from every known rival point of view. But to have remarked on this parallel is immediately to become aware of a dimension to Aquinas's account that has been so far missing from mine. For Aquinas's teleological account of the mind's movement towards the achievement of the good of truth has as its presupposed setting his overall teleological account of each human being's potentiality for movement towards the achievement of the specifically human good.

Every human being, on this view, has by nature a desire for that happiness which is achieved only in union to God, integral to which is a recognition of God as the truth and of all truth as from God, so that the progress through truths to the truth is itself one part of the ascent of mind and heart to God. Detach Aquinas's teleological account of truth from this larger teleological setting and it will appear to many of our contemporaries, and especially to those who reject teleological modes of thought, as no more than one more highly contestable theory of truth and moreover one all the less acceptable in virtue of its metaphysical entanglements. And the same verdict would of course be passed on the line of thought about truth that I developed earlier.

What this brings out is the *systematic* character of philosophical disagreement, the extent to which the conclusions at which we arrive in any one area of philosophical enquiry presuppose conclusions of a certain kind in some other areas. And one important set of differences between rival philosophical standpoints arises from the degree to which and the ways in which their adherents recognize the bearing of philosophical enquiry in one area upon philosophical enquiry in other areas. On this what we have to learn from Aquinas and what we have to learn from the encyclical *Fides et Ratio* happily coincide. Aquinas's account of truth, as we have just noticed, is embedded in his teleological account of mind and that in turn is embedded in his larger teleological conception of the human being. And *Fides et Ratio* poses questions and makes assertions about the nature of truth, but does so while also posing questions and making assertions about the nature of human beings as truth-seekers. It asks not only what truth must be, if it is the goal of practical and theoretical enquiry, but what human beings must be, if they are by nature enquirers whose goal is truth. And it shares with Aquinas the assumption that these two questions can only be asked and answered together. But, if this is so, the line of argument concerning truth that I sketched earlier is at best seriously incomplete, and not only because of its brevity and its outline character. It too needs to be embedded in a larger teleological view of human nature, one that will enable us to recognize that practical and theoretical enquiry about the human good, and therefore about truth, are essential characteristics of human beings. It is indeed, as the encyclical insists, because this is so, and only because this is so, that philosophy should be acknowledged as of central importance in human life and accorded that autonomy that it needs, if it is to discharge those tasks that make it important.

III

We are now in a position to understand why the caricature of *Fides et Ratio* that I presented at the beginning of this essay is indeed a misleading distortion. What that caricature suggested was that *Fides et Ratio*, by endorsing certain philosophical positions with respect to truth, placed constraints upon philosophical enquiry, while at the same time claiming to respect the autonomy of such enquiry. What that caricature obscures is the structure of the underlying argument in *Fides et Ratio*. It is not that the encyclical *both* presents certain philosophical positions with regard to truth *and* proclaims the autonomy of philosophical enquiry. It is rather that, just *because* the encyclical takes the view of truth it does, and the view of the human being as truth-seeker that it does, that it finds itself committed to and gladly acknowledges its commitment to the autonomy of philosophy.

For philosophy, on the encyclical's view, articulates and pursues answers to questions posed by human beings, whatever their culture. It is characteristic of human beings that by our nature we desire to know and to understand, that we cannot but reflect upon the meaning of our lives, upon suffering, and upon death, and in so doing attempt to pursue our good, making our own the tasks of rational enquiry and the achievement of truth (25, 26). So all human beings "are in some sense philosophers and have their own philosophical conceptions with which they direct their lives" (30). Philosophers by profession have the task of articulating those conceptions more clearly and of carrying further and posing more sys-tematically these same questions. Divine revelation not only provides answers of crucial importance to questions thus posed, but discloses what was defective in that questioning. Yet revelation does not, on the encyc-lical's view, thereby put an end to such enquiry. Rather it provides new resources and new direction for enquiry (14, 23). That revelation can inform philosophical enquiry is not of course a new thought, but *Fides et Ratio* gives it an added significance by its theological and scriptural emphasis on philosophical questioning as so central to human nature that, when that nature is transformed by grace through faith, it does not and should not cease to question. A life that is one of growth in holiness does not thereby cease to be a life of philosophical enquiry whose goal is truth, a type of life exemplified both by St. Thomas Aquinas and by St. Teresa Benedicta of the Cross, Edith Stein.

The autonomy of philosophy is then no more than and no less than the autonomy of the enquiring human being. Each of us has to arrive at her or his own answers to those practical and theoretical questions that we all pose and to do so not only as reason requires, but as reason is understood to require by us. External constraints on the exercise of reason are always in danger of precluding genuinely rational and unforced assent to the answers to our questions about our good that reason proposes to us as *true*. So it is as those for whom truth is constitutive of our good that we cannot but presuppose – even when we fail to recognize that we presuppose – a realistic account of truth of the kind classically formulated by Aquinas. And it is this inescapable presupposition that commits us to acknowledgment of the autonomy of philosophy. So the appearance of a tension in *Fides et Ratio* between its unhesitating acknowledgment of the autonomy of philosophical enquiry and its uncompromising endorsement of a Thomistic view of truth is the result of a misreading of the encyclical, and the caricature that I proposed does indeed distort its message. But the misunderstanding underlying that misreading and that caricature is sufficiently widespread that attention to it may be salutary. *Fides et Ratio*, like *Aeterni Patris*, instructs us that the teaching of the Catholic church commits us to affirming certain theses within philosophy and to denying others, including among them theses about the nature of truth, theses that within philosophy are not only contestable, but often vigorously contested. But *Fides et Ratio* also instructs us that it is just because we are so committed that we are also committed to securing philosophy from violations of its autonomy.

IV

Three conclusions emerge from the arguments of this essay. The first is tentative: it is that, if we begin by considering the requirements that any adequate theory of truth should satisfy, and the way in which a number of currently influential views of truth fail to satisfy those requirements, we shall find grounds for moving towards an account of truth that resembles in key respects the account formulated and defended by Aquinas. A second conclusion is less tentative: it is that we need to learn from Aquinas that any such account of truth is incomplete, and therefore more questionable than it needs to be, until it is situated within a larger teleological view of human nature, according to which truth, understood as *adaequatio*, is also understood as constitutive of the human good. A third conclusion is less tentative still: it is that such a view of human nature requires a recognition of just that autonomy of philosophical enquiry about which *Fides et Ratio* speaks to us so insightfully.

# Index